More Advance Praise for
What Everyone Believed

"Christine begins from a place of frustration and walks us through the self-carved solo process of finding herself, fueled by a yearning for and dedication to truth. For anyone who feels like something is missing inside, this book is a must-read. Through deep thought, she arrives at a level of spiritual sophistication, carrying the reader through this journey by painting a practical picture of what it means to grow spiritually, so that it feels real and understandable. She puts words to the vagueness of becoming 'deeply connected' by bridging everyday experiences with deeper shifts in awareness, teaching us that every moment of life has a deeper purpose, and is therefore perfect. By following our intuition, flowing with life's events and being open to learning from every interaction, we can come to understand what our purpose here on earth is. This book will be an inspiration to anyone searching for beauty and truth in their own life."—Elizabeth J. Agnew, Associate Coach, Bill Baren Coaching, San Francisco

"Christine has a gift to have us reach deep inside ourselves to discover a deeper reality about our lives. You will be moved by this insightful and eye-opening exploration."—Stacey J. Hentschel, Business and Life Consultant, Laguna Niguel, Calif.

"A beautiful journey from confusion to spiritual enlightenment. A must for anyone needing guidance and reawakening. Hoeflich 'connects with the infinite' and shows us all how to join her on our own quests. Inspiring from beginning to end."—Valerie Frankel, *Rambles Cultural Arts*

"Christine Hoeflich is a guide, a teacher, a student, a seer and a messenger. I can identify with her and am using her book as a guide in my own journey towards self-awareness and as a stimulus for my creative and professional work as a painter. Also, I recommended this book to my daughter, who is on her own creative quest."—Amy Cohen Banker, fine artist, New York City and Southfield, Mass.

"Christine Hoeflich masterfully regenerates the vitality that emanates from working through to the discovery of essence. The wisdom unveiled here is so much more meaningful and valuable because she courageously engages us in her painful, joyful and faithful process of enfoldment and unfoldment that leads to her discovery of what's REAL; and thereby her inestimable contribution: enabling us to glimpse the heartfelt significance of deepening our consciousness."—Bob Mang, co-founder, Regenesis Group; board member of Conservation Voters of New Mexico and World Business Academy; former president, Bay Area Greenbelt Alliance

"Pulls you in with a sense of curious voyeurism that compels you to uncover glimpses of your own soul."—Stacie Blakely-Ratkovich, president, Wa-Hoo NuShu book club, Cupertino, Calif.

What Everyone Believed:

A Memoir of Intuition and Awakening

Christine Hoeflich

Between Worlds
PUBLISHING

Between Worlds Publishing
P. O. Box 1472
Campbell, CA 95009

Interior design: Deb Tremper, Six Penny Graphics. www.sixpennygraphics.com
Editing: Valerie Estelle Frankel, www.calithwain.com and Joan C. Kirsner

Sources of written, motion picture, and lyrical works excerpted:

Michaly Csikszentmihalyi, Ph.D., *Flow: the Psychology of Optimal Experience*, (New York: Harper and Row, 1990).

Toni Sar'h Petrinovich, Ph.D., *The Call--Awakening the Angelic Human,* (Anacortes: Sar'h Publishing House, 2002), 33-34, 84-87. Reprinted by permission of the author and publisher.

Andy and Larry Wachowski (Writers and Directors), *The Matrix*, DVD. (Burbank, CA: Warner Brothers), 1999.

Jem Griffiths. They. On *Finally Woken*, CD. New York: ATO Records, 2004.

Madonna. Ray of Light. On *Ray of Light*, CD. Beverly Hills: Maverick, 1998.

John Mayer. Belief. On *Continuum*, CD. New York: Columbia, 2006.

Natalie Merchant. Carnival. On *Tigerlily*, CD. New York: Elektra, 1995.

Metallica. The Unforgiven. On *Metallica*, CD. New York: Elektra, 1991.

Missing Persons. Destination Unknown. On *Best of Missing Persons*. Capitol/EMI Records, 1987.

Alan Parsons Project. The Turn of a Friendly Card. On *The Turn of a Friendly Card,* CD. Arista, 1980.

Rush. Closer to the Heart. On *Farewell to Kings*, CD. Mercury, 1977.

Library of Congress Control Number: 2007904069
ISBN-13: 978-0-9796589-0-7

Printed in the United States of America

Contents

SECURITY IS MOSTLY A SUPERSTITION.
IT DOES NOT EXIST IN NATURE,
NOR DO THE CHILDREN OF MEN AS A WHOLE EXPERIENCE IT.
AVOIDING DANGER IS NO SAFER IN THE LONG
RUN THAN OUTRIGHT EXPOSURE.
LIFE IS EITHER A DARING ADVENTURE, OR NOTHING.

—Helen Keller
Let Us Have Faith (1940)

Preface

I t's strange to say that my intuition writes this story, but this is exactly what happened. By learning to connect with the deepest space within and consistently acting on intuition, this book was birthed, and along with it my understanding of my life challenges as well as the challenges and opportunities facing humanity today.

This adventure began around the New Year 2001, at a time when every important aspect of my life was threatened: my marriage, family, career, and even self-identity. To minimize my family's and my own painful predicament, it became clear that developing this relationship with my inner self was critical. I felt that intuition, rather than conventional wisdom, was the key to navigating this turbulence as solidly as possible.

Seemingly out of the blue, my friend Stacey Hentschel called to urge me to participate in a Soul Recognition Workshop she was hosting the following month at her home. The workshop was designed to support the connection with the deepest part of the self so that a greater awareness of the soul's yearnings, blueprint, and purpose for this life could be attained. Not having had much of a context for these ideas, I wasn't sure what all this meant, but, since I needed clear guidance, I decided to make the five-day course work. My three- and six-year-old girls would be on winter break part of that time, and I had friends near San Diego who had agreed to care for them while I was an hour north at Stacey's house. About three weeks later, I packed our bags and we drove the seven hours from Silicon Valley down to Southern California.

My Soul Recognition experience included a channeled reading from the Counsel of Light, who informed me that my soul's mission was to write a series of popular books on love and life—a "life series," books on how life works here—because "I was here to represent and make sense out of the frequently misrepresented and misunderstood dynamic of love." Love's design was going to explain itself to me through my experiences, and then I would share this understanding, first with young children, and then with people of every age. My purpose included bringing the truth of who we human beings really are. I was given an assignment for getting started: to look within for inner guidance, so I could discover who I was and what exactly I was to do here.

The reading took me by surprise because it was completely inconsistent with my education and self-image. I had a left-brain, technical background and was far from being a writer. Neither did I have much training in connecting to the inner self and following inner guidance. In fact, I had haphazardly and unsuccessfully searched for the source of my intuition and, up until that point, had mostly followed a path indicated by outer expectations—I had received an Ivy League education, worked in research and engineering, gotten married, and was now a full-time mother of two young girls.

Although I didn't understand the reading at first, I found the revelation about my mission fascinating. I sensed a vague stirring, like a little spark within, and it felt right enough that I couldn't simply dismiss it as nonsense. Adding to this was the recognition that I had been searching for my life's direction for a long time. The mission proposed also sounded important, not only from my own perspective, but from the larger world's as well. So despite the fact that the project seemed both ambitious and unfathomable, I set out shortly afterwards to prepare myself for a completely new phase in my life—myself as a successful author.

It wasn't an easy process at first, developing a relationship with my inner self, my heart and soul, so I could figure out what I was going to write or how this mission was to proceed. I didn't think I had any special knowledge about love or about how life actually worked here. In fact, I was failing in my marriage, and my husband and extended family railed against this crazy new idea, and for good reason too—we were low on money then. But because of the inner connection that I had begun to nurture and the interesting synchronicities that followed as a result, I persisted despite numerous obstacles. Once I began to feel strongly connected within (when my intuition was consistently confirmed through outer experiences), this book began to flow as if it had a life of its own. I simply listened and followed through on the guidance, while still maintaining the perspective of a scientist—an open-minded scientist who was now asking the universe to show her how things worked here.

In time, my experiences and intuition revealed to me the principles governing the process of life and the interconnectedness between all beings and forces in the universe. Moreover, by focusing my attention on my process in the moment, rather than on my rather ambitious future goals, step-by-step I discovered how to access the realm of intuition and creativity, as well as the flow experience— that often-elusive state of effortless extraordinariness. When even my physical environment provided me with clues and synchronicities that couldn't be ignored so that I could put the pieces together and solve the mystery of my life, and ultimately, the mystery of life in general, I became aware of having touched upon something magical. Also, I discovered that the people and circumstances related to my crisis—which I had previously viewed as obstacles to my goals—were in fact necessary catalysts for and co-creators of my broader mission of bringing this wisdom to the world. In short, I learned that there's a game called duality being played on earth and I learned how to play this game in its entirety.

I am not a trained psychologist or a spiritual leader, but an ordinary person who, in struggling to make sense of my own life, discovered ways to unfailingly access intuition, creativity, and wisdom. I also gained insight into life's greatest mysteries, so that we can now move with greater ease beyond the experience of duality that we're currently living, and can embrace interconnectedness and a greater understanding of love as the basis for a new way of life. (But, perhaps not before I infuriate people in the process.)

Through relating my own adventure of inner discovery and creative self-expression, I aspire to assist others to connect within, uncover their own life purposes, and experience the magic of interconnectedness. On a personal level, this story might seem like an adventure, but, on a more universal level, I believe it is humanity's destiny.

It took six years (and a lifetime's worth of growth) from the time I first heard about my mission to when this book was complete enough to be shared. The funny thing is, I had no idea I had all this within me. It is my hope that humanity benefits from my experience.

To manifest what was revealed to me in my reading—that I would explain love and life to young children first, I began my mission by writing a simple story for my younger daughter Julianne, who was then four. She had inspired me with her sense of adventure and her connection to the dreams in her heart. After all, what is life and love about if not the dreams in people's hearts?

Once we connect with that sacred space within and follow through on its urgings, life is indeed an amazing adventure.

A Story for Julianne

When Julianne was between three and four months old, I often placed her in a bouncy seat geared with pastel-colored toys. Whenever she managed to hit one of the toys with her little hands, it spun and jangled and she gently bounced back and forth, back and forth. This was, I thought, a good way to amuse her, as well as keep her secure.

One morning after breakfast, I put her bouncy seat on the broad kitchen counter so she could watch me as I unloaded dishes from the dishwasher and stacked them in the pantry. As I closed the pantry doors, a soft but suspicious "yip!" sound alerted me to turn around, to see what was the matter. Just in time, too, because I saw Julianne—still secure in her bouncy seat—bounce tummy-side down off the top rack of the dishwasher, straight into my arms.

Perfect catch(!) I thought, feeling startled but very relieved. I held her for a few moments, feeling grateful, while my mind pondered and speculated. And as I stood there just holding her, I became aware of a special connection between us. Wow, I thought. That's good.

But, feeling shock again, I made a mental note to toss out the bouncy seat and vowed to pay closer attention to her from that point on. I'm sure, however, that Julianne didn't concern herself with any of these things. She looked totally content just to be in my arms.

When Julianne was one, our family visited friends who owned two small bijon dogs. Julianne loved dogs. When they licked her hands and kissed her face, she laughed and squealed for more. One time, bored with the adult company, she toddled around the flower bushes and trees in the backyard, searching for the dogs.

Sneaking up on an unsuspecting pet from behind, she grabbed him and pulled hard on his tail. The poor, frightened dog spun around and nipped Julianne in the face, right between her nose and her right eye.

"Aaaahh!" she screamed. I ran over to see what was the matter. A bit of blood trickled down her cheek. We went inside to clean the owie. After I put on a Band-Aid, she stopped crying. I held her, relieved that it wasn't worse. Then I lectured her on always being cautious and gentle around dogs.

But before I was quite done with my lesson, she began to squirm out of my arms. "I go play," she said, brightening up with that thought. Apparently, this dog incident wasn't such a big deal, and she went back to exploring the backyard.

The following year, when Julianne was two and Angelika five, the three of us decided to go swimming one hot summer afternoon. Together we gathered our pool things: towels, water wings, goggles, and foam noodles. Loaded down with swim stuff, I opened the gate behind our house and Julianne, now free, dashed off in the direction of the neighborhood pool. By the time Angelika and I arrived a few seconds later, Julianne had disappeared. I was used to this, one moment to see her and the next she was gone.

First I scanned the pool, but saw no one. Then I yelled "Julianne, Julianne!" but she didn't answer. Perhaps this was just a game and she was hiding behind trees or bushes or in the neighbors' yards, I thought. But then I felt a chill creep down my spine as

I stood silent and still by the pool. Intently I scanned the area again, imagining I had the eyes of an eagle, and at the far, deep end of the pool, I spotted a little hand reaching out of the water.

I rushed over like mad, grabbed her tiny hand, and pulled her out of the water. Once she was safe in my arms, I said, while mentally noting to remain calm, "Were you trying to swim? It's not easy to swim if you haven't learned how. Angelika went to swimming school and soon you will, too, but now you must use your water wings and not get into any pool without me or Papa…." But after hearing such loving guidance, it was clear she wasn't interested in any further clarification. "I want my water wings," she said as she squirmed out of my arms, so she could get back in the pool.

Then one day when Julianne was three, unusual noise and laughter blared from the bedroom she shared with Angelika. It wasn't typical playing or even fighting noise but sounded more ambitious, like some kind of monkey business I ought to look into.

I opened the door and walked in just in time to see Julianne flying across the room, her forehead barely missing the edge of a table. By thrusting herself forward over her soft child's sofa, it rolled beneath her (though it was square) and when she cleared it, she flew.

Of course I wasn't thrilled with what I had just witnessed, though I was grateful that no one was injured. I picked her up and lectured her on safety. But after listening to my scolding, she didn't seem particularly remorseful about what she had just done. She wiggled out of my arms and returned to play (temporarily without the sofa, of course).

The next year, when Julianne was four, we planned a trip to Disneyland together with her friend Elvira and Elvira's mom, Ute.

All of us were thrilled to arrive at our hotel and discover Disney characters posing for photos at the entrance and Pluto strolling across the hotel lobby.

Once in our room, Ute assisted the three girls with bathroom breaks and unpacking while I went out to park Ute's minivan. The children refreshed, Ute stepped into the bathroom for only a minute or two before she heard some excitement outside. "I'd better check," she thought. She discovered the balcony doors wide open and Julianne hanging over the balcony railing, yelling "Hello!" and waving to a crowd of people watching from the ground floor, four floors below. Julianne was no doubt trying to get the attention of some Disney character.

Ute grabbed Julianne from the railing and in a fierce voice that children ought to heed, lectured her on safety. But from the look on Julianne's face, Ute saw that the warnings hadn't seemed to get through.

When I returned, Ute excitedly explained what happened, and that Julianne remained unfazed. But I wasn't surprised by Julianne's stunt or attitude, not anymore, anyway. A hint of a smile shone across my face because in that moment, the pattern in Julianne's behavior was finally getting through to me.

About two weeks later, this pattern confirmed itself once again when their dad took Julianne and Angelika camping in Yosemite. As usual, both girls were uncontainable by the time they finally arrived at the park. The tall mountains with their misty waterfalls and the groves of trees with their hiding places captivated them both, calling them to explore. "But first," Papa announced to the girls, "let's set up camp."

Then as he and Angelika unloaded the camping gear, Julianne slipped away. For a few moments they were unaware of her absence, until a man ran over to them shouting, "There's a little girl hanging from the top of that boulder there! Is she yours?"

It was Julianne, of course, about twelve feet up, holding on by her fingertips but looking calm. Her mountain climber dad took a running leap, scrambled up to the top on the other side, pried Julianne's hands off the rock, and lowered her legs safely into the other man's arms. "I'm sure she'll make a good climbing partner one day," he thought, holding her tight in his arms, wondering how she managed to scale that wall. Then he lectured her on being safe. But his impression, too, was "What's all this fuss about, Papa?"

"Okay Papa, I hear you," she finally said, and with that she went to help set up camp.

By this time it was easy to see that Julianne was blessed with some very special gifts: she was open to things new and unfamiliar, she followed her heart, lived in the moment, took risks, and had fun. She trusted herself and her world, regardless of what anyone said. The little setbacks did not really set her back. Moreover, she seemed to be so connected to her inner and outer worlds that she got what she needed at the moment she needed it. Her guardian angels always came through. With these gifts, I have no doubt she will follow her joy and live her dreams. I have no doubt she will live her life as a daring adventure. And who am I to say otherwise?

Self-Reflection

Some set sail for adventure,
only to discover that the greatest longings
are met within the heart
—*Lisa A. Blowers*

Several months had gone by and I thought this was it—"A Story for Julianne" was the one I would share with the world. I thought it expressed what I wanted to say about love and connection with the inner self and I thought it was now ready for critique from, say, a preschool teacher, a friend with a knack for words, and a family psychologist I had recently met at a party, before I'd pursue trying to get it published. Because I had some apprehension about it, I wanted the honest opinion of others, especially the family psychologist's.

For one thing, creative expression wasn't my strength. I didn't do creative writing, just as I didn't paint or sketch. In fact, I still felt somewhat irritated and incomplete with my writing experiences in college. All freshmen in the Engineering College were required to take two writing seminars, supposedly because we had horrible writing skills—at least that was the standing joke. Then there was the significant disparity between my verbal and math SAT scores. Another time, a fellow student remarked that I had the "accent of someone who didn't speak very much," the result, no doubt, of having lived in Poland for the first few years of my life and having immigrant parents who spoke only Polish.

After assessing these facts, I had enrolled in an archaeology writing seminar, expecting assignments to be of a scientific nature where, using reason and logic, I'd write about such things as the material remains of human life and activities, rather than flowery descriptions of sunsets or, heaven forbid, anything to do with my feelings. I was very reserved and quite shy.

So when I had dragged out a few paragraphs for that first archaeology paper, I went straight up to the boys' floor in my dormitory on West Campus to find a kind-looking English major I had met during Orientation Week for my first peer review. I could have asked the women on my own floor but wanted to spare myself some embarrassment.

He read the first paragraph and then, one sentence at a time, slowly and painstakingly scrutinized the placement of each word and punctuation mark. I tried to listen despite his words being blocked out by voices in my head blaring, "I don't have time for this! This will take forever! Forget it!" It wasn't exactly what I had expected—spending so much time on a few paragraphs when math and physics assignments were more important.

I let him finish his lesson and thanked him, but I didn't return for further clarification. Instead, I had resigned myself to struggling on my own by modeling my writing after the assigned reading. My first paper earned a C-, but I followed the teacher's suggestions and eventually ended up with a B in the course.

Also during my college years, I had tried to journal but got nowhere. Dissatisfied with my inadequate efforts, I promptly tore out every page I wrote. In my early teens, keeping a diary had been simple but it seemed impossible in college, as if my expectations and tendency to self-criticism had skyrocketed. Maybe it was because life suddenly became more demanding and so full of choices I wasn't clear about how to make, and I wasn't sure who I was when suddenly faced with some freedom.

I was envious of my physicist boyfriend Matt's journal, which he displayed on his tidy bookshelf. Matt recorded his daily impressions, created fantasies about dwarves and other subterranean beings for his Dungeons and Dragons games, and even wrote me love poetry. But in my dorm room, a growing stack of mutilated journals lined the bookshelf like empty bottles in an alcoholic's liquor cabinet. When each journal began to look ragged with torn pages, I bought another one. Then with a perfectly clean slate I started anew, hoping that this time I'd get it right and my writing would blossom, taking my life along with it.

I didn't understand my behavior back then. Perhaps I wanted to jump from point A to point B without having to live the learning part in between. Perhaps I knew that keeping a journal would somehow help me better achieve my potential. Maybe this is why, even years later, I couldn't totally abandon my desire to write creative prose.

After about six years of working as a research and process engineer, I enrolled in a creative writing class the summer before graduate school. For the final assignment, I handed in a short story about a national park camping adventure from New York to California and back that I had shared a few years before with my then new boyfriend W. and two of his friends from Munich. (For privacy reasons, I'm calling him W. for short.)

The adventure began when W.'s friend Michael ignored my request to bring a small, collapsible duffle bag of personal belongings because the trunk of my Honda Prelude was tiny. Michael flew in to the Chicago airport with a hard Samsonite bag filled with music and business attire, amongst other things. At the airport curb, the two engineering guys unpacked the car and arranged and rearranged but couldn't make everything fit, so they decided my personal-sized cooler had to go. I was infuriated and I was right and it was my car, and there were still four weeks to go....

Although I received a good grade for that story, afterwards I found it superficial, as if it were missing something, and I didn't know how to remedy it. So what if they had made me wade through the hip-deep Virgin River in the narrows of Zion canyon dodging slippery rocks with an expensive new Nikon around my neck for what seemed like several miles. Big deal. Bleh. Disgusted once again, I was glad to put the writing idea behind me.

Several years later, I found myself writing again, this time quite unexpectedly. I had enrolled Angelika into the Los Gatos-Saratoga Observation Nursery School, or Mountain School as it was called, an alternative school for preschool-aged children situated in the dreamy foothills of Los Gatos, California. While observing class, parents were expected to write reports about their children's temperament and physical and emotional development.

For my first report on Angelika's fine and gross motor skills, I wrote "great eye-hand coordination—check!" What could I have possibly added, not having attended courses in child development? But the teacher insisted I fill up two entire pages, so I had no choice but to get creative. And over a few weeks I got the hang of it: I paid close attention to the children and recorded my observations—their personal interactions and their possible thoughts as they, for instance, hammered golf tees into pumpkins, strung necklaces three feet long, or created art with shaving cream. And over four years, I received a few compliments from teachers and some parents.

So there it is, my creative writing past. Hardly any evidence that I should now devote myself to writing. Clearly I lacked what it took to be a good writer—the right education, the right background, and the right experience. So now, I was going to write not just one but a series of popular books on love and intuition and connecting with the inner self and how life works here, was I? It didn't make much sense.

But my Soul Recognition experience must have had me convinced that I would, that I should now forge straight ahead, though I seem to recall that I only enrolled in it in the first place to *develop* my intuition so it would help me cope with and straighten out the things that didn't work in my own life: my love relationship, for one. But that is *the* paradox, isn't it?

The main purpose of the Soul Recognition Workshop, led by Flo Aeveia Magdalena, was to open up to and recognize the soul's nudging and yearnings, thereby helping one access inner wisdom for personal growth and everyday guidance, which in turn helps the remembering of one's blueprint, or true purpose for being here right now—because right now the time is auspicious for humanity's growth and evolution. It seems like a simple enough idea, but when I did the course back in February 2001, it was like trying to grasp Einstein's theory of relativity for the first time.

Unlike academic courses, this workshop was experiential and consisted of guided meditation, exercises for connecting with the soul, including the use of expressive arts such as music and dance. Finally, once the group felt cohesive and connected, individuals took turns becoming the center of attention, during which time they benefited from the group's energy and insights. For five whole days, a group of thirteen engaged in this work at my friend Stacey's house.

At the course, a few people came up to me in private and suggested that I begin journaling to help me connect to my soul and its purpose. "There's something valuable within you that needs to come out in the open," said one participant. "You were very powerful in Celtic times," said another. Then during my individual focus, while I was under deep hypnosis, I heard Flo comment, "She's very pure." Another participant, a strong-voiced jazz singer named Brigitte Secard, told me that while I was under hypnosis, I kept saying to her, "Please help me with my voice, help me with my voice!" Flo also asked me to write, sketch, and spend time in nature to help make my soul's unfolding a bit easier, though being new to such ideas, I didn't grasp what all this meant. I didn't know what I had within me, what exactly I was to do and why, what was to unfold, or what this supposed purity was about. (Purity? Ha! My husband would have used the word naïveté instead.) I did love the feeling though, of connecting to my inner self, my soul. So a month later I made a phone appointment with Flo to receive what was to be the first of several readings channeled from the Counsel of Light to further guide my process, during which I was told that I would become a popular writer. I wasn't sure who the Counsel of Light were, only that they were from a higher dimension and were highly regarded by participants who had previously received soul readings. A year and a half later I began to work on "A Story for Julianne" and consequently began to manifest according to the Counsel of Light's guidance. I felt this story had potential; at least it might cause some people to think, as it certainly had caused me to think. And I liked that.

There was another strong motive besides: Julianne started kindergarten the next fall and I needed to find my calling. For years, thinking about my career had made me panic. This new idea of writing appealed to me. I thought that once I integrated some feedback and added a couple concluding paragraphs to the story, my first book for children would be complete and part of my soul's mission would be accomplished.

There was much more to come, of course; it's just that I didn't see it at the time. At first I believed I had written a story about my daughter, or the nature of children perhaps, but it had nothing to do with me. I continued to think this even as questions such as "Well, what about you, Christine? Are you living your life fully? It's your turn now, isn't it?" popped up in my psyche. But I remained in denial; this was after all a children's story. Besides, who in the world would be interested in me anyway? I thought my inner voice wasn't making any sense; I thought it was completely in error.

But destiny had other plans and did not care what I thought. The still small voice inside persisted, and the feeling that my daughter was trying to get my attention so she could teach me something valuable would not go away, though I tried my best to ignore it. Then it dawned on me that as long as I ignored my inner voice, Julianne would continue to try to get my attention in her own special way. So then I couldn't ignore it any longer

When I faced up to the situation, simply by asking myself, "Okay, what is she trying to teach me?" a number of questions popped into my mind, as if they had been waiting patiently for me to be ready to hear them: Have I been living my life fully? What does that mean, really? How does that look? What are the qualities associated with that kind of life? What are the rewards? Is there a tried and true method for this? How would I know I was doing it? And, what does all this mean for me?

With these questions in mind, I began to examine my life. The first thing that made itself clear was my struggle to find and trust my inner voice. As an adult, at a time when a person ought to have a strong sense of self and of solid purpose, I was still searching for that within myself, trying to discover that peace that comes from the knowing that I was deeply rooted in my self and following my true direction. I also became aware that there was an important but missing piece to my life, but I didn't know how to find it.

Then I remembered a time nearly twenty years before when, at the suggestion of an enthusiastic friend from work named Dave, I had tried out a popular faith that claimed to help you find the Creator's "will for your life." That suggested that everyone had his/her own unique plan, and I had wanted to know mine. Before Dave revealed this new information, I wasn't aware that God had specific, detailed plans for people's lives; the idea intrigued and startled me. I thought perhaps if I knew my true life plan, I'd make fewer mistakes and avoid the disasters that seemed to haunt my life at the time.

This significant discovery came shortly after receiving my Ivy League degree, when I was disillusioned with my job as a process engineer of high precision, high frequency quartz crystal resonators; was trying to let go of a depressing college relationship, and was experiencing many fiascos with my car. The old used Datsun I had purchased for my move to Long Island had begun breaking down and had also been broken into twice, when I had left it at the Huntington train station on my way to New York City. The second time the thief had shattered the auxiliary window on the driver's side and made off with my main source of entertainment then—my knitting project—as the radio had already been swiped. Thus during a freezing East Coast winter I had a hole where the window used to be. In addition, during a heavy snowstorm driving home from work, my car's windshield wipers had refused to work and, due to the buildup of snow, forced me to pull over to the side of the road, where a three-foot ditch swallowed up my car. Luckily for me, I hadn't managed to get far from work. I didn't have close friends or family nearby, and I wasn't comfortable where I lived. I seriously thought it was high time to do something about my sorry car and the sorry state of my life—get a brand-new car and a brand-new life, perhaps one with a greater purpose.

But, I thought back then, just because all this bad stuff was happening didn't mean that I would faithfully promise to follow God's plan precisely, for I didn't know what God had in store for me or whether those choices would be congruent with mine. There were some things I knew I wouldn't do—like become a missionary or join a convent, for instance. But I was curious and open, and thought that simply knowing this plan would make life easier and more rewarding.

Some months later, Dave shared another astonishing thing—that he was intuitive and knew I would help a lot of people by doing something new in the future. The idea of this intrigued me—helping others seemed so admirable—but I wondered how *that* was going to happen given the sorry state of my life. Well, I had a new car by then, but other things were the same. Besides, I knew nothing about this new thing I would supposedly do, so how could he, who barely knew me? Further, it's a little disturbing when others claim to know things about you that you yourself don't know. You wonder how and why this information had been kept from you, and if it is real. You become afraid to hear more, in case of bad news. But he seemed so sure, so smug about his prophecy.

Anyway, I developed a passion to learn more about myself and why my life seemed like such a struggle. So once when I was alone in the house, as an experiment in self-examination I studied myself in a mirror. I had been crying and my eyes were all red and puffy and I wanted to figure myself out—the eyes are the mirror of your inner state, the window to the soul, I had heard.

Looking into my own eyes, I relaxed and stared deep into them, as though I were trying to hypnotize myself. This exercise seemed soothing, so I did it for several minutes, trying to go deeper and deeper with each progressive minute. And what I then sensed frightened me and I immediately backed off because, for an instant, I imagined I felt the soul of a famous biblical figure, an ancient figure despised by humanity.

How unoriginal, how clichéd, I thought. It made some sense, too, I realized: I was raised Catholic and Catholics were always wrestling inner demons. It's just that I seemed to have picked a famous one to wrestle with, that's all. Yeah, right. Then I realized this made no sense whatsoever and dismissed this incident as a fabrication of my inventive mind as well as my religious conditioning, and I never mentioned it to anyone, not even Dave. Then out of sincere motivation I attended a few evangelical Protestant services that Dave recommended in order to discover my true life plan, even though, having grown up attending Catholic school, I had been well warned about Protestants, and even though it was religion itself that I was wary about.

But after a few services, rereading the Bible with new interest and studying a booklet or two on the topic of God's plan for individuals' lives, my enthusiasm fizzled. For one thing, I didn't seem to be any closer to discovering my life plan. Also, the experience didn't lift up my heart, and I wasn't moved. I must sound like an awful stickler, demanding and exacting, but I remember thinking that some passages in the Bible seemed to be confused, not necessarily confusing as much as confused, as if something were missing. Having lived through eight years of Catholic grade school with its daily mass, I had seen it all before and had expected more. After all, as people learn and grow, they're ready for more truth and more wisdom. The other thing was, where was the sense of humor? Biblical characters—Jesus included—must have had *huge* senses of humor to keep themselves from going mad, and this sense of humor was completely missing.

I'll insert a caveat here and admit it's entirely possible that I failed to notice something important. I know that sometimes I'm able to grasp new ideas and insights because I'm open and ready for them and other times I can't and I try to have compassion for that. But beyond the surface differences a fundamental sameness pervaded both systems of belief—believe in God and his son, Jesus, your Savior (you need someone to save you because you are too flawed and unworthy to do this yourself); adhere to some ground rules; and be rewarded with eternal life in heaven. Anyway, I failed to see how Protestant doctrine was foundationally different from Catholic doctrine, though I have witnessed both sides arguing otherwise. In my freshman dorm in college, with some Campus Crusaders for Christ as witnesses, for instance, I had ritually repeated the formula for receiving salvation—just for the fun of it—although I wasn't willing to acknowledge that I wasn't already connected to Christ or that saying those words made any difference whatsoever.

Well, I had expected more, is all. I yearned for something real, my life plan for here and now. Anyway, no need to look further in a place of worship. And although it was the mid-eighties and Eastern spiritual traditions were popular in the West, I was so turned off that I didn't pursue these either. From the looks of the world, it wasn't too farfetched to conclude that all belief systems were fundamentally similar. Surface variations existed, but it all came down to being rewarded in heaven, or in the next life, or simply accepting what is (resignation sometimes masquerading as enlightenment). In fact, how could they be otherwise? Was there a place on earth where people led fulfilled, satisfying lives? Was there a place where human beings lived in peace and harmony with themselves and with their neighbors? By the age of twenty-five, I thought I had abandoned spirituality and the search for my life plan. Then about fifteen years later, these same issues were resurfacing in my life, this time with much greater urgency.

∞

Next I reflected even further, on the times I had taken risks, had gone on exotic adventures, and had accomplished my goals—which I thought determined who I was and whether I had lived my life fully. I had been class valedictorian in high school and had received a degree in materials science and engineering from Cornell University. This means I studied all about solids—metals, glass, ceramics, concrete—the concrete things of life. Interestingly, Stephen L. Sass, my freshman advisor, later wrote a book titled *The Substance of Civilization*, where he shows how substances and civilization have *evolved together* from the Stone Age to the age of silicon. That's saying that matter and consciousness have evolved together through time.

When I first entered college, I thought I was going to study chemical engineering. But then one time when I went into Professor Sass's office to complain about schoolwork, he showed me a framed micrograph of a metallurgical specimen. I was sitting in a chair across from his messy desk, sharing with him all my troubles: my mother, my self-identity, everything; I was on the verge of crying, tears welled up in my eyes. The next moment he was holding up this photo, telling me how the properties of materials are determined by their internal structure, their internal order. That was it. I switched my major to materials science shortly thereafter, but the significance of this statement escaped my notice until many years later, after I finally began making sense of my life.

To my relatives, my degree seemed like a major achievement, considering that my parents hadn't completed high school due to economic conditions in rural, eastern Poland. My mother, in fact, didn't even attend secondary school, but began an apprenticeship as a seamstress after grade school. My achievement validated the dreams my parents had had when they immigrated to the United States for better opportunities, including education for their children.

Further, it had seemed like fate that I had been admitted to Cornell. I was the oldest of six children and Mom had not wanted me to go away to school, though I had begged her. I wanted to leave the Polish neighborhood on the east side of Buffalo where we lived and expand my horizons culturally and intellectually. My parents socialized with Polish neighbors and friends, bought food from Polish grocers, had their taxes done by Polish accountants, and attended Catholic mass led by Polish priests. Father found a job as a machinist—where a number of other Polish guys worked—making precision punches and remained in that same company until he retired more than thirty-five years later. As an immigrant who was not well integrated into American culture, Mom didn't really trust it and wanted to keep me under her protective eye. Also, she seemed always worried about my reputation and implied I seemed "easy" around boys. This confused me, as it looked quite obvious to me that my education was my highest priority.

Reputation? I suppose I did have a strange one. Once in seventh or eighth grade, I don't remember which, I had discovered that some classmates called me "Spock." I only found this out because a notebook had been passed around where you answered personal questions about yourself and other kids using a number to identify yourself. I remember being confused about this nickname and began to worry that my ears were too big, too, even though nobody had ever said anything to me about my ears.

Mom was a character. Once in early adolescence I asked her why she had so many children—six children in almost eight years was a lot even in the sixties (there was one set of twins). I was curious because as the eldest I was expected to help care for them. I had changed diapers, watched over siblings, translated letters from school, studied bus routes and maps and took my mother and siblings all over the Buffalo metropolitan area—all this from around the age of eight. Why did I have to be stuck with it?

"That was your father's doing," she said in Polish, her face showing that she didn't want to discuss this topic any further. My father wanted all these kids? Well, he had hardly ever missed a day of work in his life just so he could clothe and feed them so it must have been true. But didn't being Catholic have anything to do with it? Mom and I didn't have many open and frank conversations, so I spent a lot of my time wondering about life.

Anyway, I was a stubborn child who couldn't relate to her old worldview about how young women were supposed to behave (we needed to be more protected, had to come home earlier than our brothers) and so we didn't get along very well. I wanted the freedom to do what I wanted because I was a sovereign human being. From my point of view, gender didn't enter into the equation of my choices.

In fact, just expressing my inner feelings, my inner truth about mundane things had the potential to throw her off balance. Saying something as innocent as "Mom, I really don't care what the neighbors think about the kinds of curtains we display in our front window. Actually, I don't care what the neighbors think about much of anything," could upset her. (My parents had been discussing buying new curtains. Mom had wanted elaborate, custom-made ones and asked my opinion.) Moments later, she was on the sofa weeping, asking God what she had done to deserve this kind of treatment. I didn't understand. It's not as if I had done something. I didn't even get a chance at doing anything, except for school stuff and part-time work and chores at home. It was gut-wrenching awful, seeing her weep because of what I said about myself, about my values, and perhaps about my own frustrations with her behavior, particularly that she was much too concerned with what others thought.

Well, I did care what certain people thought about certain things—my grades, for instance. But that's part of what kept me going, what gave me hope and faith in my future. Anyway, I wanted to leave home so I could freely determine the course of my life. But since I had little money for college and Mom was against me going away, I was stuck in Buffalo. I moped around a lot my senior year in high school, aware I was letting part of me die. Then one day my horticulture teacher Mr. Nuwer stopped me in the hall and asked which colleges I had applied to.

"Uh, I just applied to Buffalo State. I think I'll stay here my first year and apply to other schools for next year," I muttered.

"Come with me," he said as he took me by the hand and marched me into the guidance counselor's office. "Would you please give Christine an application to Cornell and help her fill it out right now?" Mr. Nuwer asked the guidance counselor.

Amazed, I didn't question him or recite a list of my considerations but just filled out the application, wrote an essay that evening, got all the other necessary materials together and mailed it all a couple days later. And though it was almost two months after the application deadline, I was admitted, with a partial scholarship too.

Mom's reaction to my acceptance at Cornell surprised me—she was delighted that I had been admitted to a school with such a good reputation. Obviously, it was the neighbors who informed her of what a good school it really was. Isn't it just marvelous though, how your whole perspective changes when you learn something new? Naturally, my siblings didn't have to argue with her about going away to school. She almost pushed them out the door.

Another accomplishment was my work in Germany, which I attribute to a course called "The Forum" (presently called "The Landmark Forum"). While still working at my process engineering job after college, I attended an introduction to The Forum one evening about a year or so after my evangelical adventures. This workshop promised to improve effectiveness and satisfaction in all the important areas of life—career, relationships, family, and personal development—through the setting of specific, tangible goals, as well as the process of group inquiry. Group inquiry was helpful because it revealed often unquestioned and unacknowledged (and thus unconscious) attitudes about life, about people, about self, about anything. By listening to participants dialogue with the course leader, people realized that some of their personal attitudes and beliefs weren't necessarily true, which enabled insights and new possibilities to come through that previously were blocked by those beliefs, thus making it easier to achieve goals in the end.

Although The Forum leaders didn't specifically advertise that the questioning of beliefs was part of their work, they focused on distinguishing the domains of "what happened" versus "what you made it mean," which is similar. On the board in front of the course room, The Forum leader represented these domains as two non-intersecting circles, showing that often they had nothing to do with one another.

Like learning Einstein's theory again, at first it was difficult to grasp what The Forum was really about, as though the idea was so outside the scope of what was familiar that the connections to where that kind of information would be stored in your brain hadn't yet been made and you had to build new neural pathways for it to sink in. It required some work. But recognizing a particular belief system as one of many alternative ways of viewing things, in other words as *just another* system of belief rather than *this is the way things are,* was an important beginning step in my growth process. I experienced firsthand how, as you let go of conditionings, new possibilities come into your awareness and the old belief systems no longer impede progress toward reaching your goals. Of course, this is my current viewpoint and not necessarily the last word on this topic.

No one had to convince me that this was exactly what I had been looking for. Also, there was something about the woman who led the introduction. Though she was bombarded by a roomfull of skeptics wanting to know *exactly* what the course was about and *exactly* what happened there, she responded with quiet authority and remained poised and graceful under pressure, and I wanted that. Yet in spite of all these good qualities and my good intentions, when I mentioned that I was going to participate in The Forum to my colleagues at work, they were not supportive. Several even warned me that I was going to be brainwashed. But my heart beat hard with excitement at the thought of questioning and releasing the old and coming up with something new, so of course I went.

Interestingly, even before I participated in The Forum I had set several goals for myself and committed them to paper on the course registration sheet: to have adventure in my life, a fulfilling new job, and a satisfying long-term relationship. And indeed, it was around this time that I began to envision the possibility of working in Germany after meeting the engineering student from Munich named W. He was completing an internship where I worked. Also interesting is that I stayed at this job as long as I did—just to meet him, I am sure.

He was tall, very handsome, and an adventurer. I was enthralled. I invited him to a birthday party I gave for my sister Lydia and after that, W. and I started doing things together. Sometimes we drove down to Jones Beach at night, where he took off his clothes and jumped in the ocean for a swim. As a kid, nothing had scared me more than deep water. I was terrified of open bodies of water like the ocean, especially at night when you can't see a thing. So I just stood there, holding his shorts.

There was just one little thing: he needed to return to Munich to complete his electrical engineering degree. That's when we came up with the idea of my working in Germany. After he left, I took one semester of German at the local college and secured two possible job contacts in Munich from an old Materials Science professor. My plan was to enroll in an intensive two-month language course at the Goethe Institute in Munich (committing the money beforehand made sure I didn't chicken out) and then fly to Munich as a tourist, after which I would apply for a student visa, then find a job before the student visa ran out. Once I had a job, I would arrange all the necessary legal formalities.

Thrilled with this strategy, I shared it with colleagues at work but, to my astonishment, they weren't supportive at all. They warned me about my need for a work permit: Germany would make me return and apply for proper documents from the States. Everyone knew that Germans were famous for timeliness and correct procedure, besides having a high unemployment rate at the time. Also I had my own concerns, one of which was that I might not have the right experience.

But I had been cautioned all my life and now that I had some freedom, why would I let anyone tell me what to do?—especially since my advisers had never worked overseas. Thanks to The Forum, I also had learned that everyone has a different perspective on life, and mine was just as valid as anyone else's. The potential of my plan plainly depended on perspective—the outcome was unknowable, was unbounded, was subject to my thoughts and intentions and actions. It wasn't set in stone. Besides, W., whom I admired, supported my idea. And that was enough.

As they say: I knew what I needed to do. I proceeded with my plan and flew to Munich. Though voices in my head blared, "What the hell are you doing here, Christine?" over and over and over again as I waited by the baggage claim for my luggage, they began to subside as soon as I spotted W. He was in the back of the crowd, holding a single rose. Funny, how quickly the sight of the Beloved defends against terror. As he drove me through the outskirts of Munich, I stared at the fields as they lay bare in early February, allowing the peace of this bareness to calm me and reassure me that what I was doing was going to work out.

I stayed in the apartment W. shared with two other students until I found a place to live. About two months later, near the end of the language course, I signed a one-year contract to be a member of the staff in experimental physics at the *Ludwig-Maximilians* University in Munich. There, I would assist a physics professor and his thesis candidates by analyzing ceramic superconductors.

Ceramic superconductors were a hot topic at the time. Below certain temperatures, they exhibit no resistance to the flow of electricity, allowing for zero loss of energy. Research groups throughout the world searched for ceramic formulae that exhibited zero resisitivity at increasingly higher temperatures. The job was exactly what I had been looking for, and the German administrators promptly granted me a work permit after I had signed a contract with my employer.

Having grown up suppressed and overprotected, I was now learning what expansion was like. On weekends I could visit the Bavarian Alps with W. and, after hiking uphill for hours, enjoy *Linsensuppe* and beer at one of the many *Alpenverein* huts while admiring the array of mountains and clouds below. I could drink *Doppelbock* or *Weissbier* at a monastery, take a train to Lucerne or Prague, drive to Italy or France for Carnival or a short vacation, mingle with students from all over the world at German language courses, and take controversial personal growth seminars in a foreign language. I could order wild duck and *Kartoffelknoedel* for dinner, wander around historic towns on Sundays, could be whoever I wanted to be and this would bother no one. Before, I felt myself fenced into a small square, but now the world was my meadow. It was wonderful!

Something in me knew that W. was the one. I felt a level of comfort with him that I hadn't experienced with anyone else. At the same time, I knew he would never let me just sit around, but that's the way I wanted it—I wanted to be challenged, to learn new things, to have adventure in my life. And although he had communicated back in the States that he would never get married or have a family, somehow I knew not to take what he said too literally.

Not long after he completed his studies in electrical engineering, we moved to Santa Clara County, California, where we looked for jobs. I quickly found a job at the Philips Research and Development Center in a company called Signetics, selected by my Austrian boss because of the experience I had gained in Germany—emphasizing how fortuitous my decision to work there had been.

A few days later, after we both had job offers, W. surprised me by proposing. "Let's get married tomorrow," he said. That evening we ordered champagne at a restaurant with David and Darrah, a couple we had recently met. "So what are we celebrating?" they asked.

"We have a surprise," W. said.

David and Darrah glanced knowing smiles at each other and at us. "You're getting engaged," Darrah sighed.

"Close, we're getting married tomorrow. Want to be our witnesses? W. said. They thought we were a blast. (Presumably, conventional wisdom advises women to *always* take men at their word, especially in the case of personal relationships—except of course for those times when it doesn't apply.)

The next day, on April 20, 1990, we got married before a San Jose city judge. Then we took off for a few days of camping in King's Canyon National Park. From a pay phone at the park, W. called Xilinx to accept the position he had been offered. Life looked so promising.

And just as I knew he would, he continued to involve me in many learning experiences. For example, he taught me how to downhill ski in one day, convincing me to go from the bunny hill directly to the intermediate run because, "by European standards, it looked like a beginner's run." "You can do it. I know you can, just disregard the signs," he said. Disregard the signs? Yeah, sure! I thought. But although I ranted and cried the first time down, I made it to the bottom undamaged and skied the hill several more times that day, of my own free will.

He was skeptical of conventional thought and rules, preferring to rely on his own experience, and this is the only kind of man I could have lived with. I was also amazed by his ability to handle difficult situations, no matter where we were. Once driving through Mexico, he defiantly refused to pay fines to cops who unfairly stopped us for running a red light we had never run, who ignored other cars that went through the lights after us. "Take us to the station, and we'll pay you there," W. said to the officer.

"What are you thinking?" I thought. I hadn't planned on a visit with the Mexican police as part of our vacation. Then he asked me to write down the officer's badge number, and when I started writing, the officer blurted out, "Okay, no problem." After a verbal warning, they let us go. This happened twice.

During that same trip I learned firsthand how appearances could be deceiving and the mind could easily be tricked into believing things that weren't necessarily true. One night while we were driving, I looked to my right and suddenly saw another two-lane highway exactly parallel to the one we were on, which was strange because this was undeveloped Mexico and we were in the back country. "Look W., a parallel highway," I informed him. "That's odd, it's not even on the map. What a waste of taxpayer money…." Then a few seconds later we saw something else that was weird: a car appearing to be in our lane was heading towards us. It took only a second to realize that we weren't on any sort of parallel highway at all but were driving on the wrong side of the road. W. found a spot to get off the road and pull over to the proper side—lucky for us because until then, hills had divided the highway, making it impossible to cross over or even see the other side.

Then after a stop in the Yucatan and a few days in Belize, W. sold the used car we had bought, just for this trip, to a local government official in Belize City. (We had heard this transaction was supposedly illegal.) From there, we hopped on a bus headed to Guatemala, the bus teeming with life and filled to the brim like no other bus

I've encountered my entire life: inside was a double layer of people, though this wasn't a two-tiered London-style bus but a retired school bus from the U.S. Some folks sat regular-style with feet planted on the floor, while others took advantage of the interstitial spaces by crouching on the backs of the chairs—similar to how atoms naturally arrange themselves close-packing style in crystalline solids. I witnessed firsthand how people could get really creative when the need arose, and I wouldn't have traded the learning experience for a day of lying at the beach.

On yet another excursion, we awakened in sleeping bags to the delightful sounds of cowbells and the voices of shepherds tending livestock in the back country of Turkey. We had crashed in the field because we hadn't been able to find a hotel the night before. I remember feeling so peaceful but also slightly embarrassed as the shepherds shooed the cows away and let us be. The diversity of this planet astounded me, yet I felt a palpable sense of familiarity—as though I were lying in my own backyard. For someone who grew up like I did—overprotected in a rather monochromatic part of Buffalo—experiencing all this adventure and the diversity of other cultures with a man I loved and admired was like being in heaven.

After I reflected on these things, the following words flowed clearly and forcefully into my consciousness: "Yes, I was overprotected but at the same time I had to grow up fast, which was a challenge for me. I was the oldest of six and had to help in the way that older children have to help when the parents don't speak the language and don't know the ins and outs of the country in which they live. And I had to help care for and pave the way for my brothers and sisters, as first-borns often do." After I wrote these words on paper and took a much-needed food break, I heard my inner voice say, "Now replace the word 'country' with the word 'universe,'" and I recognized this was a clue to my life purpose for right now. (It's funny how my inner voice often announced important things when I took a bathroom or food break.)

∞

Because my travels had broadened my perspective on world problems, when Signetics closed its doors barely a year after I started my job, I was inspired to begin graduate work in environmental studies and majored in alternative and renewable forms of energy such as electric- and hydrogen-powered vehicles—my thesis topic. The many possibilities included energy efficiency and conservation, energy policy, and alternative and renewable forms of energy. I knew the energy field was right for me, but for some reason my psyche resisted being boxed in to one specialty. I knew that something was up, for instance, when I presented a paper on the methods used to determine the role of UV radiation on the incidence of skin cancer. My behavior back then earned me funny looks from some classmates, but it hadn't exactly helped that I had developed a mental block and then racked my brain trying to discuss methods of hypothesis testing in the context of the generation of alternative energy. In any case, after a while all my career choices seemed flat and monotone and nothing stood out from the rest. Even my thesis topic had begun to bore me by the time I wrote the first draft. Yet I couldn't give up the hope that once I stumbled upon my specialty, I would know.

Luckily for me, Angelika was born several months before I defended my thesis, and Julianne was born three years afterwards. My children's births exemplified perfection in timing because they staved off the day I'd have to make real decisions about what to do with my life. And for a while, the confusion and uneasiness around my life path could be safely tucked into a drawer in my mind and avoided like a bad-news letter.

But not for too long. It became more and more apparent that regardless of what my life looked like from the outside, it wasn't enough. Though I seemed to have everything a woman could want—a high-caliber, adventurous husband and two beautiful, healthy children, a comfortable home in sunny California, a good education, and a few good friends—was this it? Was this all there was? My accomplishments, though they had meant something at the onset, were scattered and not fully realized. And as the years rolled by, in spite of my preoccupation with daily matters, I knew that something important was missing, something I hadn't even begun to tap into yet. I felt incomplete, was mildly dissatisfied, and knew I wasn't living my life fully.

W. noticed my lack of ambition and lukewarm spirits and complained, especially since I had "the advantages of a good education and all kinds of resources at my disposal," as he put it. He also said that I didn't have my priorities straight and was dissatisfied because I was unchallenged in a major way. He was an electronics engineer in the marketing and applications of hardware/software emulation systems—complex, real-time circuit-testing tools for designers—and he was brilliant at determining systems problems. Unfortunately for me though, he also saw what didn't work in me. Well, I couldn't argue with him about that.

He wanted me happy, and it must have been frustrating for him to see my spirits low, but I also knew I didn't want to work simply to spin the wheels of commerce. Also, it wasn't that I didn't want to make a career decision but that each time I considered one, I felt disheartened immediately. A sinking, sickening, uneasy feeling would grow in the center of my body, along with a plummet in energy, almost like depression. It was a real bummer, and I began to worry about what was going on with me.

Yet when I developed new interests, like a business idea I had once, I noticed that I became energized. However, after a while that same sinking feeling returned and I knew that at most, these ideas were only a temporary distraction. "I can't see myself sticking with this for very long," I heard myself telling my friend Stacey. "I want to finally begin my real work, whatever that is."

It really seemed like I didn't want to limit myself or my options. Crazy though it may sound, it's as if I wanted to work on everything, all at once. But how? Besides, who was I to expect my life work to meet my personal set of requirements—passion, broadness of scope, opportunities to learn and to make a difference in the world, a connection with nature and the environment, and flexibility besides? Again, I didn't understand what my inner promptings were trying to communicate. They made little sense to me.

Over time, I became more aware of the inner dimension to life and began to see that I had mainly searched for purpose and gratification outside of myself, which could never give me what I truly yearned for: inner fulfillment. It also became clear that for much of my life, I had tried to compensate through external activities for what was missing inside. There was a fundamental separation on the inner level that I began to understand only later. Outside accolades and adventures—no matter how fun or admirable—could never give me the kind of satisfaction that comes from knowing that I was living my true course. There isn't anything *wrong* with them, but for me they weren't the main event. I also saw the formula I had previously used for success in life—setting specific goals and forging ahead with them—as empty and meaningless, besides no longer very effective.

Before I contemplated these things, I didn't know whether I was following my heart, what that really meant, how exactly to go about it, and what was possible when my inner core guided me in the moment. But how could I have known when no one provided that example for me? When it really wasn't okay to follow your heart's desire, when the subject was rife with confusion and grayness? I had lived most of my life unaware of these things, until some pivotal events occurred and I had no choice but to follow my guidance in order to make it through. Then the truth of my life began to be revealed and everything began to click into place.

The Hard Part

YOUR VISION WILL BECOME CLEAR ONLY
WHEN YOU LOOK INTO YOUR HEART.
—*Carl Jung*

Although initially I strongly resisted writing what I am about to reveal, processing through my life crises ultimately illuminated the mysteries of my life, and then the mysteries of life in general. Working through despair and dread is difficult enough in private, but you feel like such a fink when you drag loved ones into the picture and bare all to the world. I was disgusted to be a part of what I had perceived as madness.

I felt chagrin as well at the thought of having a life crammed with events I couldn't make any sense of. So although I knew that sharing my story was the right thing to do, all I wanted to reveal at first was the following paragraph. I thought it was sufficient for leapfrogging all the way to the next, slightly lighter (and more enlightened) portion of my story:

"The details of my predicament are not that important. They don't matter, really, for they're not the crux of my story. If you must know though, imagine that my crisis could be any combination of problems, one on top of another. Recall the things that hadn't worked in your own life and list your favorites right here. As far as *my* story is concerned, it's enough for me to say that it sucked."

But when the earliest draft of this book was almost complete, it began to dawn on me on a hike one morning that I was walking around with a teeny tiny little molecule of a *fuck you* aimed at the world in general, and at two people in particular. And it became slightly obvious that it was both irresponsible and very selfish of me to withhold such an essential part of my story—the interesting life experiences from which others could learn, and the contributions of those who were critical in helping me resolve *the* most important search of my life. During my hike that morning, the fog in my mind had lifted and I realized that I needed to deal with this situation like an adult. I knew I had to write this, regardless of how painful and puzzling it was. There was no way around it. Besides, was I planning an addendum on what I was glossing over once I got over my pettiness? No, there wasn't going to be a book at all without giving proper credit where credit was due.

So I started a separate *Word* file and named it appropriately: The Hard Part. Even if this chapter of my life was never included, it was still worthwhile to write, so I could process through and learn from the events for my own sake, I thought. The *fuck you* I was carrying around was reason enough to do this. But of course it belongs here—was there ever any doubt?

Back around March 2000, my life became challenging when W. began to experience heart palpitations, or arrhythmia, after a skiing trip. (This was after an enjoyable Y2K camping trip with friends in Death Valley.) At first I thought I could find some remedy so life would remain stable, because that's what I wanted—stability. Taking care of two demanding children, aged two and five, living with an increasingly irritated husband, dealing with remodeling a house, and brooding over my future career were plenty to deal with. But W.'s medical issues pushed me into crisis mode when his heart began to change towards me. I didn't understand. It didn't make any sense. But if you can understand how much he meant to me and how much I loved him, then you will understand how I felt when he began to withdraw from me and question our relationship.

After a checkup and a treadmill test, a heart specialist informed W. that his heart was in excellent shape and in fact, the office hadn't seen anyone in over six months ramp up the treadmill as high as he. According to the doctor, the irregularity was in the electrical system, the nerves to the heart. The heart-brain connection, the heart-mind connection—the way I saw it.

We were relieved to hear that his heart was healthy, but we also knew that the connections to the heart were just as critical and that palpitations could even be fatal. We were also informed that there wasn't much that could be done except to keep stress under control and go on beta-blockers until the condition improved spontaneously, which happens in quite a number of cases.

But I refused to believe that nothing else could be done. I sought the advice of alternative healthcare practitioners and combed through physicians' newsletters for anything I could find on the subject. Then I set up an appointment with a physician who practiced traditional osteopathic manipulation, a therapy that helped W. relax and settle better into his body—which he acknowledged produced subtle but positive long-term effects. He wasn't very open to unconventional medical approaches and often said, "Don't send me to any of your bush doctors." (That shows his worldview on alternative modalities of healing.) But when I explained a method and its possible benefits, most of the time he was willing to give it a try.

For instance, after I discovered that flaxseed oil is good for the nerves, W. began taking a tablespoon or two daily. Suspecting that stress and emotional baggage were also involved, a few months later I discovered a chiropractor in Los Gatos specializing in neural-emotional technique (NET) and became hopeful that NET therapy would heal emotional issues associated with the palpitations. According to

NET practitioners, old subconscious emotional and mental patterns (or memories) could become trapped in the nervous system, manifesting as physical symptoms, perhaps in W.'s case as heart palpitations. Thought patterns from negative experiences could also impair one's ability to effectively respond in similar situations unless the old subconscious pattern is first cleared. In other words, bad memories can affect your ability to deal with certain things, unless you make peace with the memory. In addition, an internal conflict between the old pattern and the new desired one could itself lead to stress, blockages, and physical symptoms. Clearing work involved changing one's thoughts (or beliefs) about memories by learning the truth about them—at least that's the way I was beginning to see it.

Furthermore, I learned that the "bad memory" in question didn't even have to be traumatic, just unpleasant or disagreeable. I remembered in my Forum a woman in her late twenties who shared that she had spent years in therapy trying to improve her relationship with her stepmother, with little success. Then at The Forum she remembered the moment when she had decided that her then-new stepmother was horrible and she would not ever accept her, because her stepmother had made her eat her vegetables. This early decision (she was about five years old then) had colored her relationship with her stepmother from then on, even though up until her insight in The Forum she had forgotten the reason behind her decision, and even the decision itself. Thus I had observed that it was often the *decisions* made about certain events that colored a person's life in the long-term, not necessarily the event itself ("what you made it mean" rather than "what happened"). In fact, I remembered saying to one couple who weren't quite satisfied with their Forum experience, "You're still mad at the decisions you made because of what happened, not necessarily at what your parents actually did to you," and they began to consider this idea.

Learning the truth about painful memories, old thoughts a n d beliefs can help clear emotional blocks and undesirable responses and eventually heal physical blockages that affect health and well-being.

I was grateful that W. was willing to try the NET, though it wasn't the easiest therapy to go through as it involved linking current emotional issues with root memories. And indeed, I had observed that some of W.'s upsets had been provoked by our children's behavior, as when Angelika cried at her sixth birthday party because a favorite (boy) friend had ignored her. Seeing Angelika cry at her own party had noticeably upset W., though from my perspective, small children crying at their own parties was a routine thing. He worked with this incident at his NET appointment and connected it to his own childhood birthday party experiences.

When, however, after a number of appointments W. quit the NET therapy, I viewed this as a withdrawal of his interest in our relationship as well. Because we had already tried a short course of marriage counseling, I felt powerless and frustrated and didn't know where to turn. (He had quit that too, said it wasn't working.) So I finally called the chiropractor for advice. The chiropractor said, "W. seems to have hit a wall around the age of three or four and doesn't want to process through it. There isn't much I can do if the patient refuses to continue. But perhaps you're the one who can get W. unstuck. And probably," he continued, "The reason he is still here is you." Then he offered me words of encouragement I hardly heard and wished me the best. Well, I thought, that wasn't very helpful, and kind of a strange thing to say to me besides.

But exactly how I was to go about helping him I didn't know, because W.'s heart condition limited his ability to cooperate with me. He withdrew further and further, often not saying a word to me for days, sometimes a week or two at a time. He even bragged about it, that he could be out of communication with me much longer than I with him, as though it were an advantage. Increasingly, he saw me as the one to blame for most anything, as though I had turned into the archenemy. Could it have been I that had caused his illness, by preparing mostly vegetarian meals? Or were the children also at fault? And…he questioned whether he still loved me, sometimes muttering vague words about leaving me. He had definitely disconnected his heart from me, so how was *I* going to help him now? I didn't have a clue.

His illness and behavior completely baffled me. Even though our marriage wasn't perfect, I thought we were doing okay, okay enough to hold on anyway. We could have used more time to ourselves of course, but that is a common complaint among parents with young children. I didn't see any major problems in our marriage. I hadn't seen it coming. It didn't make any sense.

Well, I suppose that isn't entirely true. In a way, I had known about this for a long, long time—ever since we married, ever since he started saying to me that there was something missing in me— however tiny a speck in my psyche it was. When I asked, he couldn't tell me exactly what it was that was missing, only that there was more to me than I had been letting on. Well, on the one hand it's flattering when your husband says he wants more of you, but when it's put that way you're left with the feeling that you are treading on shifting sand and sooner or later, the charade will be up.

I remember sitting on W.'s lap several times, he discussing these things with me, and I trying to respond to his complaints, all to no avail. How *do* you discuss what you don't know that you don't know? It always terrified me when he brought this subject up. I would squirm in his lap with my heart in my throat, fight back panicky tears, vow to work on it. "Just give me more time," I would say, not really knowing how I would fix this lack for him, or for myself for that matter. I couldn't just deny it because I knew it was true. And I knew that one day, this would have serious consequences in my life. I had no choice but to take this stuff seriously, yet I had no idea what to do about it either. Understandably, I tried to block the whole confusing thing from my mind, pretend it was nothing, and hope it would work itself out somehow.

Well, I did have fleeting glimpses that there was a part of me that was completely opposite to the reserved, composed, and aloof person I presented to the world because it showed itself at times, briefly, before being stuffed again. This was understandable though, considering that from childhood on I had lived in an environment and society where that free, fearless, and expressive part of you is suppressed to the point where you no longer need anyone to control you, you become your own best jailer. You might think that you are free, but are you free to be yourself fully? You may think that you are free, but free to do what, exactly?

To free myself of this concern about my husband leaving me, I had repeated The Landmark Forum about a year after W. and I married. Standing up from my seat, I had admitted to over a hundred people that I harbored an irrational fear that my newlywed husband was going to leave me because he was always finding fault with me and hinting that there was something missing, some aspect of myself, of who I was that wasn't present, as though I were keeping something important from him and the world, something without which he couldn't much longer go on.

The Forum leader and I had a short, clear dialogue and I was able to see how unwarranted and absurd my concern really was. I sat down feeling satisfied; much of my fear had lifted. Then in a moment of insight, perhaps, he addressed the group and said, "Can you all hear the intelligence in this woman? Christine, your husband wouldn't leave you if you held a baseball bat to his head."

I was relieved to hear that; certainly it was good news, as my experience with Forum leaders was that they were pretty much "right on." Yet I also knew there was still this other reality waiting for me at home. And now, after over ten years of marriage, it was really coming true—he was planning on leaving me after all.

During the summer of 2000, which I call the summer of the Heart Problem, he had announced that he'd make a decision about the future of our relationship at the end of the year. But then on New

Year's Eve he must have postponed this decision because he went to bed at ten o'clock without a word to me. He was stuck all right, stuck at the age of three or four, or at least the prevailing personality, the one that engaged with me, was. I still loved him, could see only him in my life, but no matter what I did I couldn't reach him; I couldn't make inroads into his heart. I worked harder to make things better and less stressful for him, but working harder wasn't working too well. According to him, there was no connection between us—it had been torn apart. I tried to connect, but he didn't buy it. "You are just faking it," he insisted. I tried to get him to talk after the children were asleep, but most of the time he wasn't in the mood.

"Why can't you talk to me now?" I asked him one evening.

"Leave me alone. I'm tired and I want my rest."

"But I don't understand. You said years ago that I could wake you at any time, even in the middle of the night if I needed to talk, if it was important."

Nothing.

"Talk to me…"

"I said I need my rest. Why couldn't you ask me earlier? Leave me alone or I'm going to the guest room. Don't make me get up."

That night I cried myself to sleep, but he wasn't moved. Instead, he had moved himself into the guest room. I no longer knew who he was. Frankly, I had begun to suspect that he had somehow turned mental on me, which was very difficult for me to accept. Somehow, I also knew that it would take something really big to snap him out of it, but that eventually he would. I tried to deal with all my fears by detaching myself from him and giving him more and more space. It wasn't easy to detach, to let the emotional ties wither like torn-out weeds, but I wasn't left with much of a choice. For over a year my efforts to connect with him had failed. I had to let go, even if it hurt like hell.

So when Angelika's kindergarten year was over, I thought I ought to take a two-week camping trip to Oregon with my girls to avoid being around much the summer of 2001. I also thought a change of environment might be good for all. Still giving him the benefit of the doubt, though, I invited him to share a long weekend with us. But he viewed this camping trip as a bad idea and said, "Why are you going to Oregon? There's nothing interesting up there."

"Why do you say that? There's lots to do in Oregon. There are dunes, mountains, a famous country fair near Eugene, and on our way up we'll stop in Mount Shasta, one of *your* favorite places."

"What's so interesting about a country fair in Oregon? You never go to country fairs here."

"Well, it's an alternative kind of country fair, not like a typical *county* fair. It was highly recommended by someone from the Soul Recognition Workshop."

"You mean one of your weirdo friends who need to do those strange workshops."

"They're not strange, not stranger than you, anyway. I'm sure I'll find lots of interesting things for the girls to do and they'll love it. It's one state we haven't explored, you know."

"We didn't go there because it isn't worth it. There's nothing there."

"Well, I guess I'll have to find that out for myself."

"It'll be a total waste of your time, but I know that's not an issue for you," he snarled.

I stopped for a moment to consider things, then said, "Well, you're welcome to join us anyway. You could take a couple days off from work, and I could pick you up at the airport in Eugene. It's up to you; you can think about it." We left it at that and he went to tinker in the garage or something. It was the beginning of July, a few months after my Soul Recognition Workshop and I could already see its positive influence on me.

I planned our camping trip and began packing the car with gear. Shortly thereafter, another wonder: W. decided that he would, in fact, fly out to meet us for a four-day weekend. He also made us promise to hike at least as far as Heart Lake, which is on the way to the summit of Mount Shasta, California. On a solitary retreat the previous summer, he had fallen in love with the secluded, heart-shaped pond after swimming in its waters. Finally, the familiar feel of adventure suffused my days, and there was a chance for love and harmony to triumph after all. Perhaps becoming more detached was a step in the right direction, I thought.

The girls and I drove to the beautiful high country of Mount Shasta and ate spaghetti marinara at a pasta-making shop in town. We set up our tent in an undeveloped campground at the foot of the snowcapped mountain and washed our hands in a stream, perhaps only two feet wide and a few inches deep that snaked through the campground. The children screamed as I scrubbed their feet in the ice-cold water, then giggled as I struggled to carry them back to the tent, one on each hip, where they crept into cozy sleeping bags and fell asleep within minutes. The reddish-orange evening light had vanished, exposing a sky dense with twinkling stars. I was enthralled by the exquisite beauty and serenity and noticed another effect of the Soul Recognition Workshop: I had listened to and acted on my inner guidance in spite of the objections of my husband, who was now going to meet us after all. The earth filled me with a deep, deep peace.

The next day my kids begged me to stay in Mount Shasta and eat pasta again for dinner, but we continued north to Oregon so we could meet W. on time, after a tour of the Oregon coast. I assured them that we'd return for a few more days on our way back home.

Although chilly even in midsummer, the Oregon coast was beautiful with jagged cliffs, vast beaches, dunes formed by crashing Pacific waves, and quiet, friendly fishing towns. We drove at a quick pace, stopping for meals, bathroom breaks, bakeries, hikes to dunes and caves and other touristy attractions, and camping in the evenings. We were headed to Deadwood, a very remote rural town (if you could call it a town) located roughly halfway between the coast and Eugene. In Deadwood was Alpha Farm, an organic farm also recommended by my workshop acquaintance. I had called ahead and received permission to visit for four days. I planned the farm as a "base camp" for our excursions, as well as a fun experience for my kids.

Upon arrival, I was given a short tour and inquired about my chores. All visitors were asked to do some work in exchange for meals and lodging, as was only fair.

We slept in our tent near the main house, where we ate community meals with the twenty or so residents and farm interns. My children made new friends, chased dogs and hens, climbed trees, hunted for frogs in ponds, and made the most of their freedom from the normal restrictions of home. Late one afternoon they ran to me so excited, I could almost see the sparks flying. "Mommy, Mommy! Can we help bring in the hay? Can we ride on top of the hay truck? Oh please, *please*! We'll do *anything* if you let us!" they cried in unison.

Two days later we drove to the Eugene airport to pick up W., and all the way there I fidgeted, wondering what he'd think of our "base camp" or some of the lodgers, who seemed to be happy just floating around, wearing hippy clothing. He was on time, as usual, and then there I was, driving this industrious and sharp-looking man who when patronizing the arts in Munich wore a trench coat and hat like Humphrey Bogart in *Casablanca*, to a place called Deadwood. We drove on tortuous dirt roads tens of miles deep in the hinterland of Oregon to a farm that consisted of a hayfield and a vegetable garden. I was also nervous he'd think I was now going to wear long, gauzy skirts, and our children would run loose, looking unsanitary, feet black with mud. Also, I had forgotten to mention there would be chores in exchange for his board, which was vegetarian, of course. Just how did I get myself into this? Was it such a good idea to have invited him?

Once on the farm I let the other folks give him the tour while I made plans for the next day. I would show him the dunes (he liked plans that included nature) and take him to a nice seafood restaurant (he liked to eat). (It was revealing to observe that even while trying to detach from him, I was still trying to accommodate him.) To my pleasant surprise, he seemed to enjoy his farm experience and even fixed a couple of rusty machines with tools he found lying around in the barn. But the next day at the dunes and the restaurant he seemed irritated again, in spite of my effort to promote harmony. Perhaps it was just I who so irritated him?

Looking at this from a purely logical point of view, our fights didn't make much sense. They weren't about serious, weighty issues but about trivialities, compulsively blown out of proportion. And whenever I tried to sort out an argument so I could learn something, to manage better in the future, my mind would go blank. I couldn't remember how it got started or even what it was about, which was very annoying. I know that sometimes the mind conveniently forgets; it doesn't want to know things that might make it ill at ease, the fear of being wrong, perhaps. Well, this I most definitely knew: we were both first-born; we were both stubborn, and like aikido partners, we butted heads a lot.

Well about the trivialities, here is a good example: we had different ideas about giving proper directions. I would say, for instance, "Next, go east on Route 80, which is coming up in a few miles." Those were the kinds of directions I'd give myself if I were driving. But my directions annoyed him; he demanded them to be like so: "Make a right turn at this next exit"—which seemed to me the way you'd direct a child if they happened to be driving and didn't know how to read the signs; you'd have to be with him every step of the way. Yet I would have indulged his whim if he hadn't made me wrong, if he had asked for what he wanted with courtesy and good humor.

Many such fights had occurred in Europe where he did most of the driving, especially in the messy cities of Italy. This was one typical formula: when we got off-the-track on our way to our destination, usually the *Centro*, he'd pull over to the side of the road (barely), snatch the map from me, and somehow make out more information than I was able, though usually our maps weren't detailed enough to make out the city streets. "Do I have to do everything?" he'd bark, stashing the map on the driver's side. I'd reach over and grab it back. I thought he ought to be grateful, not critical, since I was still willing to give directions in spite of incomplete maps. And like the *Centro* signs to the Italian destinations I was always on the lookout for, there were signs that pointed to our central problem: the direction of the vehicle—literally as well as metaphorically, I can now see.

These fights quickly became so boring, at least to me, that at times I entertained secret wishes to provoke a serious argument— one that would split us up for a while—just so the high cost of our compulsive behavior would become obvious. (But I wondered whether that would yield the desired outcome.) In fact, once my secret wish almost came true and I almost separated from him during a vacation in Turkey. I was so mad, I wanted out of his VW bug and demanded to be left off in the city we were driving through. In my momentary frenzy, I was actually thinking I'd rather find a bus to take back to Germany than endure his presence one minute longer. But he refused to stop the car and my sister Lydia was with us, which put a serious damper on my plan. I forced myself to be civilized—it was her vacation too—and let the incident pass.

He was extra irritated with me that time because I had acciden- tally bent the passenger side headrest of his beloved VW bug (the pair of stainless steel prongs that attach the headrest to the seat back). We had been sightseeing in the interior of the country, admiring limestone terraces that reminded me of frozen, cascading waterfalls like the Minerva Terraces at Yellowstone National Park, except in Turkey the tourists were oddly enough allowed to trample all around those magnificent natural formations. I had innocently gone back to the car to get my camera. Leaning my left arm on the passenger-side headrest, I reached over to the back seat where my Nikon lay and before I knew it, the steel bent back, as if by magic. Strange too was that I heard it kind of click into place at an angle of about forty-five degrees. I tried to bend it back but it wouldn't bend. This incident startled me; it was something I would call a phenomenon.

I caught up with Lydia and W. at the terraces and informed him that something was wrong with the headrest of his car. The three of us rushed back to have a look and indeed, it was still bent. But it was W.'s reaction that surprised me the most: instead of being interested by the odd unexpectedness of this and perhaps curious as to the cause—maybe a flaw of some sort—he got very angry with me. He started yelling and screaming, "Why did you do that? You put your whole weight on it, didn't you?" and we weren't even married yet.

"I didn't *do* anything, something must be wrong with it," I tried to explain. But he dismissed my explanation.

I protested: "I weigh a hundred and twenty-five pounds, and even if I did put my whole weight on it, which would have been a pretty sight and which anyway I most certainly did not, I shouldn't have bent that stupid thing!" Were the properties of stainless steel so variable, so unreliable that if you were to lean on a safety structure of an automobile, it might collapse? I was a materials scientist after all, on staff at the Department of Experimental Physics of a prestigious university; I mingled with Nobel laureates in physics at staff barbeques, and I didn't have a rational explanation. Yet he had the nerve to pin the blame on me, as if I had done this on purpose just to spite him.

W. tried to bend the prongs back, but they wouldn't bend. Then he lifted the whole contraption out and tried to bend it against the ground, but it wouldn't budge. So we took it to an auto repair shop, where the three of us stood around waiting for it like strangers at a train station. I saw a mechanic put it into a vise, but it wasn't easy to bend. I noticed I actually felt guilty about it, as if I were a child who had done something wrong. They might have wondered how it got bent—a bad car accident, maybe. Maybe they viewed it as some sort of practical joke. There must be practical jokes in Turkey, I would think. Well, I am just babbling on self-importantly here because I'm not so sure they wondered about it at all. They didn't ask any questions, and we didn't volunteer any information; they just continued fixing it as if a bent headrest was completely normal. And now that I think about it, perhaps calling my experience a phenomenon or a wonder is a bit grandiose for what could after all have been a common occurrence in Turkey.

In any case, after it was fixed W. and I didn't discuss this incident further and nothing of this sort ever happened again. Maybe we figured that if we had actually discussed this, it might have come to seem real, so we avoided the topic altogether. Years later I discovered a possible clue about the area in Turkey where the supports got bent—the "veils between dimensions" are supposedly thin there. I read this once in some book, but I'm not sure it explains anything. However, perhaps one reason why the European Union is reluctant to admit Turkey is that the basic natural laws of this dimension (meaning this planet) can't always be counted on over there. But maybe our understanding of physics is currently incomplete?

But I am trying to explain how easily W. and I misunderstood each other and also, how certain events—natural and supernatural both—conspired against us. You know things are pretty bad when even inanimate objects turn against you.

Anyway, I thought that finally things were going to turn around for us in Oregon. The day after the dunes we drove to the Oregon Country Fair, where we admired carnival-attired fair goers—Blue People with blue skin, for instance. We enjoyed live music, an African dance show, a play about space aliens with huge rear ends that made the children and me double over with laughter, and homemade food and crafts. The kids and I loved it all! It was a blast! Then the day after the fair, we drove east from Eugene towards Willamette National Forest. Near Leaburg, we picked tasty blueberries and raspberries at an organic farm. Next we visited Belknap Hot Springs and splashed in a warm pool supplied by a natural hot spring—which

W. enjoyed a lot. Finally, we camped in a lush rain forest at the Paradise Campground, a postcard-perfect vision of moist evergreens and ferns. It seemed that nature's serenity had rubbed off on us as we climbed into the tent, feeling peaceful. And I thought from that point on, things would finally move in the right direction. After all, he did join us in rural Oregon of all places.

∞

The rest of summer vacation, W. continued to join us on Sunday outings, such as riding bikes to "Music in the Park" concerts in downtown Los Gatos. Though things were still strained between us, he hung around us, no doubt wrestling inner demons. Anyway, it was at one of the concerts where I experienced another interesting encounter. My children met a little girl and they danced and played together. Then the girl's mother came over and introduced herself as Jahde, "But you can call me Jed," she said. Then she said something that caught my attention: "You're an author, aren't you?"

"Well, not exactly," I replied, "I just started thinking about it earlier this year when I did a spiritual course. The leader and a few participants recommended I write, but I haven't written anything yet." I didn't mention the Counsel of Light's prophecy, which I thought might be viewed a bit too far out.

"Maybe we can support each other in writing our books. I need someone to help me organize my material," she said. (It *was* true that if motivated, I could organize things quite well.)

I didn't know how this woman could have known this. I asked her. She said that she just knew that she'd meet an author that day. I don't know about these things. People don't just hop out of bed in the morning thinking they'll meet an author that day. But I found it interesting that I was struggling with the idea, and yet she somehow already viewed me as one. We exchanged phone numbers. Jahde and W. also exchanged cordialities and after the concert we biked home.

I took Jahde's perception of me as a mystical sign. I think sometimes you are shown the way by signs and symbols like these. Her idea of me also boosted my unsure inner state and not long afterwards I informed W. that I would attempt to write. Perhaps something *would* come from it. Thus, I thought that I was settling into my correct role: my true life plan. I thought he would finally settle in too. Weren't things moving in the right direction?

But you just don't know; you don't ever know for sure what's buried in people's hearts. Not long afterwards, he began to look for another place to live. It just goes to show you my enormous capacity for self-deception back then.

He announced his departure on a Friday the first week in October, the day before his planned move. Although by then I knew he had been looking for another place to live—a woman just knows these things you know, that, and the newspapers he carelessly left lying about the house (a publication we didn't subscribe to because we didn't get our news from newspapers but where we found the latest scoop on sales and other matters of commercial importance), because when I sighted this anomaly in our home I became very suspicious, so much so that I flipped through its pages, opened to the rentals wanted and spotted the circled ads and notes scribbled in his handwriting—it was still a shock.

I didn't want him to leave; I still didn't understand what troubles lurked in his heart. We hadn't talked much for many months. But now, with him moving the next day, the dam that had held my emotions in check finally cracked. I had had enough and was going tell him what I couldn't have told him for fear of upsetting him, of making things worse, of causing further discomfort to his ailing heart. I was going to make this last-ditch effort and have him see me fully.

I don't remember exactly what I said that day. I had babbled on and on for hours, had caused him to stay home from work. I don't think I ever spoke so many words in one day. Tears flowed in my voice and then real tears, loads and loads of tears. I laid bare my confusion, anger, sense of betrayal, disappointments, and fears. I let him know how it had been for me the previous year and a half, how we needed to get to the bottom of it, that I wanted us to stick together as a family, that I still loved him. He listened to my outburst, attentive and silent. And after I talked and pleaded and cried myself out, I felt I had said everything I needed to say.

Then I went to the master bathroom to splash water on my face. "Okay," I thought to myself, "I think I said everything; I feel empty inside now. Anything more would be redundant and futile. It's up to you now, because I'm done." Immediately, I felt that something had loosened; something inside my brain had eased into place. I want to say that something had spelunked in there, if that makes any sense. The terror I had felt earlier seemed to have released its grip. I remember standing in our bathroom that afternoon, in a split second realizing that no matter what happened, I was now prepared for it and could move on if necessary. A split second is all it takes to change the course of a whole life, to propel it forward along its path as if down a cascade of successive waterfalls (or, if you will, down a terrace of frozen emotions).

I didn't know what he was going to do the next day. He had asked earlier to borrow my station wagon for the move, so I went to him and said, "You can borrow my car if you want. Just let me know." But he didn't say a word.

He slept with me in my bed that night, or at least *I think* it was my bed at the time. We had changed sleeping arrangements several times the previous year and I don't remember if it was I sleeping in the guest room then or the master bedroom. This had caused some confusion in our children as well. (Some mornings a bedroom door would slowly creak open somewhere, revealing a sleepy-eyed child in her pajamas, and on her face a look of surprise, or of reassurance… were we together? Were we apart? Who was where?) I mean that he chose to stay with me in the guest bed. It felt nice sleeping with him once again. He was more attentive and loving than in a long time.

The following morning in bed, I asked him again: "Do you want my car keys? I can take the Audi and leave my car for you." I needed to get up early to get the children ready for Saturday German-language school. He mumbled something I understood to mean no, so I got the children up, fixed breakfast, and, taking my own car, dropped them off at school. Then I drove to a nearby park where I usually meditated and wrote in my journal. I had butterflies in my stomach about was he or wasn't he going to leave, but at the same time I felt a deep peace.

When we returned home shortly past noon, everything was as we had left it that morning. I found him outside, sweeping leaves off the back patio. From this simple act of housekeeping I understood he had changed his mind. He also seemed to have a more peaceful air about him, as though something had spelunked into place in his head as well. Relief came over me, relief that the children and I wouldn't have to go through unpleasant adjustments. I was wildly thankful for some stability too.

He didn't say much, and I didn't ask. I thought I ought to let things come as they will. Anyway, time would tell.

∞

But I'll be the first to admit that I also wasn't an angel, or a superwoman. As I had mentioned, there was something missing in me. W. had more than once tenderly aired his frustrations about not being able to reach me, and about my excluding him from decisions. And the times when he told me that I could do anything I wanted, that I could have my life any way I wanted it, that I have the resources—our resources—to accomplish anything I wanted, I felt so cared for and understood. He is a sensitive guy who cries easily at sentimental movies and in front of me, too; I didn't cry very much. This sensitive, tender side of him melted my heart and that's why I fell for him.

Yet sometimes his grievances frustrated me because I didn't know what to do about them. I couldn't even reach myself and didn't know what to give him. For a large part of my life, I wasn't free to express myself without the fear of judgment or reproach. Either you live in an environment that's open and accepting, become strong within, or you keep to yourself. Then W. began to press me to fling open the mysteries I somehow sensed were hidden in my subconscious. But how do you access your subconscious? How do you change your most ingrained qualities?

Another one of my issues was keeping our multilevel townhouse—four levels to take care of—neat and orderly enough. At least one stack of articles, papers, and books I was reading was always somewhere—on the floor on my side of the bed, on the kitchen counter, or on the empty chair in the dining room.

I couldn't seem to manage my stacks of refinement and knowledge, though to him I always seemed to be reading. As I've already confessed, I was a bit scattered in direction, but planning on finding it one day. Meanwhile, you just never know when you'll have need of an article on the geometry of hyper-dimensional systems, or the pedagogical and persuasive effects of Native American lesson stories, or when a Lynda Barry cartoon saved since college might come in handy. This cartoon, for instance, illustrated why you should never try to find yourself: because what you'll discover is that you are a jerk. Relinquishing any of my stockpiles of information was unthinkable to me, as it was entirely possible that the key to my life direction was right under my nose.

Then there was the problem of saving vegetable peelings for compost. Throwing them out in the trash was unconscionable to me, especially since the organic matter was so beneficial to our vegetable garden. Besides, keeping compost was a habit I had picked up while living in his country, from his people. Large bins for compost were kept in the community trash room of our apartment building, and I used them religiously. It was a good habit, or so I thought.

But the occasional fruit flies annoyed W. to no end. On our clean glass kitchen cabinet doors he left fat fingerprints and the remains of squished flies just to spite me. As an alternative, I offered to bring on board special garbage-eating red worms, kept in a bin in the garage, but he quickly nixed that idea.

Yet another thing: most of the time I didn't dress the way he would have liked. In my stay-at-home, "mother duck" stage of life, I favored comfort and practicality over style and spotlighting my "bodacious attributes." But I did tell him I was willing to work on my wardrobe, in my spare time. I discarded some dark-toned clothes because, as he explained, navy was the color of Polish peasants lacking a flair for fashion.

For a long time, I remained confused and self-conscious about my wardrobe. So once when W.'s father visited from Germany, I tried to make myself presentable for a whale-watching excursion by wearing a colorful and flowing Scandinavian-style Oilily sweater. But instead of getting the compliments I expected, W. said, "Get rid of that impossible sweater!" Then he confessed that his father, loathe to hurt my feelings, had expressed the same sentiment to him in secret. I was appalled and puzzled at first, but then I finally caught on, changed into an old, inexpensive but tight-fitting T-shirt, and received the compliments I expected. "Much better," they said, grins on their faces.

Another issue was that I was tired when I finally slipped into bed for the night—*not a good thing*, seen from the husband's point of view. This behavior pattern was viewed as a withdrawal of my interest in him, which it was, of course, and also as going against convention and expectations even though, in reality, he and his offspring, who paradoxically were the natural and for the most part irreversible outcome of the dalliance being disregarded, were the primary sources of my fatigue. Yet he attributed this problem to my Catholic upbringing and the influence of "American society," in which case it was already too late for me. Beliefs and opinions color everything, yet one is powerless against them—that is what I'm trying to show here. People believe what they want to believe; you might as well have your hands tied behind your back. I mean if a person decides to deny that it's the antagonism that's killing a relationship, that keeps two people from love and intimacy and happiness, then let him wither in his own bed. But if you are to lead a life of striving towards truth and love, of growth and freedom, you can expect opposition and obstacles and mistakes sometimes.

Well, you get the picture—trivial, Mickey Mouse complaints are what I thought they were. I, on the other hand, was increasingly feeling the pressure of real, not pretend worries.

∞

Opposition rather than openness and inclusiveness had prevailed for as long as I could remember, back into my childhood, in history books, and beyond. But since my family was different from those of most of my schoolmates, having come from the Old World, I projected the old ideas back to my parents' home country, to the time when they grew up in small villages where everybody knew everybody else's business and was required to behave in a narrow, rigid manner in order to be accepted. Back then, it was already spelled out for you what to think, what to do, where to stand, when to eat… and that was the way it was. You didn't question why things were the way they were; some people told you some things and that was good enough for you. Especially if you were a kid.

So I wasn't perfect, having come from a simple background in an imperfect world, but I was open and willing to work on the things I knew how to change. If only W. and I had been more like partners instead of opponents, perhaps then things between us would have been different. And I did work on myself; I searched my soul. It is clear that the happier you are within, the better it is for everyone around you. I knew that was the key—that's why the course on Soul

Recognition. Because even if only one person took heart-felt steps to change, it altered the whole relationship dynamic, which could help transform the entire situation.

But even before the course, I had wondered why I was in this relationship, with this man, on this planet, in this galaxy, at this time, and why life around here hadn't exactly been going very well. Depression and embarrassment were what I felt, are what I still feel, looking at the state of my world, the state of the world. So I tried not to dwell on the negative too much. I tried to think of other things— today I must remember to put windshield fluid in my car, and make sure I have costumes for the kids for Halloween. And we really need to find those two overdue books and return them to the library. But the bigger questions snuck in between my other thoughts. With life so turbulent, the existential question of why I was in it suddenly grew in urgency, if only to focus on something of larger consequence than relationship drama and everyday routine. Because if my deeper life worked, if I were clear and confident in my bigger purpose, I could face anything more effectively, regardless of others' opinions or what they were going to do. Anyway, that was my logic.

In hindsight, if I knew what I know now, I would have let go sooner. I wouldn't have let him get away with behavior that was so clearly out of line. But everything seemed so stacked against us: he feared that he had already escaped his own death for a decade. His biological father had passed over at the age of twenty-seven, before he was even born. His mother was terrified. I had all these concerns and dos and don'ts running through my head, instructions about what I should or shouldn't do, advice from doctors, from his mother. ("Perhaps it is you who could help him," the chiropractor had said.) And still I sounded like an insensitive daughter-in-law, not worried enough. So I avoided putting additional stress on him. Ultimately, I couldn't be present in the moment and I couldn't be free to just be me. I couldn't view him as the capable being I knew him to be, and I certainly couldn't call him on it.

Another constraint was that I was still living under the presumption of *if only*. If only I had my own act together, or knew my purpose here, this wouldn't have gone on for so long. If there's anything I feel I failed in, it is this: I failed to be powerful and detached and free; I failed to be unaffected by what occurred in my relationship. Therefore, I failed to be effective in this situation.

I had already learned firsthand that detachment was the key to being effective, because years ago I had been more independent and wasn't so affected by his ways. When we got married, he bragged to his friends and family that he couldn't have married anyone else because no one else could have handled him as well. He was what you might call a difficult person, very opinionated and headstrong. He didn't need to brag though, they all knew.

I knew life with him wouldn't be easy. But I also knew it was my job to teach him about love and relationship, and that we'd make great partners and teach each other many valuable things. How I knew this I don't know. I just knew. That's why when I had first moved to Germany, one of my goals was to have W. enroll in The Forum, of his own free will—which wasn't easy because he thought he was going to be brainwashed. I was going to teach him about love all right, but I planned on letting others teach him the fundamentals first.

We had had several conversations about The Forum over the course of a few months and I thought I finally had him convinced that there wasn't any brainwashing going on, that on the contrary, it would be a wonderful and freeing experience for him. He would be free of his conditionings and the power they held over him and wouldn't that be great? He'd be free to repair his relationships, set new goals previously unimaginable; the sky was the limit. But then, several days before The Forum not only did he refuse to participate in the course, he said he was rethinking our relationship as well. On a park bench near his apartment in the trendy part of town called *Haidhausen*, he poured his heart out and cried for a couple of hours about how things couldn't work between us because I had been seriously brainwashed and we would never, ever understand each other.

The funny thing is, I had no recollection of what he had babbled on about during those two or three hours. Except for the part about things not working between us—which I had clearly heard—I hardly heard anything else he said, as though he were talking at me in a language I didn't speak, as though it had gone in one ear, and, without registering in my brain, out the other. Or perhaps my mind had been temporarily hijacked. Oh, who knows. But at the same time it seemed that my awareness was heightened and I sensed the importance of this moment. This was a moment of truth for me. Anyway, I allowed him his tantrum and didn't react one iota—because who would take personally those things that had as much to do with yourself as, for instance, the shifting of the earth's axis? So I just looked at him, blinked, nodded, and smiled understandingly from time to time—what else could I do?—as though I were a psychiatrist and he were my struggling patient. Well, maybe I also shook my head occasionally, said a few words here and there, asked a couple questions. Then he broke up with me.

"As you like," I said as I gathered up my personal belongings from his apartment, surprised with myself because I felt a strange inner peace. Then as I walked peacefully towards the bus stop I became aware that the full reality of what had just occurred must not have had a chance to penetrate my brain yet, and also that I had forgotten my monthly transportation pass. So I returned to his place less than ten minutes later.

"Uh, I forgot my bus pass," I said good-naturedly as he opened the door. "Can I please get it?" But by then he was a changed person and asked me to stay; this time it turned out for good. He also asked me to warm him because he had been shivering, so I did. The next day he took the plunge and enrolled himself in the upcoming Forum, completed the entire course, and even convinced most of his family to enroll in the following one, with the ease of an expert sales-man. Even his relationship with his mother had been transformed. Immediately after the course he had gone to speak to her, to renew their relationship after many years of conflict and struggle. I remember his parents and us at a *Biergarten* just days after his Forum, his mother shedding tears of joy, grateful for "having her son back," as she put it. And things went relatively well between us after that, I thought, at least until his heart started acting up....

Now I know that I am not responsible for other people's happiness; I can't heal them; it's up to them, and there is nothing I can offer except my love and presence and steadiness. I'm only responsible for my own health and well-being. I'm only responsible for myself and for my children. I'm not responsible for anyone else. And other people's personal issues have nothing to do with me ever.

But even if he were to heal his heart issues, would that clear his difficulties with me? Would I ever receive from him what I wanted? Would he be more loving, less judgmental, more free? Was I really the one who could get W. unstuck, as the chiropractor had said? Perhaps he wasn't getting what he needed from me. I hated to consider these things; the prospect wasn't very comforting, and nothing made much sense. But what else was there to do? Perhaps remain grounded and steady a while longer? Steadiness and stability sure sounded good.

∞

But stability was nowhere on the Event Horizon. Less than three weeks after W. did not move out of the house and my consciousness did expand in the master bathroom, I experienced another fateful encounter and connected with someone, just like that. Apparently, he had been trying to get my attention for a year, but it had taken that long for me to catch on. It just goes to show how lost in my own thoughts I had been those days.

For several days before, he had begun to crystallize from the blur of people who came across my everyday field of view—his wavy, almost shoulder-length brown hair, his easy stride, and his warm smile were what I noticed first. Anyway, one ordinary school day Julianne and I were walking Angelika to her first grade class. Ordinary, that is, except for the air that felt lightly electrified and the sun's rays that rebounded here and there off the school grounds. Then I spotted him. He was returning to his car after having dropped his boy off at school, his younger son at his side. Other days he had greeted me with a smile and a wave when driving by, but this day our eyes met. We walked straight toward each other without a word, held each other's gaze until we crossed paths, focusing on the business of the children. That is not so strange, I know, but when the connection was broken, what startled me was the scream I heard that seemed to originate from the center of my chest. The scream was one of... what? Recognition? Premonition? Yearning? It definitely took me by surprise, this new dimension to my inner resources.

Then the same thing happened the next day. Well, when something out of the ordinary happens two days in a row it's bound to get your attention, and it sure got mine. Thus began a certain magnetism between us, a fascination, something familiar and yet unfamiliar at the same time. I would spot him easily across the schoolyard, and notice that he saw me too. I would turn around on a whim and see his eyes on me, as though we both had radar. This new thing persisted for days but we didn't acknowledge it, didn't say to each other more than the usual, as if nothing had happened. After several days I decided to ask him whether he knew what was going on, because that's exactly how it had occurred to me then: that something was going on.

I tried to talk to him at Pumpkin Walk, an annual family fundraising event sponsored by the elementary school the Saturday evening before Halloween. I spotted him as I walked the costume parade with my costumed children. Later that evening when I stood directly before him and looked into the erotic radiance of his eyes, he smiled warmly and put his finger to his lips, barely. "Well, I'll see you around. Hope you're having a great evening. It's lots of fun, this Pumpkin Walk," we said something of the sort as we sidled past each other. I suppose it wasn't the right time to discuss what was going on—his boys were holding his hands; his wife was around somewhere, as were my girls.

Then around mid-November when I crossed his path at school, I handed him my email address. He seemed startled, but two days later I received his email:

"Hello Christine, How are you? I'm sorry I have not gotten back to you sooner, but I have been very busy at work and have had no time for myself. Nice to see that you have time for me!! I will definitely make time for you!! When would be a good time?...Just tell me where to go and I will be there."

After I read his email, I was overcome with a warm glow and a spinning sensation in the center of my body, as if I were floating on a cloud and the sun was beaming its warmth and energy into me, which made me dizzy. This mystical experience threw me off balance so much I had to lie down for half an hour to regain my composure.

I emailed back to let him know, very matter-of-factly, that I seemed to have developed an attraction to him, almost overnight, that I didn't know what to make of it, and did he know what was going on? I was serious about this. There *was* something going on, I could feel it in my bones, something I'd have to figure out, something I'd need to investigate, something soul-stirring and intriguing but also something that made me very suspicious....

At the beginning of December we got together at a small, quiet coffee shop one morning after dropping the kids off at their respective schools. He drank coffee with cream and sugar, which is the way I would drink coffee had I ordered it; I had peppermint tea, unsweetened. We talked. Well actually, he did most of the talking.

I was attentive and curious, listening for an inner impression as to what our being together was about.

First we talked about our experiences living in Europe. An American (let's call him "J."), he had moved to Europe not long after I, had lived in Switzerland for several years, had married a Swiss woman, and had two boys, also three years apart. He had learned some German during that time and had visited some of same places I had. At this point, I began to notice that we had a number of things in common—my first clue, I thought.

"What are you doing with yourself at the moment?" J. asked. I wasn't exactly sure how best to answer his question and I must have looked uncomfortable, because before I could respond, he said in a calm, reassuring voice, "It's okay; whatever you're doing is okay."

I told him that I was preparing to write a book. "I don't know what I'm going to write about, perhaps something about love, about explaining love and life," I said. "I'm in the process of looking for the right subject matter at the moment," I went on, "I'm waiting for inspiration to show up so I can write about it."

About two and a half years later, I am writing this, remembering our conversation in the coffee shop as I hike up St. Joseph's Hill in Los Gatos. I carry a pen and paper with me wherever I go, as I cannot stop writing now. And as I recall that day, the 1982 hit song "Destination Unknown" by the Missing Persons is playing in my head:

> *Life is so strange*
> *Destination unknown*
> *When you don't know*
> *Your destination*
> *Something can change*
> *It's unknown*
> *And then you won't know*
> *Destination unknown…*

I know this song was a hit back in 1982 not because I'm good with music trivia, because I am not, but because when I turned on the car radio after my hike that morning, it happened to be playing. I had tuned to the "Ten at Ten" show on KFOG, where ten big hits are played from a selected year, which happened to be 1982 that day. I think this song fits the mood perfectly right here. Life *is* strange, especially when you don't have a clue about your destination.

I found it strange in any case, sitting in the coffee shop with J. that morning, telling him I was waiting for the right timing, for inspiration to come along so I could begin to write my book. This brought up the topic of books, and then he began to discuss *The Celestine Prophesy*, a book he had read. We also learned that neither of us could imagine taking the time to read fiction now—there was just too much to learn in real life and not enough time. "But even though it's fiction, *The Celestine Prophesy* made a positive impact on my life," J. said. (*The Celestine Prophesy* is an adventure novel about an American who finds himself in the rain forests and mountains of Peru, in quest of an ancient manuscript containing nine essential insights about life—secrets that will expand spiritual awareness and change the world.)

"I didn't like the way it was written," I said to J., "Parts of it seemed too contrived, too predictable, and I didn't like how it ended—that ascension scene left me feeling a bit weird; I mean it almost gave me the willies. But by far its biggest flaw is a book like this really ought to be nonfiction."

"That's interesting. My sister felt pretty much the same," J. said. Then he talked about his stacks of poetry and song writing, telling me that he had written the lyrics and sung the lead to a song called "Reality," which had been played on radio stations in Europe. A curious thing: we had discussed living in exotic places, fiction, and the writing of books, songs, and poetry, but we didn't bother to discuss the reality of the moment—what we were doing together in that coffee shop.

Anyway, I knew that he knew that sometimes people meet for a bigger reason—one of the key insights in *The Celestine Prophesy*. In fact, at times I felt I could read his thoughts, as though they were being beamed, without background noise, into my consciousness. We also seemed interested in similar things, as if we were on the same wavelength. From these points and from my internal gauges, I realized our meeting at this time was significant somehow; I just didn't know how significant.

A few days after our coffee shop meeting, J. invited me over for dinner when his family was away. He was warming up tomato soup and fixing a green salad with pecans and blue cheese when I arrived; I stood in his kitchen watching him. We managed to finish a small serving of soup and salad but weren't very hungry so we talked, mostly small talk. Then he said, "You make me nervous." That's when I reached over the table, touched his hair, and kissed him. And well, what can I say? If we had been single I would have stayed, but fortunately—or unfortunately, depending on your point of view—I had to leave rather early. And near the end of our time together that evening, something interesting occurred when we kissed: in perfect synchrony as in a mirror, his left palm suddenly pressed flat against my right, we clasped fingers around each other's hand and squeezed firmly. It caught my attention because this wasn't exactly what you'd stop and think to do in the middle of an embrace, to break off a kiss this way. My investigative leanings perked up and I sensed there was some meaning behind this act, as though some ancient pact was nearing its time to which we, with our parallel gesture, were now recommitting, and it felt good. I sensed this, yes, but it was the most fleeting of glimpses; I had no evidence for this whatsoever. And I didn't share these feelings with anyone, not even him.

My life brightened up like a rainbow after a storm. Even though I knew our situation was potentially problematic, as did J., I wasn't going to just drop it. Perhaps I also imagined that he'd help make my heart feel right and I could go on, steadfast and fortified. And if I were happier I'd breeze through my days—my house sparkling and uncluttered, my children like angels with faces radiant and clean, my books on love written. Perhaps we imagined we would be so discreet that our little thing—whatever it was—would go unnoticed. I thought we could continue this adventure if we were cautious and set up some boundaries. A big part of me didn't want to be untrue to W., not necessarily because he had been so kind to me but simply because of my word. And I definitely didn't want to cause any grief to this man's family. More or less J. felt the same.

∞

Around the same time, near the end of 2001, more changes loomed on the horizon. W.'s company was downsizing drastically and the entire marketing department was going to be let go by the end of the year—a development that actually pleased him. He planned a three-week trip to visit his family in Munich immediately after Christmas, then informed me that after he returned, he wasn't going to look for work right away because it was now my turn to support our family. He thought it would be better if he stayed at home with the kids. He had planned on relaxing, mountain biking, and also doing a better job of keeping the house in order and the kids in line than I had.

This sudden change of attitude confused me because before we had had children, he had insisted, and I had agreed, that I should be with them until they started school. In addition, I wasn't ready to go to work yet, or to go somewhere to do someone else's work. Granted, not knowing exactly what I intended to do with my life or what I was going to write was a major issue for me, not just a financial concern.

If it had been time for Julianne to enter kindergarten and I had found myself without direction, sitting at home would have been like being in purgatory. Going shopping or having lunch with friends would have made me feel worse because I wasn't so easily fooled. I would have known I was using tactics of distraction and compensation to avoid my real issues (which I must have wanted to avoid so much I wasn't even conscious of what they were). I would have felt as if I had a hole in my heart so big it couldn't ever be filled, and that there was indeed something wrong with me—I was a failure. The hole would grow bigger the harder I'd try to fill it with other things, and the harder I'd try to compensate, the bigger it would appear to be, my spirit spiraling ever downwards because the truth is, what you feed grows.

I never expected that at this point in my life—after some impressive jobs and grad school and kids and all—that I'd be thinking such tortuous thoughts. But maybe W. knew I was thinking them. Maybe by pushing me to go to work, he thought he was helping me out.

But I didn't see it his way. Julianne was in part-time preschool for another year and a half; I had plenty of time to figure things out. Furthermore, I had begun taking this writing idea seriously. It gave me something to strive for, something to live for; it gave me purpose, even, though the idea terrified me. He knew I wanted to, so what was up with him? He certainly knew how to upset me.

It became apparent that I needed to tell J. about my messy situation—shaky relationship with husband, life unstable, inner turmoil, just trying to hang on for the time being. It wasn't easy to tell him, perhaps warn him is a more accurate way of putting it. I emailed him knowing full well I could frighten him off completely. But I couldn't keep these things from him; my heart told me to tell.

But of course the news scared him and he backed off. He viewed himself as another "potential destabilizing factor." "I want no part in it," he emailed. This was a smart move on his part, but now there was a chasm where my heart used to be that couldn't easily be mended.

That same week, when W. was in Munich after Christmas, I called to tell him that I wasn't sure whether I wanted to continue our relationship, though I wasn't yet ready to make changes of any kind—I needed time to sort out my issues first. I had already demonstrated during my college years that I was capable of acting in ways that were contrary to my best interest, and I had changed my mind about things before. I knew all this intellectually, yes, but my insides held no illusions about my predicament.

The news scared W. "I'm coming home, I'll catch the next flight back home," he pleaded with me.

"Don't bother, there's no need to, I'm not going anywhere for the time being. I just need to figure things out."

It wasn't easy to tell him these things but I needed for him to know. I needed *both* of them to know that I had had enough. So I told them both what I told them, all within a few days. I don't know what I had been thinking.

∞

After W. returned home and things became somewhat semi-normal, he returned to insisting that I go to work. "There's no evidence that you can write, and gambling on some future success is a luxury we can't afford," he said. He had the annoying habit of pointing out, with some measure of truth, both the drawbacks and my shortcomings in most any situation.

From my point of view, I saw writing as my only hope for a life of inner harmony. Besides, a job at this point would have been just another terrible demoralizing insult. But I needed time, as even a simple children's book could take many months from start to finish. So how could I have justified something that wasn't even started? All

I had was the guidance from the Counsel of Light, some measure of trust in myself (otherwise, why would I be thinking about it at all?) and my daily practice of listening to my thoughts, feelings, and dreams, and writing them into my journal. I tried to explain that I had been guided to write, that it was important that I did, but he found that idea hilarious. "*Who* says you're supposed to write? I don't like those words, *supposed to*. You're doing it again, listening to what others tell you to do. You're *so* naïve." And how could I have convinced him that it was I who wanted to write, if I didn't yet know what about?

Anyway, he refused to return to work and hung around the house too much, bugging me constantly because money was running out. The pressure to support our family financially mounted daily. It got really bad; I mean I even put off buying tires I needed.

I saw it coming like a rattlesnake that refuses to budge on a narrow trail; you have no choice but to go around it, sometimes in a serpentine way, rather than confronting it or stepping over it. By the way, I actually did encounter a persistent, unyielding, coiled-up, ready-to-strike, juvenile rattlesnake on my hike the morning after I began this paragraph—my first time ever to see one in the wild. I had desired a perfect metaphor to describe my special circumstances, had written a note to myself to look for a metaphor, which the rattlesnake then the following morning so promptly delivered: a metaphor of real-time significance, an actual, *defacto* obstacle. The rattlesnake with its poisonous bite I also viewed as the beginning of my demise—if I had reneged on my commitment to writing.

Be like water, Christine, I would tell myself. Find the path of least resistance around the obstacle and collect yourself on the other side. Water flows downhill; it always searches for the easiest way to go, for the lowest ground. Water doesn't care if there's a rock in its way—it simply flows around it. And over time, water smoothes rock until it becomes round and non-irritating.

In the short term, this meant that I'd have to at least pretend to look for temporary, part-time work. Paid work, I mean. As a domestic laborer, family logistics manager, tutor, chef, chauffeur, and laundress I did plenty of work, but it wasn't formally recognized, as is the case in most of the world. And of course when you do things your heart's not into, they don't usually turn out well. But at least the bomb was defused. At least that. But even after all that, I wasn't unsympathetic to W.'s wishes. I just thought his timing was off.

One morning during these difficult times, I awakened from a vivid dream. A woman was casually slicing small pieces of flesh off her right arm (her writing arm) using a regular kitchen knife. Strangely, as she examined her arm there wasn't any blood and it did not bleed as she cut it—maybe because by that time she was already bled dry. And she was wondering, this anonymous woman in the dream, how much more she would need to cut in order to be free. I awakened from this dream feeling strangely casual, but its message was not lost on me.

It wasn't easy, but I went around his demands as best I could. I wasn't about to return to work full time simply to appease someone who'd tried to make me do what he wanted me to do, even if that someone happened to be my husband. And *I don't even like you,* the way you've been lately, I thought to myself.

∞

Anyway, this whole miserable, out-of-control debacle, this series of unfortunate events was enough to make anyone come undone. But I walked that knife-edge, struggled to keep it all together though it hurt and the pain didn't go away. I didn't know when or if it would ever go away; I carried it around with me like a scarlet letter that had been pinned into my heart. And when I awakened mornings I was exhausted from restless sleep and a dread that infiltrated even my deepest dreams. And for what reason, exactly? I wanted to ask the universe: what kind of cruel joke did heaven play upon me? Who in their Infinite Wisdom thought this whole drama up?

Yes, this is exactly how I felt: as though I were an actor playing a role in a cruel and absurd soap opera, or some crazy play, except there wasn't an easy way out of *this* performance. I couldn't just scream, "Cut! I quit!" exit the stage, dissolve my contract, and leave this drama—this was my real life.

I hated it. It thought it was totally unfair. I had done inner work; I had grown emotionally, and I thought the tough part was over. I thought I'd be comfortably married till the end. It's kind of funny, now that I think of it: I had imagined myself fairly aspiring; I had imagined myself contributing to the world's betterment, to peace and harmony and understanding. Not this. Hopelessness and depression hung over me like a low foothill fog.

I tried to use logic to reason things through, but that proved futile and only left me more confused. Rather, thoughts that I had been set up by some universal powers hung around my head for months. I mean my mind was obsessing that those guys had set me up!

So what was I to do now? Could a new story line be created and acted out impromptu? Could my contract be altered? Maybe, but I couldn't merely inform my supporting actors that this theatre was over and I wanted to act in a new, more carefree and happy story— perhaps a romantic comedy of some sort, or a new genre of love story, or even a mystery solved by an unknown but brilliant investigator. I considered it, but this cast acted out their parts *so* convincingly, as though all this craziness was real, that I didn't think I could convince them otherwise. ("Wait you guys! This isn't real, we're just acting in some crazy play!")

So there was no way back or out. The only way was through it—no running away from anything—because the only thing I felt I had any control over was *how* I would perform the rest of my part of this story. I had no other control over the situation, and any control I thought I might have had was an illusion. I wondered whether I had control over my own self, even, over my own feelings, thoughts, and reactions. The personality, the identity *Christine* didn't seem to be in charge here.

Further, I didn't think I had gotten myself into this predicament because I had made some bad choices, and neither did I view this as punishment for being stubborn, naïve, or just plain stupid. No, I began to feel there must be something else in charge here, and that the picture was bigger than I was able to see at the time.

Trying to be helpful again, W. suggested I consider medication as a temporary measure to jump-start me out of my depression. But I knew this wasn't right for me and that it might even block the kind of "medicine" I was seeking—real answers to my puzzling life. His intentions were fine and good, but there was nothing wrong with me physiologically, nor was a chemical imbalance in my brain the cause of my depression. It's just that I had gotten myself into a bind that no one could help me out of. There was nothing that could comfort me or save me. I felt completely on my own in this. This is how I viewed my reality.

But why would I have wanted anyone—other than myself—to rescue me or save me from this craziness? As if I needed to be saved. Saved from what, anyway? Of course I wanted the issues in my life to be resolved, but I sure didn't feel that my soul needed to be saved, as though I had done something terribly wrong. I admit to no wrong. I wanted to participate in my own comeback and in the lifting of my own spirits; I wanted to save myself. Even if others had decided on giving me a break, what would it say about me if I did nothing to help myself? What would I have learned? How would that have helped my process as a human being? How would it have helped others? Besides, it's just dawned on me as I write this: if I had had it easier it would have made for a much less interesting story....

So if there were a way to solve all these problems successfully, I would commit myself to finding it. I also decided I needed to accept full responsibility for how I was going to proceed, and perhaps begin being responsible for what had already occurred. And since it was clear to me that nothing or no one else could help me, I had no choice but to search within for my own truth and my own answers— that was the bottom line, the point of it all, I realized.

I also called Flo Aeveia Magdalena in Vermont to set up a phone appointment with the Counsel of Light because I didn't know how on earth they expected me to fulfill my mission and write about love when my life was dread and despair. Delightful little children's books about love did they want? Well let me get right to it! What a joke. What was love anyway? I had no idea. The idea of an important assignment was fine and great but, frankly, what I really wanted to know is why my life was in such chaos. If I were going to write books, I expected real support and real answers.

The day of the spring equinox of 2002, Flo channeled a message from the Counsel of Light. The way the channeling worked was like so: Flo connected internally with the Counsel of Light and then they began speaking through her voice, which I heard over the phone. She also recorded everything on cassette tape, which she then sent to me. I didn't need to tell Flo what was going on in my life; the Counsel of Light already knew. They just began to talk and questions were left to the end of the session. They also went on for about an hour but I chose only the most concrete, the most helpful passages, to share here.

That day, The Counsel of Light suggested that I see beyond my immediate external circumstances and pay attention to my inner core to access the deeper meanings and learnings about my life situation, so that I could learn about how life works here, about the underlying rules of life. "What you're learning about now is how the pattern of human existence works and how it evolves…You're learning how you, Christine, transmute pain and suffering and therefore how pain and suffering can be transmuted—because that's what you came to teach, that's your wisdom. So you're getting hit over the head and you're saying that you can't figure this out—what's that saying to you? It's saying you're just like everybody else. Why are you like everybody else right now? Because you want enough compassion to be able to help people who can't find their way out of a paper bag. Because you know it's just a paper bag. (They must have been trying to be funny here—I was in that "paper bag" myself.) You're a very wise person, but it's just that you can't find your way out right now, you know. You're really depressed. So what do you do? You change the pattern. You focus on what you know will create the balance you need, and that's all you can do right now. And pretty soon, the commitment that you made to honor All That Is, and to rest in that and to trust that, starts to emerge as a way of being...and this is the time to integrate that wisdom so that you can go out and share it with the world...What we're saying to you has to do with your innate wisdom—your innate wisdom is so strong that it will guide you, but you have to let yourself get into that innate wisdom and that innate wisdom is accessed through your heart and soul right now....

"You have pain because you're human. You came in to be human because you can't help human beings without understanding what they go through, so you're going through what you're going through partially to help you to return to the wisdom of what's real and what's true, and also because it engenders compassion in you so that when people get really stuck, you'll be able to say, 'I know, I was stuck myself, I absolutely understand.' And we're not meaning to sound ruthless; we're meaning to tell you how it is so that you don't delude yourself into thinking that there's something that you could do outside of being at one with your own wisdom or your own being that will help this, because there isn't. Going into the deeper quest for your own wisdom gives you answers that have to do with all wisdom, and then you put things into place....

"This time for you is a time of coming into your power; it's coming into resolution with the world's issues and realizing that nothing that happens in the world can really affect you. It's hard to believe sometimes but yet you know that's true. And when you're unaffected you can act from truth, you can act from wisdom, you know what to do. You've had that experience before…

"And nothing is going to resolve in your outer world until you keep the commitment to be in love with and married to and organized around your own evolution. And that's really what all of this is about…To speed up the process of resolution, you come into unity with yourself…This is all about who you are, and we want you to go inside and see that so the bubble bursts, so you can get clear about this and you can say, wow, I've got myself back now," they said.

Well actually nothing was clear to me yet, but I was open to receiving clarity by paying close attention to my inner core and continuing my quest for answers. And like a good student, I asked the Counsel of Light pertinent questions about my assignment, questions such as "What is the best way for me to connect?"

The Counsel of Light prescribed a special meditation for connecting to my inner core and impressed upon me that receiving this meditation was the point of my call to them, as well as the key to everything else. "It's very simple: you take your hands, you put them on your body, you start the wave going, and you stay with that as long as you can and the more you do it, the less afraid you'll be, the more wisdom you'll have, and the more you'll understand. When you make the choice to live through wisdom and creation you begin to see with different eyes," they said.

So I dove in and worked on this meditation diligently: I lay down and closed my eyes, put my left hand on my heart and my right hand on my soul seed (at the center of the chest), breathed slowly and deeply, and went inside. I placed my attention on my heart and soul and with each downward count 10, 9, 8, 7, 6, relaxed more and more and with each breath 5, 4, 3, intended with all my power to go deeper into my heart and soul, 2, 1, because I knew there was nothing else for me to do and nowhere to go—except within. Then I got the wave going by imagining a circle going around my left hand and then around my right, together forming the figure eight, connecting the heart with the soul right under my hands.

I went to my innermost space without any resistance. The path within felt strangely comfortable, as though it was familiar to me from eons ago. After a few minutes, I noticed a subtle but tingling warmth in the center of my chest where I had placed my hands, and sensed a surrendering to my inner core. It felt so comfortable to be within, with a peace that wasn't present in my everyday life. And when I was deep within my core I asked, why is all this happening? And then I screamed silently to myself: what is all of this about? What is my life really for? What am I to do here and when?

The answers didn't come immediately, but I persevered, returning to my inner core as often as I could, often before falling asleep. Sometimes in the middle of the night when I found myself in that dreamy state between sleep and waking, I became aware of having been in the void, feeling the deep, deep peace of the nothingness within. This place became my safe harbor, a refuge of rest and restoration during these troubling times.

I practiced this meditation during the day as well. On extra challenging days, I visited the sauna at the association clubhouse. The sauna was a perfect place for de-stressing and private dialogues with myself as it was almost always empty. After turning up the heat and sprinkling water on the hot rocks, I would undress, lie on a towel, and then argue with myself in peace. Sometimes I argued with myself, sometimes with God. I repeated the questions I had screamed into the void, pleading out loud why all this was necessary and what was the point. Being naked with sweat pouring down every inch of my body helped my tears flow easier too.

The Counsel of Light had hinted that what was happening in my environment was helping me discover what my purpose was, but I couldn't see it yet. Furthermore, this sounded like too big of a project for me. I wondered if they had gotten the right person; perhaps this was simply a case of mistaken identity. Even though I had imagined them to be the "command control" of the universe and they happened to be aware of my life circumstances, how reliable were their messages? The other thing was, they used terminology I didn't understand, terms such as *levels of being, formulae of consciousness,* and *foundations of truth*—which I was going to write about. It took many months for my brain to register portions of what they had said. The topics were so abstract, and they often jumped from one concept to another without any transition. Finally, how reliable are messages from other realms that tell you that you'll write a series of popular books on love and life and you haven't demonstrated any of these gifts as yet?

This fear of being misled was a major obstacle to my progress then; it paralyzed me for months. But I also worried about being misled by my own self—a crazy idea to lead yourself down a black hole with, to then have to slog through. For if you can't trust in your own inner self, in what you feel rings true for you, in your deepest intuition and heart spaces—then where are you? What else can you live by? It would be like trying to drive in a blizzard-filled night in a vehicle from which the headlights and windshield wipers had been swiped, with nothing to guide you except the awareness that thick snow blocked your view. So you pull over to the side of the road, straight into a ditch.

But ultimately these uncertainties didn't matter anymore because the idea of becoming a writer was now permanently lodged in my head and wouldn't go away. I started to imagine that one day I'd be known as a successful author. Wishful thinking, some might say, or else I had been brainwashed.

Anyway, this whole thing was extremely annoying. Just what did they expect of me? *What did everyone want from me!* So in the sauna I told myself and those listening in their other dimension (the sauna being as good a place as any for getting a hold of them, I thought at the time) that if I were being misled into something I, the person whose name was Christine Hoeflich, did not want or could not accomplish, *I would not go through with their fucking plan.* They were counting on me to fulfill my life plan, and I thought this gave me some leverage over them. But then it didn't take too long for me to realize that my leverage was like dust in my hands because it was stupid to remain at a standstill when my life was so uncomfortable. And then, slowly, I began to realize that it *was* my life plan I was acting out, a plan I at one point fully and knowingly accepted, even jumped at the chance to accomplish. (*What ever was I thinking?*) They were simply doing their job trying to help me remember, that's all.

From my Soul Recognition work I understood that with the help of guides, the individual soul makes a life plan for itself while still in the heavenly realm, before incarnating on earth. The plan defines the agreements made with others and the learning that will be experienced so that the individual will grow, evolve, and come to know who he or she is. In other words, the earth experience we choose is mainly for our learning, the type and direction of which is dependent on our individual "soul blueprint."

I understood these ideas and knew in my heart they were true. But it's one thing to mentally understand the concepts and another thing altogether to live your life plan effectively and graciously once the soul has incarnated into the body. The soul knows it's infinite; it has the answers, it's safe; it is security itself. It knows the bigger picture, why the life plan ultimately makes sense—not only for the individual's own life but also in the larger context of humanity and the universe. But for a human living a human life, it's a whole different story. We forget what this earth experience is about; we don't have our life plan spelled out for us, we're not born with a manual, and also, learning the lessons necessary for growth is hardly ever easy, as learning often involves change. In addition, sometimes it requires us to stand alone while the pressure to conform to society's norms or to meet the expectations of others is enormous.

But who would have known it would be this difficult? Who would have known our paths wouldn't be strewn with rose petals, that perhaps it would be way more challenging than anticipated when we had first planned this whole adventure? After all, there's only one way out of a life plan. The other thing is, once one is here, one can't just change her mind about what she wants in life, think positively, recite some simple affirmations, give off some positive vibrations and…abracadabra—her life is transformed. Our life plans might be much more involved than that—which is what I was realizing about my own.

While my life plan involved a great opportunity—which the Counsel of Light would remind me of during my phone consultations—now that I was in the middle of this "opportunity" I didn't find it so wonderful. When things got tough, I admit that I felt like screaming at anyone who had anything to do with my current circumstances, be they from this realm or not. But as tempting as that was, blaming others wouldn't help my situation, and it could even prolong my discomfort and confusion by extending the learning experience.

Anyway, grains of sand going down an hourglass is a good metaphor for my diminishing spirit as the months went by and I would think about not having actually written anything of value yet. At the beginning of the summer, I was scribbling random journal entries and trying to use my inner voice to write a little story for children called "Who Are You?" but this story was turning out to be nothing really new or exciting. I was trying to push my inner voice to do what I wanted (*make it* write a children's story) rather than trusting it. I wasn't quite ready to trust it yet. How could I have been?

How could I have trusted anyone or anything? With such results, I constantly had to talk myself into persisting, telling myself that at least I was showing up, at least I was making an effort and preparing myself for eventual inspiration.

Sometime around then, I began to realize that the only way to gain peace in my life was to begin implementing my soul's plan. I also came to feel that deep down, my heart *couldn't* be misled, and that I would eventually keep my soul agreements, the promises I made to myself and others, though I hadn't a clue as to what those were yet. Cultivating that deep connection with my heart and soul helped me make this leap of faith—that, plus having no better options. This is when I committed to listening to the inner voice that seemed to come from my heart and soul. I surrendered to it and let it guide me, not just part of the time, but whenever I became conscious of its cues. For example, if I had a hunch to call a friend, I would do so as quickly as possible. Besides practicing my meditation, I also cultivated the habit of being silent and still for a few moments several times a day while paying attention to my inner core, meanwhile listening for inner promptings—which helped me become more aware of them and not let them pass by unnoticed. And then just a few days thereafter, during a hike up St. Joseph's hill, my inner voice spoke up clearly and gave me an idea for "A Story for Julianne." I jotted down a few words and kept the note for future reference. At that point, we hadn't even taken our Disneyland trip yet. (And actually, we wouldn't have gone if my sister Lydia hadn't offered us the tickets and a hotel room stay.)

∞

About a week later in mid-July, wanting guidance again, I received another session with the Counsel of Light (through Flo via the phone, as usual) where they asked me not to care too much about how I felt, but to connect within and get to work on my creativity.

"Part of the next few weeks for you is a curve of learning in which you are consciously aware of your solar plexus, of your soul area, and of your heart area. We call this the sacred space. Where is it taking you?…In each moment, you're alert and aware and you're following your guidance…

"Your whole job here in a sense is to bring the communication with the source or with the creative or with the interconnectedness into a frame where children talk about it. You want to teach the children how to make the connection with the sources and the guides and the expansiveness of their own intuition so that they can begin to develop their sense of ground, stability, and strength. So you're making bridges between what has context in the heart but has no language in the mind; you're providing a map for children to find their way through life, you're retraining the children who have been conditioned through fear; and you're healing that which has been taught to children from the illusion rather than from the basic premise of the way this universe is run…Part of what you're really doing besides teaching the children and giving them different ways of viewing everything is you're bringing spirit into matter…You're here to literally change the systems that exist here, and by doing that, you're instructing them how to live in harmony and in cooperation with all things…How do we express truth to children?—that's the number one question you're asking yourself….So you're very much dedicated to revealing aspects of consciousness that no one seems to understand…

"So don't focus on getting a job. Focus on how hard getting a job is when you don't want to get a job and when you want to be free and your situation doesn't allow you to be free. Find the freedom in the situation anyway….

Near the end of our session, I asked them, "How do I know when I'm following my guidance?"

"Excitation, when you get excited. You want to ride the wave of creation, so when you're riding it it's as if you're living in the moment and there's nothing else…What you're doing, distinctly, is providing a deeper relationship with your being, and when you're in this deep relationship with your being you feel better, you're more alive, you're healthier, you're clearer. And when you stop, everything stops, everything gets kind of stagnant…And you pay attention, and you spend time doing what you get excited about."

They must have sensed my worry about what I was supposed to do because they ended our phone conversation saying, "Have some faith here; don't worry so much, because it's not about worrying, it's not about whether you do it right or you do it wrong—it's that you are being creation in moments and in ways that you haven't seen people be yet. In other words, you're doing something new; so there's not a template for this. You're not writing a book about, oh, you know, the Civil War. You're coming up with a new genre of a book. You're writing a book about how you live in a dimension where the spiritual energy is separate from the practical experience and how to bring them back together, because that's what's causing people so much pain. So you're doing something new. So don't expect it to look like something old. Allow it, because you don't know any better—how can you be so worried about something that you don't know anything about? It doesn't make any sense! You're being very incongruent! You're being very human, but you're being very incongruent." *Chuckle chuckle.* (They laughed light-heartedly here—at me I suppose—because I certainly wasn't laughing with them.)

"You're worried that you're not going to do *this* and you're not going to do *that*, but you haven't started yet! So you start and you let it flow and you let it flow and you let it flow and pretty soon, you'll wake up one morning and it'll all be done and you don't know how it got done but you kept track of it and you wrote about it and then you read it and then you get it. Sometimes you'll write it and you won't even get it until you read it, until you go back and you realize—wow!—this was really what was happening, but I was too involved or enmeshed in it to understand it. So now what you're going to do is put it together and look at it, but in a literal sense it's much more important for you to be a part of the process than to get a result. And you of course want a result but the most important thing is to be part of the process. If the result is what you're focusing on, it's harder to get a result. So you do not want to focus on the result; you want to join in the essence of creation and unfold. All right?" they said.

All right, I suppose. Yes I heard them, but since there was no context in my mind for what they said, I was still worried, especially since it was apparent to me that there was a big disconnect between my inner life and my outer identity and circumstances, as though my inner and outer reality were out of sync, or something.

The weeks continued to go by and my efforts slowly began to pay off, though it certainly seemed like two steps forward and one step back. My resistance began to dissolve, and I developed more trust in my inner self. I liked the idea of listening within for direction, and the more I paid attention to my sacred space, the better I seemed to feel. Besides, what really mattered is not that weeks and months went by, because they would have gone by anyway, but what I would have to show for it.

Still, fear and reality crept in, muddied my mind, and I became unsettled when I tried to explain to others what I was planning to do with my life (become a successful author). Then also thoughts about my own sanity lurked in the back of my mind and pounced like a tiger uncaged in the middle of the night: "Did you really agree to this? You don't actually remember, do you? Perhaps W. is right about you after all. Seems, anyway, like a case of you against him. We'll see who's going to win in the end, won't we? So what will become of you? What will happen to your children? What if you never find your inspiration? You're no writer, and besides, you've got absolutely nothing to say and you know it too; you've known this for a long, long time. Perhaps you *are* just like everyone else and perhaps if you're lucky, you'll take a job reading endless boring reports on government policy, pretending your efforts will make a damned difference. So what will you do? Where will you go? Can you trust the Counsel of Light? What will your mother think? She will just die, your poor mother. What will everyone think?"

"The people who know you, your friends, they think you're out of touch with reality," I could hear W. saying. I registered this phrase over and over again in that part of my brain reserved for terror and adrenaline and reptilian instinct. He never told me who these friends were, who saw me so full of lofty delusions. I, of course, did not wish to be seen by others, especially by my friends, that way.

There seemed to be no end to my angst, and my mind reeled crazily through the night, even though the Counsel of Light told me not to worry, that I was "playing with a full deck." (I wasn't exactly reassured.) It bothered me that these obnoxious thoughts would visit me at these dreadful hours, at a time when I had little capacity to deal with them except to let them run wild like children on high-fructose corn syrup, until, totally exhausted, I'd finally collapse back to sleep. Even though I was basically sane, I had obsessions enough to keep me awake nights.

But the next morning, dreads having faded, I again made a sincere effort to rely more and more on my newfound relationship with my inner core to get me through the day. Besides, taking my children to school and seeing all those sane teachers and sane parents and conversing with them on sane, ordinary everyday things made my night tossing seem foolish.

But anyway, I had begun to give my inner life at least as much attention as my outer life. That's what I think made the difference; the relationship with my inner core became at least as important as everything else going on around me.

Then gradually I noticed that sensations of joy and excitement began to stir within, sometimes when I least expected it, such as when I awakened at night or when I was driving. I experienced these feelings—which I began to recognize as triumph and indestructibility—more and more often, regardless of my basically unchanging outer life circumstances, as though my inner happiness no longer depended on them as much. W. was still bugging me: "If you refuse to work, we're going to have to reverse mortgage the house," he claimed. And except for some "hellos" at school and a few mostly uninteresting, curt emails such as, "How are you? I'm fine," J. was still avoiding me. Despite these things, I didn't have to try to manipulate my feelings but was genuinely beginning to feel better because I was developing a relationship with my inner self.

∞

Then in October in another channeled message (I thought things weren't moving fast enough), the Counsel of Light told me that it was very important for me to more deeply forge the connection to creation and to trust that there was a process unfolding, because in the next few months I'd be "getting in my power." They said, "You know something that it is time to take the recipe for and give the recipe out so everybody can cook the same meal, in a sense…You don't have an agenda in this lifetime. You didn't come here to learn anything in particular. You came here to activate the consciousness of the new world, and of course you have to activate your own consciousness on the way in there…Your job is to foundation and contain the structure for the new world, and to support the children in bringing it forth, to call the consciousness into being so that the children understand that it's now time for that consciousness…So let's show you how you can make sure that everyone who's here—particularly the children—remembers how creation works and begins to create a new world…

"So what you'll do is root the Christ consciousness, the energy of that—there is only oneness, and it's time for oneness—that idea. You'll root that idea—that's the Christ consciousness idea, the Christine idea, the Christ-ine idea," they went on, as though they were trying to have me get something, but my mind was a brick wall then. "This energy is, you know, really important and very consciously being orchestrated right now…

"What you're being given is an opportunity of a lifetime…You're sitting on a pot of gold…This is about something so big that everything changes because of this and you want to find that place within you that knows this is your mission. You want to find and get in touch with and be aware of and live through the energy of that much freedom and that much connection with truth" (and "embrace all of it," I suppose, if I felt like using New Age, positive-thinking jargon, which I don't, and can't seem to be able to pull off).

"So you rest, and relax, and de-stress yourself, and not worry about where you're going to end up…You just let yourself be, you just let the flowing occur, let the energy unfold. As you rest and relax and open and receive and in some ways, trust the process—not trust that the universe is going to do something, but trust that there's a process unfolding. And as you trust the process you are more and more available to a responsiveness because you're not worried. And worry stops the creative process…

"Who are you? Why are you here? How can you activate the hugeness of your consciousness?…It's not about trying harder. It's not about giving things up. It's about connecting, and as you connect, everything starts to make sense. All right?"

Well I was certainly trying to connect all right, trying to understand, though I don't think I was quite ready to trust the process. Anyway, I realized that I needed to continue to cultivate the connection with my inner core so that the wisdom I'm carrying can come into my awareness. The commitment to myself and to my own evolution and expansion would need to come first. And regarding my life situation, I slowly began to realize that the point wasn't how I resolved the chaos so I could live more comfortably and get on with my purpose, but how were my life circumstances *already* part of my life purpose? How were they already forwarding my life purpose?

What were they trying to teach me? So I asked the universe: assist me in my life purpose; assist me in serving humanity. And it was not long afterwards that I began to notice that the uplifting feelings were sometimes accompanied with words and new insights. The further along in my process of connecting within and listening, the more I could express my feelings with words that came from within, and could write them on pages. Like an investigator to a mystery, I wrote whatever insights came into my consciousness, and tried to set aside about a half hour each day for this practice.

∞

That same month, another interesting occurrence: while walking back to our car after dropping Angelika off at school, Julianne and I were startled by a walnut that landed near us from clear out of the sky. I stood for a moment and looked around. An old lone almond tree stood by the road, but there weren't any walnut trees in sight. J., who happened to be strolling about a hundred feet behind, caught up to us and explained that a blackbird had dropped that nut. "Blackbirds fly up high and drop nuts onto hard surfaces so that the nuts crack. They know exactly how high they need to fly and they know to drop it onto the pavement. They've learned to do that," he explained. "But *how* do they know?" he asked, looking straight at me.

"They just know," I replied, as though it were obvious.

"It only takes one of them to learn a new behavior. The others follow, and soon thereafter, they've all learned it. Just like the 100th monkey theory. That's how evolution works," he went on. "It just takes that first one—the one that will begin. Everything depends upon that first one."

At this point the investigator part of my brain kicked in because something he had said had caught my attention. "Do you really think it's important which one of them is the first? Does it really matter, which one?" I asked.

"Yes," he said, looking straight at me, "It's very important."

We reached my car by that time, exchanged "have a good day," and then off he went to his. And after he was gone I thought to myself—what exactly did you mean with those words, using those words? Where did you get them from? Why did you tell me those things? I was agitated because I knew he had given me a message, just like the characters in *The Celestine Prophesy*—the book we had discussed several months before—kept on doing. They were always giving each other secret messages and having intense discussions about it as well.

Well, I knew *what* the message was, just not the *why* or the *how* of it. But I never asked him any of these questions; I don't know why. Maybe it's because he might not have known the answers, might not have had a clue. He might have even *denied* giving me any secret messages. I also thought it might be a good idea, at least for the time being, to keep my investigative activities a secret.

Keeping things to myself, I thought about blackbirds for the next several days; thoughts of blackbirds and their ways filled my head. I thought blackbirds know what they know because they're connected to that infinite intelligence in the universe, and because of this, they instinctively sense whatever they need. They are somehow able to read the landscape and the energy, somehow they sense the hardness of the earth below, and they "know" that dropping a nut from a certain distance will crack the shell. They have all they need to perceive their world and act accordingly so that they evolve and thrive as individuals and also as a species because they're connected to all of creation—through a web of interconnectedness.

Determined in my role as secret investigator, I continued to pose questions about birds to myself as I went about daily life…Two months later in mid-December, those pushy blackbirds were still on my mind as I flew to a winter solstice gathering in San Jose organized by Father Charlie Moore, an unconventional Catholic priest (a peculiar bird, some might say). Father Moore was a slim, soft-spoken man who looked like he was in his mid-to-late sixties. (He wasn't wearing a priest's habit as he had been "excused" from his vocation.) The topic of the discussion was "Nation Building—or How to put our Country Back Together Again."

Father Moore addressed the flock gathered to hear him that evening, first by saying that eagles are heavy birds, seemingly too heavy for flight, but they are able to fly upwards with ease by finding updrafts using telepathic power. "Ducks do the same thing," he quacked. He viewed telepathy as "internal technology" and the use of telepathic power as "magic." It is well known among his followers that Father Moore is a gold nest of philosophy and scholarly knowledge and I scribbled and chicken-scratched pages and pages of notes that evening—I know investigators do this all the time.

Then he began to crow about spirituality and the role that true masters play in spirituality: true masters never tell you what to do or what not to do, what to believe, or to believe in them. They only help you try to figure it out for yourself by helping you get in touch with yourself. They help you get in touch with yourself so you can access what you know deep inside your heart because your heart already knows everything; it knows exactly what to do. In other words, by "remembering" what's in your heart, you access your inner knowing, your inner wisdom, crowed Father Moore. Which means that by connecting to your heart, you simultaneously connect to the whole universe, I thought. (!) I was excited because I was finally beginning to make heads or tails—bird tails, mind you—of these ideas. My connecting and investigating activities were finally beginning to pay off.

Father Moore continued: "In true education, you are questioned until you remember what you already know. In conditioning, you memorize what you are told. The difference is, we believe what we are conditioned to believe but we know what we remember…Jesus never claimed to save us from our sins. He only said, 'You are the master.' Look in the mirror—you are originally innocent…" Then he said that "some belief systems require people to believe unconditionally things that are totally unbelievable; they require you to believe the opposite of what you remember, the opposite of what's in your heart—which is what induces schizophrenia and mental illness." I saw another way of putting this: some things we have been led to believe are for the birds. Curious about schizophrenia, I looked up the definition: "a psychotic disorder characterized by loss of contact with the environment and disintegration of personality expressed as disorder of feelings, thought, and conduct." Ahem. I supposed that "loss of contact with the environment" included loss of contact with reality.

The evening lecture went on and I chicken-scratched another revealing quote that got my attention, this one from the Gospel of Thomas: "The one who seeks will find, and the one who finds will become disturbed because of the conflict between what he is told and what he remembers." (Oh no! Was this fate being spelled out for me?)

Father Moore elaborated on the role of the master: "Masters help you use your power. Masters say, 'The power of the master is in every one of us. Do you remember that you have the power? Do you remember that you are a master?' So instead of worshiping God, use the powers you were given and *be* the glory of God."

I interpreted this to mean that this power is innate but since we aren't aware of it, it remains dormant. Come to think of it, it's a good example of something we don't know that we don't know. There are things I *do know* that I don't know: cosmology, for instance. The difference is, I *do know* how to learn about cosmology. And then there are things—like telepathic power—that I didn't even know that I didn't know. I mean, people don't go around saying, "I can't seem to find my inner power. Where's my inner power?" They aren't aware they have such a thing in the first place. But when this new idea (for example, telepathic power) enters into the domain of possibility for you and you connect to your heart and "remember" what you know deep inside, then you begin to have access to that power.

When you listen to your heart, you begin to have access to the power of a master.

Father Moore suggested asking your inner self for guidance. "The answer to any question you may have will be whispered in your heart," he said. He also spoke of Pocahontas's prayer for help—"Listen, listen, God please listen, until I hear you hearing me. For I know when I hear you hearing, I shall be well."

Lastly, Father Moore said, "When you begin to do really truthful things, you're going to make a lot of people mad." Well, we'll just have to see about that, I thought. And then I remembered that in a previous lecture, he also said that people on the discovery of truth get hooked on something called the ecstasy of the heart, which sure sounded good to me.

I found this bird philosophy fascinating and uplifting and, feeling on top of the world with my newfound insights, I took wing and soared home. And although I attended a lecture on nation building, on dreaming the American dream, on building our nation on the principles of Thomas Jefferson and Benjamin Franklin, who used the golden rules of freedom, equality, and brother/sisterhood, principles originally inspired and borrowed by Jefferson and Franklin from the Iroquois nation—many Native American tribes were matrilineal and based on women's wisdom, so why not?—I got my blackbird questions answered: I learned that "the power" was intuition, or telepathic power, or inner voice, and that the DNA was a kind of radio transmitter and receiver for this telepathic energy. I learned that this power was accessible through the heart and soul (or the sacred space, as the Counsel of Light called it), that your inner voice whispers, never commands, and that it always sounds like yourself, not like someone else. Sometimes you get your questions answered if you wonder long enough, I thought back then—even questions about blackbirds and their ways.

I wrote a few paragraphs about what I had learned and emailed it to J., who sent me additional material on blackbirds, including a photo of one, and told me that my writing flowed well.

∞

Now that I look back, I realize it didn't take *that* long to connect within and establish a pattern of steady progress, which gave me some trust and confidence in my inner core. I had started my meditation practice at a low point in March. In July, I had been inspired by an idea for "A Story for Julianne." In October, I had written the first draft, and became fascinated with blackbirds. In December, I had written what I had learned from Father Charlie Moore. By now life looked more promising, and I thought that *perhaps* I was on my way to becoming a writer after all.

Meanwhile, W. had found an interesting job and returned to work around the end of October, so we didn't have to reverse mortgage the house. He also wanted us to stick together, but I was in a completely different space internally and required more independence and the freedom to write—which was at odds with his idea of what I ought to be doing. Well, it's not that I suddenly had become so brave, but I was bolstered by my strengthening connection with my inner self, and even by occasional communication, mostly by email, with J.

Though J. didn't reveal much about himself, I had a feeling his life wasn't exactly rose petals either. A few days before the blackbird incident, we had crossed paths at school. He seemed to be in good spirits that morning, so I emailed to let him know that he looked bright-eyed and bushy-tailed, then asked, "So tell me, what's your secret?"

He emailed back, "I don't know what it is that keeps me going. Maybe I have some kind of nuclear reactor inside of me. Well, I would say that my love of nature and the shopping mall keep me going. You have had my motor going. Wanna start up my motor again sometime?"

"What can I expect when I get your motor up and running?"

"You can expect a long drive," he wrote.

Naturally, I wanted to know more—for one thing, how long a long drive was ("as long as it takes").

Okay, so we had had some fun and games via email sometimes but, other than the occasional encounter at our children's school, we didn't meet for an entire year and a few months into the next, not even for coffee. Not that I didn't want to, but that's just the way it was. Like secret friends, we helped each other go on in our duties and our pursuits, but from a distance.

Interestingly, after I noticed a greater sense of spiritual strength and inner confidence in myself, these uplifting energies began to be reflected in the outer world, as well as in my dreams. On the last morning of the year, I dreamt that I was going up a skyscraper in an elevator, except that the elevator didn't move in a straight line but went up and around the outside face of the building in the configuration of a loose spiral that reminded me of the DNA helix. I pressed myself into a corner with my arms flat against the walls since I am seriously afraid of heights. I was with a man whom I did not recognize to be anyone in particular, though he definitely seemed familiar. We got off at the floor with a food court. The multitude of colorful food stands, which reminded me of Quincy Market Colonnade in Boston, were abundant with huge assortments of fruits and vegetables and even Polish *kielbasa*.

Together we walked into a brightly-lit diner where my companion tried to order for us a romantic Italian meal with wine and the works despite it being the wrong place for that—on the menu were dishes like gefilte fish soup. To me, it was clear what was or wasn't on the menu, but my companion, insisting on Italian, began to argue with the waiter. I felt awkward; I didn't want to be there. And while my companion is fighting with the waiter, I'm thinking I really ought to get out of there—forget about the pasta—and get back on that elevator and continue spiraling upwards.

I awakened in high spirits and interpreted the dream to mean that I was on the right track, that I just needed to continue to cultivate that connection with my inner self and not pay too much attention to all those things and events in my environment, in other words, to not get myself distracted by secondary life matters such as pasta or gefilte fish, or even men. After all, romance wasn't even on the menu at the time.

Was I ever glad to have the last few years behind me, especially 2002. 2000 through 2002: The Terrible Years. I took my old calendar from 2002 outside and set fire to it a few minutes into the New Year. "Burn," said the primal goddess in me. And it burned.

Moving Through

AND THE DAY CAME WHEN THE RISK TO REMAIN
TIGHT IN A BUD WAS MORE PAINFUL
THAN THE RISK IT TOOK TO BLOSSOM.
—*Anais Nin*

It wasn't very clear to me then, but by connecting to my inner core and listening to my inner voice, I had begun the journey "home" to my deepest, truest self. Slowly, I began to live and express from my heart and soul—by "dropping down" into that sacred space and letting it guide me. It began with little things like writing an idea, calling someone, going to a book reading, or even going shopping with energetic Julianne. I acted on whatever inner messages or hunches I received and often, noticed interesting things or gained new insights as a result of following through.

I suppose to some extent I had done this all along, but what was new was having more conscious attention on it, and also, I didn't dismiss the inner voice as readily—I followed through deliberately and immediately. Not a whole lot in my situation had resolved itself, but now I was more connected to my core. That was the difference, and also the way I began to make changes in my life.

Sometimes I experienced fear, which sometimes made me procrastinate and other times actually catalyzed me into action. But when I got connected to my inner core, my fear lessened because I felt connected to something bigger than my limited identity. I actually began to feel this connection (as an exciting or uplifting feeling); it was real and palpable, and so I began to trust it.

This is the core of what I think happened: except for my inner core (and beings from another dimension, with whom I spoke only occasionally, like a couple times a year) I didn't receive much encouragement and support for my writing or mission, not even from my own mind (which at times was in a panic about it). But the more I connected, listened to my inner voice, followed through, and saw results in the form of serendipitous events, signs, and valuable insights, the more I trusted the process. And when I began to trust my self, my mind then began to calm down.

My core guided me, though I had worries and doubts galore, though I didn't have the answers, though my actions didn't always make sense from others' points of view. Sometimes I'd have to tell my mind to calm down, that my core would take care of things. That's how I got through—I set aside the crazy thoughts and placed my trust in the core. And it guided me; it took me to the next step, though in the beginning I didn't see my next step until it was right in front of me.

In February 2003, I got a hunch to call Flo again to set up a talk with the Counsel of Light. They asked me to keep doing what I was doing. They said, "It's important that you understand that you're going through a particular time period where you have an opportunity to choose to sustain this kind of experience for the rest of this lifetime. So it's not automatic. Is this something that you feel comfortable with?…This is choice time. It's a time to really ask yourself—is this energy that you're working with in terms of creativity and in terms of connection with the invisible and in terms of feeling the core energy being much more important than the outer relationships of your life and really understanding who you are for the first time—is this now what you choose?

"This time of awareness is extremely important…What the choice is about is bringing together the potential with the actual and marrying the course of that consciousness within the body, and opening to formulate a whole new dimensional reality, and opening out to that dimensional reality as if it were this reality. So when we say 'bringing heaven to earth,' we're really talking about changing the existing vibrational quality of consciousness.

"And the good news is that the fear is much less strong than the connection to the core. You have really made amazing inroads into that consciousness, and there's really nothing that you need to worry about in terms of the process that's unfolding. It's truly an amazing experience for you to go forward without knowing what the answers are…What causes the fear is the not knowing. But what's so amazing is you're not in a place energetically of fear. It isn't about the fear anymore. It's really about, wow, this inner amazing and very gracious space of creation is so important to you and so strong that you now choose to live from that place." (I didn't know what they were so amazed at, because I hadn't written anything amazing yet.)

"It's not about 'what should I do?' It's more about: what is my consciousness telling me to do because, it's hard to describe to you, but what you want to think about Christine is that when you listen to the knowing (within), the actions that support the knowing make peace wherever you go. They help to bring awareness to each situation and to clarify and acknowledge things in ways that really support life, and happiness, and health, and wellness, and so forth. So part of what you're learning to do is to support the knowing because you realize if you do that, then even if you don't know how, the outcomes will be much more positive for everybody. And so you really make a choice to do that…

"So instead of asking questions about survival and about the outcome, you're asking 'what's being told to me today? What am I aware of right now? How is the foundation designing itself from my inner yearnings so I know what to pay attention to, what to strive for, what to affirm and intend and connect through?'...You're following this very clear guidance and as you follow it, it brings you everything you need in the moment, it gives you the awareness that you need, it opens the doors to everything that you'll need...It provides the keys to the kingdom in a sense...the secrets of how life really works here...

"Really there's not anything you need to be worried about...It's challenging because you've never lived this before, you don't have a guide for this, and it's not like you're waking up knowing that everything will be the same; you're waking up knowing that everything's going to be different...And what you're learning in the next few months is that the inner connection will get you through...

"So what you're learning is that there is interconnectedness... When people know that, they're not afraid anymore. Whatever they need will come. It will come as soon as they let go and let it come. It's trusting the interconnectedness and knowing that everything is already woven together and when you live from that place everybody will benefit because they're also part of the interconnectedness. That's why you called us today—so that we can tell you that the interconnectedness is real."

∞

Around the beginning of March 2003, W. and I had a heart-to-heart talk and decided it would be best if my next step were to look for another place to live. Though I didn't have anything figured out yet, I felt I had little choice. I knew there was a bigger picture to everything that had happened (and was still happening) and it was my job to discover what that was and bring it to resolution.

About three weeks later, more pain and confusion entered our world when W. found out about J. Apparently, Angelika first tipped him off after noticing that J. talked to me too much for her liking. She found his name in the school directory. Then W. had discovered a couple emails and confronted me about the relationship. "I want you out of this house, and fast," he said to me.

I admitted to an emotional attachment, and of course he wasn't pleased. And though he believed me when I told him that we hadn't slept together or even been getting together, he was more upset about the emotional bond (the heart connection, I suppose). A one-night fling would have been more acceptable to him. "You could have had your fling, and it would have been done with," he said.

Later that day I heard him crying; sitting on the bathroom floor with his back against the locked door, he was shaking and sobbing, and he wouldn't let me in. It was just too much to bear. I would have reversed this mess if I could have. The only thing that saved me was my heart, which told me to move out and write for the benefit of all—which gave me something to live for.

Yes, when you listen to your heart for guidance, maybe it works out best for everyone involved—at least that's what I was intuiting, grasping with, praying for. Of course, the truth of this isn't so apparent in the midst of a painful tragedy. The pain of the children was a very big concern for me, but also the very real pain of the adults who, unlike me, didn't know there was a much larger picture playing itself out. I knew there was a larger, deeper explanation for this apparent disaster, but I didn't know what that was yet, and there's no way I could have explained what little I knew well enough to alleviate the concerns of others, or that by trying to explain it, it would have made a damned difference to anyone anyway. Would it have made a difference to anyone (except for maybe the children, who were more trusting and open-hearted and impressionable) if I had said, "Trust me, I'll get to the bottom of all of this; I'll take care of things. And W., just trust me, will you? Because—I promise you—I'll get to the bottom of the business behind this alleged affair." Yeah, right.

The year before, the Counsel of Light had encouraged me to think this, with their message of wisdom that all of us have chosen this experience, that it applies to everyone, every single one of us involved, even the children, and that I was going to make sense of it and share what I learned with the world. But who would have believed me? "This is a natural evolution that you've all chosen," The Counsel of Light had said. "They may know at different levels and that's how it gets a little tricky…because most people don't have the spiritual understanding to know that they've chosen to be in the situations that they're in. So the one who is conscious needs to deal with that part, because they can't." So there I was, walking that edge between two worlds again, between this reality and another reality.

I did my best to understand and tried to explain as much as I thought my family could grasp, as much as I understood. I wasn't smug about it, didn't tell them this was something that everyone chose, did not mention that part at all, or anything about growth and evolution for that matter. I tried to calm everyone and to keep believing in the heart and in love and in truth. I tried to explain my course of action to my children, but other than "I'm following my heart," "mom and dad don't get along," "mom has to write so that everything will be fine in the end," and "you will always be loved by both of us," I could not tell them anything else.

Further, I tried to release my fear, keep stabile and strong, and continue connecting and listening to my core. I knew I was the catalyst for everyone's growth and development. And since remaining at a standstill was a betrayal not only of myself but to others as well, I went ahead with my inner guidance, because at least I would still have myself, and because I really needed to resolve this situation. By following the guidance of my inner core, I knew that ultimately I would make it up to my family somehow, regardless of how my actions were perceived at the time. Making it up to everyone involved, especially the children, was my very intent.

∞

The next few months, I went house hunting for a place for myself and my children. First, I came across a two-bedroom guest house on a large property in Monte Sereno that had a pool, a dog, and was close to school—good qualities as seen by my children. I developed a rapport with the landlady and discovered her uncle was a former neighbor—more pluses. On the downside, the cottage's ceilings were only seven feet high, which made me feel slightly claustrophobic, though I hadn't noticed my psychological responses to ceilings until then. The rent was also somewhat out of my budget, which meant I'd need a part-time job or to pinch pennies—not possible with children. I told the landlady I was interested but, just to be sure, I needed to sleep on it and I'd get back to her on Monday morning.

But Monday morning came and went and I hadn't made a decision. I didn't feel connected, couldn't hear my inner guidance but instead was consumed by anxiety and a feeling of "not rightness." How could I trust myself then? Where was this connection that had guided me before?

So I emailed J. for advice, writing, "Hi J., I found a possible place to live, but I can't feel or hear my inner guidance because I'm anxious and scared. I don't feel right, so how can I know what is best to do? Help! I need to make a decision right now."

J. emailed back immediately: "Hello there. I'm sorry you're feeling anxious. Try to take an hour or more to relax. Get as calm as you can and try to sleep a little. That should help you with getting some guidance. Let me know how things go. Talk to you later, okay? Got to go now." Sometimes I could depend on J. for some wonderful stuff but I never knew for sure.

I took his advice, lying down on my bed in the guest room and relaxing as much as I could. I also added a little prayer, just in case: "I ask the universe to give me a clear sign about this cottage, because I know I can't trust myself at this time to pick up subtle messages that can be interpreted one way or the other. So I'm asking for a clear sign that will show me without a doubt what is best for my family and me. And thank you God for assisting me."

About an hour went by, time to get Angelika home from school, but I hadn't received any clear messages yet. I got into my car, trying to be as quiet and calm as possible, still patiently waiting for a sign from the universe. Then without thinking, about half a block from school I turned the radio on to almost blasting. At that moment Bono (of the Irish rock band U2) sang "I still haven't found what I'm looking for."

That was it, the sign I had been waiting for! There was no way I could misinterpret it; it was clear and I was pleased, not only with the guidance itself but with its form as well. When I returned home, I emailed the landlady to let her know that I decided not to rent her guest house. She emailed back, "No worries. A former tenant came by this morning and asked if the cottage was available." It was even more pleasing to find out that this decision had worked out for both parties.

About a month and a half later I looked at a mother-in-law unit on a large property in Saratoga. Although the unit itself was small, the rent was reasonable, the exterior was beautiful with a picnic table under a large evergreen tree and a covered patio, and there were cute pets—a tiny white long-haired dog and a bunny, which delighted my children.

I thought I could make it work for a year or two. I was determined to live in a house or a cottage with a nice yard rather than an apartment building, even though two bedroom cottages were almost nonexistent, and houses in the area were way beyond my budget. W. reminded me that my wants would be impossible to be fulfilled where we lived, especially since landlords preferred not to rent to mothers with small children. "That's reality," he said, "and you're just being unreasonable."

But still I didn't feel 100 percent right about this place and noticed as I filled out the application that I was sloppy and careless with my handwriting—rather unusual for me. That should have clued me in but as usual I dismissed my body's subtle responses and blamed my anxiety instead. So what was going on with me? Was I being unreasonable, or just plain chicken? I don't know. The whole time I was just trying to follow my intuition.

Again it was time to communicate my decision, but I had none. I didn't feel good in our home and needed to begin my work of resolution, but I didn't want to make a mistake either. This was a huge decision and I wanted, oh I don't know…a sign from heaven I guess. So again I tried to listen for guidance. As before, the time came to pick up Angelika from school. This time though, I turned the radio on as I pulled out of my driveway and the same song by U2, "I still haven't found what I'm looking for," was playing again.

I knew this wasn't merely a coincidence. This song had been a hit a few years before but wasn't being played very often anymore. Anyway, the message was clear and it helped relieve my anxiety. (I suppose messages from heaven, from higher dimensions, usually do.) Later that day, I found out the owners had second thoughts about renting their cottage anyway, so the decision was again right for both parties.

These two experiences taught me something important: I had requested clear guidance from the universe because in my state of anxiety, I couldn't trust myself to interpret subtle inner messages, and this is exactly what I received. In retrospect, had I been more experienced, I would have noticed that the guidance I sought had been with me all along—in my body's subtle responses and my sense of "not rightness"—but I wasn't quite ready to trust it yet. But even blind people can receive clear guidance when they request it of their higher selves and even the unenlightened can learn. Another interesting point to consider: it's certainly possible I wouldn't have experienced these interesting "signs from the universe" had I not bothered to ask for them (I might not have noticed them, for one), and I might not have bothered to ask for them had it not been for the fact that I was an "intuition novice." I might have been conditioned to think such things were impossible, or that "this isn't the way things are done." After all, when your intuition is already strong and your connection unfailing, for what do you need such over-the-top guidance? And indeed, it probably was taking me so long to find a place because I might have needed to learn these things first, as part of my process. Also, it was becoming evident to me that when you listen to your heart for guidance, it seems to work out for everyone's best interest.

∞

Yes, everyone's best interest, everyone's highest good: the reason for my moving out, rather than my husband, was that that decision, too, was based on searching my heart for guidance. On a walk one day, I got inspired to leave our house to him and my children. I got a very strong, positive feeling about this and this feeling came up again on several occasions. From then on, the memory of those feelings gave me comfort and confidence in my choice, even when friends and relatives advised me against what they perceived as an unwise decision. It was an easy decision, and I was glad of it. Well, maybe the small, self-righteous part of me wished to say "Here, take your house since you've earned it," but mostly, I wanted him to have it and I knew that one day, I'd have a house at least as nice.

Besides, W. had put a lot of work into our townhouse. He had installed maple Kahrs floors in our kitchen, dining, and living area; built a custom bookcase into a wall nook; laid slate tiles on the patio, and built our dresser and bed; had done it all impeccably. In German high school he had majored in physics and minored in art, and he loved to create things with his hands. We had remodeled our townhouse in modern European award-winning style. (I say "award-winning" because shortly after I moved, he submitted a photo of our kitchen to a local home magazine and won first prize for the "best design for a small space," for a "clean and simple" design.)

Well, he may have designed it, but I'm the one who had searched all over the San Francisco Bay Area for the items that added color and creativity, including the tile backsplash, lamps, stemware, and most appliances. In the magazine spread featuring the prize winners, he leaning nonchalantly yet self-assuredly against the kitchen counter, hands in pockets with warm smile, the judges had "applauded the homeowner's unabashed use of color" and felt that the "most striking feature is the bold tile backsplash"—my contributions, though I had thought that color-coordination hadn't exactly been my strength.

And now that I contemplate this, I realize that the source of my inspiration had been an image in my mind. I told W. about my vision and he had agreed to have me do the backsplash, though he had asked me more than once when it would be complete. So we weren't just about disagreements—sometimes both of us worked together like an award-winning team.

Anyway, it felt good to leave the townhouse to him and the kids; I thought he'd enjoy it more and do a better job with its upkeep. And I knew that somehow things would turn out fine in the end.

∞

Late one evening in July, my children and I came home from a barbeque at my friend Marianne's house while W. was away on business. After my children were tucked in bed, I was tired, but as I passed my computer on my way to bed, my inner voice told me to turn it on and look at the rentals listed on Craig's List. I had been doing this daily, sometimes a few times a day, for about four months and the day before, I had placed yet another "rentals wanted" ad.

Do I have to right now? I thought to myself. I mean it can wait until morning, can't it? I just wanted to go to sleep, not to power up my snail-paced laptop, which took several minutes to boot. But as I had already mentioned, I was getting good at hearing my inner voice and following through immediately. Well, if I were in the shower and got a hunch to call someone, it would have to wait—you use your common sense with these things, of course. But being tired didn't count as an emergency or a major inconvenience. "Okay Christine, just do it, just so you could say you did." (By this time I was talking to myself fairly regularly.)

I logged onto Craig's List and immediately found a new ad for a small house with a very reasonable rent only one and a half miles away. It seemed like the perfect place, and as I scrutinized the ad details, I astonishingly received an email from the owner of this same house, asking whether I was still in need of a rental. Well, that was an interesting coincidence, I thought. (Actually, I hadn't believed in mere *coincidence* for some time already, but hadn't begun using the word *synchronicity* with regularity either.)

My children and I met with the owners that weekend. The house had everything we needed for the time being—two bedrooms, a small bath, a living room, kitchen, dining area, a laundry/storage room, and even a compost area in the backyard (which would enable me to continue my composting habit), as well as two friendly neighbors and a dog that lived in the back cottage. The house was bright and it felt right.

When I expressed my interest to the Vietnamese landlady and asked for a rental application, she said, "You're the first person we show this house to. It's not in move-in condition yet, but if you like it so much you can have it. I won't show it to anyone else then. I'll tell them it's taken." I almost started crying then as I had been looking for so long. I thanked her for her confidence in me, and we made an appointment to sign a month-to-month lease about two weeks later.

When W. returned from his business trip, he was pleased that I had finally found a place to live—and just in time, too, since I was so past my original target date that, before he left, he had decreed that he would find a rental for me if I didn't have one by the time he was back. (That's when I went to that barbeque with my kids.) I understood his point though—he wanted me to do what I needed to do and not prolong the painful situation any longer than necessary. But at the same time, I knew he wasn't pleased *at all*, especially after I received an email of the correspondence between himself and J., forwarded to me on the same day by them both:

"Subject: Well done

Yesterday I had the dreadful task of explaining to my children that their mother will move away and our family will be separated.

This probably was one of the worse weekends for me, seeing my little ones shattered and damaged in their trust and relatedness to their parents. Angelika was very resentful of you and Christine, and she is painfully aware how you are damaging her family. Her bond with her mother is severed.

The short-term and long-term emotional and financial effects on my family are known to be detrimental. It's appalling to me that, despite my warnings, you continued to engage with my wife, who is struggling to find herself and is trying to pull herself out of her inherited depressive tendencies.

I hope you feel terrible that you were the catalyst to rip into our challenged situation. Educated and respectable men are aware that women are more likely to leave a relationship when another man is present. But you seem to possess neither education nor deserve to be respected. Despite already having caused great harm to your own family, you chose to intrude into others' families as well.

People like you should stay away from society. My children and I will reject you always, as well as many friends who know Christine and are very disturbed by the situation. I will make sure others get to know about your despicable and immoral character.

W."

J. felt terrible about this. Through email, I tried to explain to him that he wasn't the cause of this mess and confusion and that one day in the not-too-distant future, all of this would be healed, we would see the truth of what happened, and this learning would be helpful to others as well. (Okay, I admit I was stretching reality a bit here because I didn't see *how* all that was going to happen, just that it was my job to make it happen.) But I'm not sure he believed me. He responded to W. as I thought he would:

"I regret to see this situation digress into the determination of an individual's social worth, intelligence, and integrity based on a minute portion of one's history. Are not your reactions as deplorable as those you describe to be mine?

Is vengeance a socially accepted form of behavior?

Is close-mindedness a socially accepted form of behavior?

Is denial a socially accepted form of behavior?

Are these characteristics any less socially distasteful than those you so descriptively label as mine?

I have no desire to judge or label you, but through your actions I easily could. Nor do I feel this overwhelming desire to slander and insult your name simply to quench the desire for retribution.

The problems that stem from this conflict were there far before I was. Denying this and using me as a scapegoat have only allowed this to escalate. Your problems lie between you and your wife, not me. I was simply the catalyst that got what was already there to boil over. I simply made a bad decision at the wrong time.

If you feel that name calling and stone throwing are best for you, this is not my concern. For your ignorance will never have a profound affect on my life.

Before judging another human being, judge yourself. For I'm sure you are no saint.

If you have any other concerns or issues take them to the source, your own relationship! Do not contact me again for any reason.

I'm very sorry about all of this!!!!!"

To me J. wrote: "I'm very sorry about all of this. It saddens me greatly to see such an innocent meeting of two people, no different than that which happens tens of thousands of times a day, has evolved into such an unruly and resentful affair. No matter how unfortunate this is I think we need to discontinue contact for an extended time to allow for some normalcy to retain a foothold. My presence is that of a catalyst, getting what is already there to come to a boil. At this point in your life, you need to focus on what is important, without the disruption from unnecessary, problematic sources. I feel that this is mandatory for the peace of mind of all concerned. I'm very sorry for any harm that I have caused, it was never my intention."

Yes, focus on what is important, on the important work of my mission: that is certainly what I did and what I knew would get us, including me, through all this.

∞

On our last night together, W. and I slept in the same bed. He wanted to make love one last time before I left, and I welcomed the closeness, knowing that it would be some time before I had this again. Even while he was saying to me how fucked-up I was (for going ahead with my plans), I lay in his arms as all the painful events of my life—the disappointments and misunderstandings—flashed before me like a movie. It was so heavy, this pain, that it was hard to breathe. So much hurt and disappointment and none of it made any sense. I was afraid, too, but at least my fear felt noble, like the fear felt by tree-sitting environmentalists in old-growth forests. My tears tried hard to dissolve it all away.

How could so much hurt and misunderstanding be of any use? How could all these painful events bring any good? Yet that's what I tried to believe in my heart and what I eventually came to understand. There are gifts greater than the hardship when you come through the hardship.

∞

Several days before I moved into my new place, I ran into a neighbor at a supermarket where I usually didn't shop. Brenda knew things hadn't been going well for me and we talked about my move, and also about our children and the new school year fast approaching. Then she said, "Your girls can have Lauren's bedroom set. It's a trundle bed. I'm getting Lauren a new set for her birthday." I appreciated her generosity, as now that W. and I were separating, there would be significantly less disposable income available, especially since I was going to be an author. About a month later Brenda called, saying, "Do you want my side-by-side refrigerator and the antique table in my kitchen? I'm remodeling my kitchen." Because the refrigerator in my house was small and I could make use of the letter table, I gladly accepted her offers.

When the fridge and table were available for pickup, I mentioned this in passing to Lisa, Angelika's friend's mother, when we picked up our kids from school. Lisa said that maybe her husband could move it—they were having their kitchen remodeled and had a truck, a dolly, and extra help available that afternoon. We followed Lisa to her house and in about half an hour, the fridge and the table were delivered to my house. Well that was interesting, I thought.

Some time later, I needed a washer and dryer at my own place. I had used the washer and dryer at our townhouse for about two months after my move, but W. wanted me to have my own. Though I was partial to my programmable Miele German-engineered washing machine, I had to move on and let go of that attachment too. So many things to let go of.

After pricing new appliances at Sears, I logged onto Craig's List and emailed two or three sellers. But before I had a chance to check out even one used appliance, Keri, the neighbor who lived in the back cottage, knocked on my door and asked me to consider her proposal: she was offered a relatively new washer and dryer that she would pass on to me if I would let her use it one day a week. There was no hookup in her cottage, and she didn't have the space. Of course I agreed and soon the washer and dryer were delivered and set up for me. I had done nothing except open the door to my house and help Keri install the aluminum dryer duct.

In the same manner, I fell into a perfect part-time "job." Through Lisa, I met Julie, whose children belonged to Angelika's swim club. Because Julie worked full time, she needed help to get her children to swimming practice. It was ideal to be compensated for caring for two cute kids while being with my own, and it supplemented the support I received from W. without taking time away from writing.

It seemed to me that the things we needed in order to be relatively comfortable were appearing effortlessly—furniture and appliances, dependable, low cost car maintenance from Lisa's husband Frank, and now added income. All of this came so easily that I started to wonder what was going on. Perhaps this was because I trusted my inner self enough to listen and follow through, because once you do that, synchronicity begins to work in your life. Perhaps, also, it was the universe taking care of us, because in spite of challenging circumstances, I was going through with my soul's mission, what I had come here to do. This is the best explanation I have.

∞

While I was moving and cleaning and organizing my new place, I was thinking about the guidance I had received from the Counsel of Light the week before I moved: "Well we would like to begin by congratulating you on your determination, and on the presence you bring to all that you do and the energy that your consciousness is carrying in each moment as you unfold. One of the things that is important perhaps to understand as a human being is that there is a *way* that you do things that's just as important as what you do... Sometimes people are very either results-oriented or success-oriented and it's not always easy to experience the consciousness outside of your own dimension, in other words to live in the world when things do not appear as if they are moving in the direction that one wants them to move in and to have patience and presence is a very important thing in those times. So it's regarded in terms of your experience very directly that you are bringing a certain quality of consciousness into everything and that's a very important part of what you're experiencing and also what you're imbuing and embodying. And this is of course what you're bringing into the work that you're doing—that there is this quality and the quality carries with it a very strong resonance of truth…that can be like a sword….

"Keep trusting in the soul's expression and where it's guiding you and keep opening out to that consciousness. Trust that the truth is influencing and informing the expressive soul level and that the truth is underlying the whole project…But it doesn't just come because you want it to; you're going to end up someplace much bigger than you thought because you're not using the willpower, you're using the energy of your potential to support you…

"You're writing for individuals who are going to grow from what you've written no matter how old they are, because even though somebody's a particular age they may not be psychologically or spiritually or emotionally that particular age…You've already thought this through. We're just reading this for you from your record. This is not something we're trying to convince you about…So what you've already written, what you've already done, just go back over it. Take that one (story) that you really want to succeed, and just go back over it and add a few ideas…until it feels like it's written as a part of this huge endeavor to support the unification of humanity with its potential and with its wisdom and with the ending of the suffering, the ending of the separation…

"And you're real close, real close…"

"Real close, huh? Well, I hope that I will be able to bring it all the way through," I said.

"Of course you will. Just put the energy of your soul purpose behind this and it will fly."

Once my home was scrubbed clean and furnished, I felt comfortable and knew it was time to begin. It was the beginning of November when I sat down at my kitchen table, a table W. had built from pine over ten years before. A perfect place to begin, I thought, as I remembered the remarks of two friends who helped me move in August. One was an electrical engineering Ph.D. and the other the head of maintenance at the 107-acre townhouse association where I used to live. They noticed the craftsmanship of the table with its perfectly equidistant brackets underneath, some straight, some L-shaped, some angled, about two dozen brackets in all to support the table. They looked at each other and then at me, shook their heads, and then both Doug and Chuck chuckled.

"What's so funny? W. built this table about thirteen years ago. It was our first kitchen table," I explained. Both of them knew W. well, and Chuck had previously worked with him in the same company.

"Well if there ever is to be another earthquake," advised Chuck, "I'd recommend that you get yourself and the kids under this table."

So I felt lucky, privileged even, to begin my work on such a solid foundation, despite the fact that except for "A Story for Julianne," a small number of journal entries, and some random notes written on scraps of paper, I didn't have anything amazing yet. Besides, that short story hadn't exactly left me feeling confident. What kind of story was it, one that encouraged children to slip away into pools or steal away to scramble up rock faces; one that suggested, if you really wanted to see it that way, that I was an improper, irresponsible, or even a neglectful mother? What genre of children's story would that fall into? What would a famous baby doctor have said about it? Would he have been sympathetic to my cause? Furthermore, most children wouldn't need encouragement to run wild and free, would they?

But these were days of fear we were living in so maybe, just maybe, some *would* find a refreshing quality, a balance perhaps, in this creative work? Yes, a bit of balance in the world would be good right now; yes, some balance in the news, in people's lives, in my life. Well, perhaps I should submit my services for the purpose of holding the opposite end of the fear spectrum for balance. Balance fear with fearlessness. Or maybe courage or love or inner power is the opposite of fear?

Hard to believe that only a decade before, I had been basically against balance. "You need balance in your life, you're too extreme," my sister Lydia often said to me. (Referring to my previous bouts with evangelical Christianity, The Forum, and stuff.)

"No, I don't," I had said to her. I thought the term "balance" was a "politically correct" concept, just like the term "political correctness" itself, conveniently made up to control people. I had been away in Germany in the late eighties, and when I returned to the states everything all of a sudden seemed to be about political correctness and balance.

Okay, sometimes I saw the world differently but that was hardly encouraging. Certainly, I wasn't commended for my different point of view. On the contrary, it often brought up uncomfortable feelings between myself and others. So now I was to write about my consciousness? I supposed so.

Anyway, I had a basic idea for how to proceed because cleaning my house like a compulsive helped lift the fog in my brain and allowed some fresh ideas to come through: I would write a few more paragraphs about Julianne, about her growth through various stages of life, and what was now going to be possible given her strong sense of self. I thought it would take perhaps another two thousand words and then I'd be done; book number one for children would be complete. After all, children's books can't be too long.

About two hours later, with Julianne in mind, I had written what turned out to be the initial foundation for this book. Then after that, my writing quickly petered out. The reason was that I was resistant to writing about myself, even though my mind was being bombarded with thoughts of "living life fully." I pushed those thoughts out of my mind and then…nothing. For a few weeks, no writing, no words, I guess I could say I had writer's block.

But then new, more powerful thoughts began to trickle through: it occurred to me that using real life experiences would be very helpful in explaining ideas as the protagonist grows and evolves, and who else could I write about anyway? Moreover, where was my credibility if I were to fabricate even a small portion of this story? Of what real use was it if it were simply made up?

All right then, perhaps I *could* use some of my own experiences and adventures to illustrate the protagonist's growth. That would be fine with me, no big deal—anything to begin writing. But then as soon as I let go of my resistance and gave in to the inner voice, it took liberties to say whatever it pleased, all kinds of tall notions about itself and about the world. I wrote some of this material down (in my "Self-Reflection" chapter and some other places), but, frankly, I thought it went a bit too far, and it was arrogant, too. This was disturbing news, as I had always thought myself unpretentious and reserved, not arrogant at all. In fact, one of the things that most annoyed me about W. was what I perceived as his arrogance. He came from a well-educated, well-to-do German family, thought that he was better than others and that his opinions counted more, but now it was clear to me that I was that way, too. And then it dawned on me that not only I, but, more appallingly, my own soul was arrogant.

So then I tried to tone down the arrogance so others wouldn't see it and then begin to think things about me. *What would other people think?*—especially considering the seriousness of the matters I just so happened to be writing about. (Yes, I'm feeling adventurous now, sitting alone in the sparse kitchen of my little rental shack, laughing boldly at what I just wrote.)

But after another few weeks of wrestling with my arrogance and almost nothing to show for it, I suspected I wasn't going to win this standstill. So I surrendered again to my inner voice and let go of my personal opinions about my soul, for it appeared that it would win out eventually anyway—there wasn't a question about that. And why not? I mean I had gone this far and had already given up control to my inner core, so why not let it have its say? Besides, I knew my soul's expressions were just words on paper and words in my software program, and if I really didn't like them, I could always delete them later.

Finally I began to write about my struggle for direction and how things would be different for Julianne and Angelika (and other children as well) given a strong sense of inner self. I was still thinking—though I had a sneaking suspicion that my mind's conclusions weren't very reliable—that my efforts would culminate in a children's book "meant for all ages." The Counsel of Light had informed me that I would write for adults as well: "Adults, children, it doesn't matter," they said.

But as usual my soul had other plans and wasn't particularly impressed with or concerned about what I thought. Eventually, I gave up control altogether, letting go of any preconceived ideas of what kind of book this was going to be and simply listened and wrote. So what's another thousand words? No big deal. It's not like I knew what was to come, but what else was there to do? Around Christmas I felt that something was different—my internal struggle lessened and writing got a lot easier. In fact, I actually became a bit excited about it.

From then on, my story revealed itself to me from one day to the next, as though it had a life of its own and all I had to do was listen. Various parts of my psyche seemed to open up simultaneously, stirring up memories, feelings, and knowings in a nonlinear, random order. But my thoughts came out individually and clear so I could capture them all. It felt like I was piecing together a valuable, but shattered, vase.

Wave

Early one Monday morning in January 2004 I awakened from a dream feeling that I was on a wave, similar to the feeling of being on a roller-coaster or on a raft, with just enough distance between crest and trough to make my stomach drop. I recalled from my Soul Recognition Workshop that there was an expression called "getting on your wave," which meant getting in touch with your deepest self, your essence, and consciously living from that sacred space. I felt I must now be on this wave and that things would fall into place according to my original life plan, my soul's purpose for this lifetime. And if I learned to *stay* on my wave, life would flow because, I intuited, being on your wave was about aligning your intentions and actions with your soul essence, in other words, about attaining congruence between the inner and the outer worlds.

You might say that I started to ride this wave, the wave that I was. I also continued to learn how to read my feelings, my inner guidance, and the signs and symbols around me. Waking to that wavy feeling was a sensory confirmation that I had this "wave effect" going. Synchronicities and serendipities were already occurring regularly. I could get used to this, I thought. In fact, I did get used to them, as if there were nothing unusual about them and I could rely on them more and more; I also viewed them as signs of support from the outer world for my mission.

For example, the weekend before this Monday morning, at Angelika's first swim meet, I saw that I needed to get her a long, warm parka for after swimming since her swim club, the "Wavemakers," practiced and had meets outdoors year-round, and the fleece jacket and pants she wore didn't keep her warm enough. Then on Monday afternoon, I lugged Angelika's swimming equipment to school. Passing vehicles waiting for school kids, I saw Brenda sitting in her car and stopped to chat. Brenda noticed the equipment, told me that both her daughters no longer swam competitively, and said, "I've been looking for a swimmer who could use their parkas because they've been taking too much space in the closets. Could Angelika use them?" Later that week, we received not one but two swim parkas, and other equipment too. And the interesting thing is, I didn't pray for a parka, didn't even ask. I simply asked myself the question: "How can I get this for Angelika before her next swim meet?" with the intention to do this and then went about my day. The very next day, I was offered what I needed for her.

Awakening later that night, my mind focused on what had happened. I understood that when you follow your core, when you're on your "soul wave," you're connected with all beings and things through the interconnectedness (your inner core is your access point to the interconnectedness) and your questions, intentions, thoughts, and prayers are heard more easily because they often come from this sacred space and therefore they're in tune with a natural order to the universe. When you live from the inner core, you're in tune with yourself and the universe simultaneously.

Furthermore, I realized that all of us (Angelika, Brenda, myself) had benefited, and this confirmed for me that when you live from this sacred space, when you benefit so does everyone else who's involved, because they're also connected to everyone and everything through this sacred space.

Many things I needed I received in this way. Sometimes I asked for what I needed, but often it just appeared after I became aware of the need, especially the things I needed to continue my soul's purpose of writing this book. I also learned that prayers, intentions, and even thoughts, when aligned with your inner core, are very powerful, for they spark and magnetize the magic of interconnectedness: synchronicity, cooperation, co-creation, and so on.

∞

Aside from doing my meditative practice regularly, I didn't practice a religion and I didn't pray on a regular basis. I prayed only when I was inspired to, either because I needed divine intervention and felt God might be helpful, or because I had a strong inner urging to do so. When things were going okay, even when they weren't, I hardly prayed at all. I felt that God wasn't overly concerned with my individual life; I was one person out of billions, a mere spot in a universe of unimaginable proportions and what difference did my one life make anyway?

But sometimes I was nudged from within to pray, and one prayer in particular stands out—a prayer said several years ago when my bright red Honda Prelude, a car I had owned for fourteen years, was stolen. The car, which I purchased new shortly after I drove into that ditch near Uniondale, Long Island, was very reliable. It took me from one coast to the other three times without any problems, except for one flat tire. And even though it had close to 200,000 miles on it, it still had all its original major parts.

On the day of the crime, Annette, W.'s cousin from Germany, borrowed my Prelude, parked it at the Sunnyvale train station, and boarded the train to San Francisco for a day of sightseeing. Then around ten o'clock that night she called us all shaken up because she couldn't find the car. W. drove over and together they searched the station. It was definitely gone.

The next morning I called the Sunnyvale city office to inquire about my car, as it was certainly possible that Annette had parked it illegally and it had been towed. It wasn't recorded in their system yet, but still likely to show up. Sunnyvale in fact boasted one of the lowest crime rates, if not the lowest crime rate, of any town of that population (about 135,000 residents). Later that afternoon, I filed a police report. Two days later, it was obvious the car had been stolen.

Right before I went to sleep that third night I was inspired to say a prayer: I thanked God for having given me such a wonderful car; it had been so dependable for so long. I told God that the person who stole my car probably did so because he had met some unfortunate set of circumstances and couldn't see another option for himself. And if that car wasn't going to turn up, I asked that it provide for the new owner the same kind of reliability that it had provided me.

That was it; I was done with my prayer. I went over to W. who was working late on the computer that night, gave him a hug and a kiss, and went to bed feeling serene. I didn't know it clearly then, but this is what it means to say a prayer: you speak what is in your heart, you let things go (you become detached to the outcome), you send it off into the universe (by simply having that intent), and then you allow the prayer to do the rest. (This is especially true in the case when there's nothing you yourself can do about the outcome, i.e., you can't just go out on your own looking for your stolen car.)

Around one in the morning the phone rang and a woman asked to speak to me. W., still working on the computer, said I was asleep and asked her to call back in the morning—didn't she realize what time it was? But she insisted so he woke me up and I spoke with an investigating officer from the Mountain View Police, who informed me that my car had been found about two hours earlier (suspiciously right around the time of my prayer). Apparently, the car thief had asked a couple of unsuspecting youths for assistance in pushing my car to a gas station because it had unexpectedly run out of fuel. Then when a police car turned the corner and headed in their direction, the thief got out of the car in a flash and ran off, leaving the youths standing with my stalled car. Wow, I thought as I put down the receiver. That was quite interesting.

I suppose I stand corrected on my problem-free car—my fuel gauge had been reading inaccurately for some time. But the thief, of course, had no way of knowing this, and neither could he have known just how reliable to me my car really was.

The next day I drove W. to work and then I went to the Mountain View police station. My car had been towed to a nearby auto shop where the key entry was being fixed. Everything else was as good as before.

We drove that car for another good year, after which W. sold it for thirteen hundred and fifty dollars. He had been telling me that he still spots it on the road from time to time. I believe him, but also suspect that W. must be blessed with some special visual powers to be able to distinguish my old car from all the other old red Honda Preludes in the populous South Bay area. But then again, when his fine Swiss watch stopped working, he fixed its mechanics with a regular old soldering iron on the workbench in our garage, so who am I to say otherwise? The car is now over twenty years old.

While I cannot prove that my prayer is what made the difference in this situation, I knew back then that there was a connection and when said from the place of the heart, prayers were powerful indeed. And now my life experience was showing me that when you're aligned with your inner core, thoughts and intentions are just as powerful.

∞

I thought many thoughts and sent a clear intention to the universe that my mother *not call* to discuss my current life circumstances, but amazingly, that didn't prevent her from calling me anyway a few days after Angelika's first swim meet. I admit I had been avoiding her because I hated discussing my present life with almost everyone, especially her. After our phone call I was saddened, not because she had given me advice I couldn't use but because she was unnecessarily worried about me. I had known this would happen and had dreaded it all along, this feeling of being responsible for other people's upsets about what I was or wasn't doing with my life.

Anyway, she had delivered to me (again) a story of a woman in Poland who left her husband and son for another man. Years later, when this woman visited her grown son in a hospital after he broke his leg, hoping to repair their relationship, he rejected her. The woman was devastated, according to my mother's account of the tragedy. (My mother had bizarre disaster stories for every possible occasion.)

This strange and silly story was irrelevant to my life, but that didn't prevent her from making me listen to it for the third time. Her fear that I was making a wrong move I would one day regret was more powerful than my own views and faith in myself (or what little I was trying to scrounge up at the moment). She went on: one day my kids would reject me, and W. would grow impatient and reject me too. My leaving him, this whole thing, would be a huge mistake and without a doubt I would never forgive myself.

She tried to persuade me to do what she believed was right, what she would have done—return to W. and find a job—using whatever method she had in her repertoire: guilt, pleading, scare tactics. Well of course, I had expected this—how could she possibly comprehend my point of view? I wanted so much to explain that I was fine, that everything would work out well for me and for my children, in fact everything would work out fine for all of us because I was listening to my heart and soul. But I didn't say that part because I knew this would have upset her. I knew that she knew that I was prone to new ideas, that I believed in the self and in the heart, and hearing about my alternative philosophies would have alarmed her all the more. Perhaps she would have decided that I got sucked into some terrible new thing—a huge terror to her Catholic heart. I also knew—as someone who stands trial well knows—that if I had said anything, it would have been used against me as fodder for yet more questioning, pleading, and opportunities for boring, irrelevant stories.

Another thing was, my mother and I weren't fluent in each other's language. So how to conduct a meaningful conversation about, say, the multiple levels of human experience, or even about my having an important purpose here, part of which was to help people who feel terrorized and incapacitated by their fear. (Yes, that's a good way to put it; I see it now.)

And it's not like I knew exactly what was going to pass, how all this would come about, so how to alleviate her worries? What else to do except listen to her concerns: when was I going to work? When return to W.? All the sacrifices made and the hard work and the money spent for my expensive education at Cornell; the thousands of dollars I was now wasting; that she couldn't share this with anyone because it was a disgrace to the family; the mistakes I'm making with my own family....

But her concerns were not my concerns and she did not know me. (Well, I had other concerns, ones I wasn't about to share with her...like that now I would actually have to pull this whole thing off.) Much more than three thousand miles separated us—our whole way of perceiving and responding to life did, as well. So what more could I have done besides listen patiently and say, "Just trust me Mom, everything will be okay." But of course that didn't prevent her from continuing to worry.

After this phone call, I made a couple calls to friends for support, but they weren't home, so I went to the loveseat and plunked myself down on it. I sat in my sparse and deserted living room with its matching sofa and loveseat, mini-trampoline, thin rug, and television. (So glad Mom wasn't one to hop on an airplane and visit me in my humble abode anytime soon.) I sat and felt my upset. I did not turn on the television—not that that was likely, as I had never even seen an episode of *Friends*, *Seinfeld*, or almost any of the recently popular reality shows. This isn't necessarily because I disapproved of the TV, it's just that I didn't even know when which programs were on. And neither did I put the radio on or try to distract myself with cleaning or eating things like chocolate chip cookies. And I most definitely did not pick up a copy of *Evolution, Creationism, and other Modern Myths: A Critical Inquiry*, or *Children of the Matrix* and begin taking notes. I did none of those things. Rather, I sat and sat on the sofa like an old abandoned person idling away on her porch, staring off into the distance while it grew dark all around, not bothering to switch the lights on.

I sat and felt and listened and paid attention to my sacred space. All that practice of being alone and cultivating that inner connection made it natural and easy for me to avoid distractions and just be with myself. Then, after a while, I noticed that my upset slowly began to subside, replaced by a warm, pulsing energy at the center of my chest and with it a distinct, strong feeling of being supported. I took this as confirmation for continuing to do what I had been doing and went to sleep filled with a deep sense of peace, as if in an altered state, though I had spoken to no one. The odd thing was, I found this experience much more sustaining than trying to be comforted by others. It was absolutely true. Complaining to those who couldn't do a thing about it was a waste of time, while receiving support from my inner core felt more empowering and more real (and much less painful than eating too many cookies). That my friends weren't around to talk to me that evening turned out to be a blessing.

But that wasn't all. Later that night I was awakened by a warm inner glow and a feeling of indescribable joy, along with the now familiar feeling that I was floating on a wave. My mind and heart were also full of new ideas and insights, so I picked up the pen on my nightstand and wrote them down. By the next morning, I realized that I was now learning how to *stay* on my wave, thereby remaining on purpose: simply experience whatever there is in the moment, whether favorable or unfavorable, and trust the inner core to get you through it. Distracting yourself, blaming others, or trying to relieve pain or upsets by searching for answers and support from outside yourself isn't as empowering as going within and trusting the inner core to get you through the moment. Further, the inner core can teach you something valuable and take you to the next step.

That day I experienced a richness of creativity and a feeling that I was in love, in love with life, in love with the world. Almost effortlessly, I wrote many paragraphs composed from a stack of notes scribbled over several weeks, while I was in the car, on walks, in bed, or in the bathtub, notes I knew fit somewhere in my story. Most of the time I knew where they fit and how to organize my thoughts into a cohesive story, but sometimes my inner self had provided me with precise instructions; for example, "By so and so, put in such and such." I emailed the following to J. that day: "There are slumps, and after the slumps come the moments of creativity and flow. I'm in the middle of a creative time at this very moment!"

Hard to believe that only the evening before, things had looked very different. So although it's wonderful to have support from friends and family when you need it, in this instance being alone helped me comprehend a profound truth—that experiencing my emotions in the moment, trusting my inner self to get me through, and listening to the inner wisdom would reward me with insights and inspiration and creativity (besides the feeling of love). The deeper you plunge, the higher you fly; that's sure how it seemed to me.

∞

Now that my creative capacity had been activated, I knew it was time to write about the difficult part of my story—"The Hard Part." Even though the universe seemed to be encouraging me, and W. was supporting me financially, my recent past was still too dreadful to even think about, and my future was equally disturbing. I mean that whenever I actually allowed my mind to examine the rational basis for my future plans to be a successful author, it felt like it was hitting against the edges of insanity. Therefore, because I didn't want my mind getting all charged up about these things, I avoided thinking about them. I just wanted to *get on* with things. I could for one thing hide my panic behind my preoccupation with this book—just let me continue this work in peace; leave me alone; don't ask questions and don't make me explain anything, was my attitude.

Anyway, I knew I had to write about the difficult times. There was no way around it. I also needed to do it from a more detached perspective in order to analyze it as accurately and as objectively as possible. I was determined to make sense of my life and to glean whatever learnings and truths could be uncovered, not only for myself but for others as well.

So I began to write about my confusing past. Then after a few hours I thought I had sweated enough out, so I emailed J., asking to be temporarily distracted, but he wasn't at his computer, so reluctantly I continued writing. The next morning, after what I thought was enough toil, I emailed him again, asking him to "distract me, please!" then kept on writing. The third morning, feeling a bit miffed, I emailed him again after sufficient labor for the day: "Where are you when I need you to distract me!" When still he didn't respond, I continued writing again. Then about two hours later I emailed him once more: "I think I've got it done, the main gist of it at least. Faster than I thought. I must admit you did a good job of not distracting me all along. Can't exactly say I am grateful, but at least I went where I was supposed to go."

Click. Something inside my psyche clicked into place when I wrote that last email. I realized that on some level, he must have known I needed to do this on my own. No one else could have done for me what I needed to do for myself and nothing else could have substituted for it—the journey within, after all, was best done solo. And as a result of my efforts, I began to discover what I thought were truly fascinating and profound things about my personal life and, I was beginning to suspect, about life and the laws of the universe in general.

For example, when I got on my wave, I noticed it became less of a struggle to examine my life and write, even about the rough times. I didn't always have to have the prerequisite cup of tea that usually helped dissolve the inertia I felt at the onset of each day's endeavors. Once I got into it the momentum kept things going, but beginning something so thick with confusion, angst, or fear of failure used to be much more of a challenge. Then suddenly, it became noticeably easier. My housecleaning quit calling to me and I didn't occupy myself with trivial concerns such as the next day's meals. At times, I even turned down offers of coffee or lunch with friends, preferring to advance my book. "I'm sorry, but I have plans with *Microsoft Word*," I said. That's because it was exciting to see my work beginning to take shape.

So then I was writing and writing and things were going okay. But still, I was impatient and wished the story would just write itself complete already, because I thought I'd had enough. It was an emotional roller-coaster ride, up one moment and down the next and up higher again and I wanted off. I'd be feeling high from progress and then get an email or a phone call or else someone would come along and drop another bomb on me and knock me back down to reality. Enough of the waves, already. Each week I'd tell myself I'd finish the first draft the following week or two. It was near the end of January 2004, and I had planned on finishing it by Valentine's Day.

But as Valentine's Day approached, it clearly wasn't going to happen—there were gaps in the narrative wide enough that even I couldn't make sense of my own story yet. So I upped the ante, conscientiously and faithfully listening and writing. Reluctantly, I also let go of deadlines or expectations; I changed my mindset once again. Remembering the Counsel of Light's words, "It's all about changing the mindset, isn't it?" I realized that moving forward often requires changing the mindset. I also vowed to remain open to whatever was next and let my soul know I wouldn't let it down; I would go through with it to the very end. Subsequently, I filled in those gaps from the thoughts I scribbled down throughout the day and night. I didn't need to deliberately focus mental energy on the remaining issues but only listened and the ideas just came, often when I least expected them, often when I wasn't even thinking.

So although "I" was writing this story, it wasn't done the usual way of beginning to end; I had no outline. Rather, the story was writing itself from the inside out, and I simply pieced the thoughts together and synthesized the puzzle of my life piece by little piece. Well, I suppose when you finally do begin to tap into and unveil your deepest self, your true essence, you don't all of a sudden get snowed under by an avalanche of self-enlightenment; it comes to you incrementally.

And when I began to rush back from my morning hikes just so I could sit in front of my glorious computer and write, I knew I was touching upon something beautiful. One morning I flew down that hill simply because I had let go of my Valentine's Day expectation the previous day, and had promised myself to carry this work through to the end. Basically I said, "Okay, you win. What is it that you still want to say?" Then, during my hike, I was rewarded with a level of creativity and revelation I hadn't yet experienced. That's when my story began to grow by three- to four thousand words a week—a big change from just two months earlier when I had struggled with preconceived notions and expectations and accomplished, in terms of writing, almost nothing.

∞

Two days before Valentine's Day, I spoke with the Counsel of Light for the first time in my new home. They asked me to "clear out the cobwebs" and fine-tune the connection with my inner core (they called this the "vertical connection," the connection between the above and the below, or heaven and earth), so that the core attracts the things I needed so I wouldn't have to think about doing it in the real world, or "horizontally," as they put it. "Fine-tuning the vertical connection and deepening the circuits will vibrationally align you with the core of your choices and decisions from the blueprint that you're carrying, so you can expect to have more synchronicity, more flow. Then you will be standing in the design so that you affect the world around you from a pure, clear vibration that is so authentic that it comes from the source itself." When the vertical connection is strong, "this supports a level of truth, communication, cooperation and co-creation that isn't possible when you work from the will, when you just work from your own personal decision…Get that vertical strong, then you send it out, and then you watch what happens as a result…

"Part of what you get used to as this unfolds is using the universe as a partner in the co-creation. So the doubts, the worries, the concerns, the anxiety, the level of separation that you might feel sometimes, the loneliness, the sense of working on your own and having to overcome certain pre-set conditions—this is the time to erase those imprints from your psyche and begin to feel that you are working with the universe, that there's continual support inside that consciousness…

"The world that you want to create is within you. If you tap that world strongly enough it will flow out into the world around you and then the world around you will reflect that back…

"So know that we are always with you and that we are loving you very much and that we are very excited about this time for you because this is where you anchor in the true vibration of who you are and send that into the world. Know that we are with you and we give for you and yours our blessings now and always," they said.

I interpreted the "cobwebs" to be those imprints mentioned above, as well as my beliefs, expectations, and other demands of myself. I was to keep releasing those "cobwebs in my closet."

∞

The day after Valentine's Day, I was driving home from shopping with my children. We were in good spirits, and I felt the now-familiar warm glow near my heart. By then I had noticed that this feeling was often a precursor to a message from my inner core. Suddenly, an idea entered my consciousness: if connections with the outer world can be made easily through the inner core, and if the interconnectedness between all beings and things is not just metaphoric or mythical but real, then when my story was ready to be released to the world, wouldn't all the connections I needed show up naturally as well? After all, back when I thought I was going to write children's books I had unexpectedly met a woman who not only had been a children's book editor for the local newspaper, but also had read children's book manuscripts. And back then, the relationship with my inner core was not nearly as strong or as consonant. Since things appeared to be working better, why couldn't this apply to any area, any process in life? Why couldn't I connect to whomever I needed through inner guidance, serendipity, and synchronicity as opposed to the more conventional way—getting out there and pounding the pavement?

This insight lessened my fear of having to handle all the details all by myself, and I anticipated that in this new way of doing things—accessing the magic of interconnectedness through the core—everything was already on its way. Then I prayed: "So God, show me. Show me that the interconnectedness is real. Help bring me the people and the connections I will need to have this book be a success."

I sent this prayer into the universe and let go, having faith that when it was ready, it would already be on its way into the world.

Flow

IMAGINATION IS MORE IMPORTANT THAN KNOWLEDGE.
—*Albert Einstein*

After learning more about interconnectedness, I began to notice that even trivial things I randomly came across in my environment awakened my consciousness and imagination and helped me write. A book caught my eye in the bookstore or at the library, I read a paragraph I happened to pick up, a casual conversation with a friend, an email, a song playing on the radio, junk mail, a school field trip, animals that came across my path, the weather, a rainbow, a storm drain: all these activated my consciousness and provided inspiration for a sentence, an idea, an insight, or a metaphor.

Perhaps my psyche was more alert now, picking up previously unnoticed data from the environment and rather than dismissing it as coincidental or irrelevant, allowing it to spark insights. Perhaps my awareness and actions were more in tune with the environment, with interconnectedness. Perhaps the environment itself was speaking to me, wanting to be involved in the writing of this story. Well, before I'm invited by friendly readers to get a grip on my imagination, isn't this what Native American shamans claimed to be able to do—read the landscape, converse with animals and rocks, interpret signs of nature, tell nature's stories? Anyway, these experiences helped me understand that we live in a world of magic that's available to anyone just for the noticing. Knowing that my surroundings had the potential to trigger helpful ideas further motivated me to pay attention. Yet I didn't have to pay attention to *everything*—I automatically knew what was important. My heart and my body would let me know somehow; there'd be an increased awareness or animation or excitement or something like that.

My story was now unfolding and developing, seemingly effortlessly, and I even took corrections and made refinements in the same way, by listening. My heart leapt at the thought of this, that it would just write itself, that I wouldn't have to put a whole lot of hard work into it. Well, that just goes to show my mentality back then—to get it done as quickly as possible. In early 2004, I didn't yet understand that my commitment would grow as the project developed, and that it would actually be much bigger than what I originally had anticipated.

I suppose this book wasn't going to be handed to me from the universe on a silver platter, or on stone tablets, either—I would still have to work diligently and learn the ropes of writing. But I was not complaining. Once the importance of this project became clear, a bigger commitment followed naturally as the next easy step, and then I actually enjoyed transforming rather mediocre writing into something increasingly readable. Anyway, given my circumstances, this project unfolded with as much grace and ease as could be expected—which I attribute to my connection with creation.

∞

My connection with creation became apparent as I hiked up St. Joseph's hill one day in late February in unusually inclement weather. The night before, sheets of rain had pummeled the earth and crashed against my window, waking me periodically. In the morning, the storm raged on as branches of oak and eucalyptus and even whole trees, toppled over in the mudslides, lay on the trail. And though I carried a good umbrella, the wind whipped the rain around so it soaked my feather-light fleece pants until they hung heavy on my hips.

It was immensely beautiful, this morning of the opening up of the skies. I felt hypnotized by nature's wildness and unpredictability, its innate force. The world seemed radiant and charged with energy, clarifying my vision and intensifying my feelings, as though I were on a tropical island for the first time. I sensed an uplifting and an enlivening. No hikers or bicyclists were anywhere around. I had the whole hill to myself.

I paused by a one-foot-wide storm drain rushing with muddy water. For a few moments I stared at this powerful flow, and then it occurred to me that not only was I solidly connected to my inner core but also strongly connected to the environment, to interconnectedness, to creation, to All That Is. For many months I had cultivated this connection and based my actions almost solely on trust, on trust of the soul. I trusted that in due time, something would come from my efforts, though I had little evidence of this strong connection ever materializing. And if there actually were a test, I realized this was it, and that I had passed it.

Interestingly, years ago people used to tell me that I was "very connected" but I denied it, had doubts about it then. For instance, my friend Stacey Hentschel, a woman I met my first day in Silicon Valley, is a business coach who is very intuitive. She can go in, switch some internal circuitry and click—a moment or two later she gets her intuitive answer. Well, she told me that I was also very intuitive but I had no idea what she was talking about. I didn't *feel* connected, and thought that perhaps she simply empathized with me. I, on the other hand, viewed her as a member of an exclusive club I could only *hope* to get in one day. Yes, "hope" is the correct word in this context because *exactly how* I would go about it I had no idea. Yes, I thought, one day I'll be capable of that too; yes, I'll have a circuit to turn on too someday; yes, it's definitely a possibility, at least I hope. I'll work at it, work, work, try…After all, I knew I was still searching for this kind of connection.

But now there wasn't any doubt in my mind. Standing by the rain gutter, I could suddenly remember what it was like to be ultimately connected, when everything was unified, before things got separated. I remembered the moment before creation, before motion, or time. I had the inner knowing that I had been there. My soul recognized this immediately.

There was another interesting thing Stacey had said to me—that I was always a spiritual warrior for truth and freedom. I used to wonder what that really meant, but I hadn't asked her—I thought I ought to discover these things for myself, in due time. Then she had also said that it would be a good idea for me to spend as much time as possible in nature and near running water, a river, or the ocean, to listen to spiritual music, and to pay attention to symbols, metaphors, images, and sacred geometry. And now it seemed that all these things were coming together.

Still standing in the downpour by the storm drain, I realized the channeled messages from the Counsel of Light were finally beginning to make more sense, which excited me. And it wasn't because they told me something was so and I simply accepted it, but because of my firsthand experiences and the "remembering" I had been doing in my own heart since then.

Then I remembered the first time I had received a channeled message in March 2001. Their first words to me were "We are glad that you have come." I could sense they truly were glad. They didn't say who they were or where they were from but explained that I used to work for them and with them. Of course I didn't have any conscious memories of this, and I knew they must have been referring to a previous time, not to this lifetime. I thought, well, that could be possible; that might be true. I felt a bond with them from the very beginning and I listened.

Further, they talked to me about the particular vibration of love I am contributing to the world. My purpose, they said, was to honor this heart connection. "In the next several months, watch what happens and write down what you experience…It would be helpful for you to write a very simple children's book about the principles that you learn." They asked me to return when I had learned enough to ask some real questions. Finally, they said, "Know that we are always with you in each moment as this unfolds and that we are part of the wave that you're carrying so we will become very familiar with you and you with us in the next time and know that we are loving you very much and that we give for you and yours our blessings now and always."

They would always be with me, they said, and I was to call upon them when I needed them. I was moved and thanked them for their message and support, and they replied: "You are very welcome. There is much gratitude that you are here being the eyes and the ears and the touch and the spoken and written expression of this experience in the world. It is very beautiful that it is so, and we are also grateful to you that it is so." And I was grateful for having been given an opportunity to contribute something to the world.

I also remembered that they said I was going to fulfill the design, and that "all" I needed to do was to connect and remember, because then I would get in touch with who I am and in touch with the truth. They said, "This is your time; it's your time of birth, it's your time of initiation, it's your time of restoration…"

"Who I am": an interesting concept. I really thought they meant who I am in general terms and I, being intelligent about who we are, could have proudly recited: I'm a child of God, a fragment of God, a divine being, part of the interconnectedness, and also the star of my melodrama. But I already knew that, by the way. So what was I still missing? I didn't know back then that they were referring to who I was as an *individual*. I had been conditioned to think that who you are as one person in this world doesn't really matter in the larger scheme of the cosmos. If you thought otherwise, you came across as arrogant, egotistical, even worse. But now, standing completely alone on the hill, I had learned that the individual did matter.

For three years I had been instructed to "cultivate, nurture, and pay attention to my inner core, so that the wisdom that I was carrying could surface." And if I followed my true course, I would succeed in this endeavor, because I am the one who "wrote" the story of my life. Another way to describe my mission, as I understood it, was to ground the energies I was carrying onto the grid system of the planet and write the book of truth and wisdom, to write the truth of the underlying rules and laws of the universe, which the Counsel of Light stated were: "the laws of karma, detachment, order, commitment, truth, union, and harmony."

So standing next to the overflowing rain gutter, I was finally getting it; it was all becoming clear to me now: all that time when I thought I was in deep trouble it was really that I was a special agent on a highly sensitive, secret mission. Secret because I couldn't tell anyone, not even those who were intimately involved in this assignment with me, even if I had wanted to—they wouldn't have believed a word of it anyway. I wasn't entirely sure myself what the assignment involved, since the information came to me in bits and pieces on a need-to-know basis. Also, I took my instructions (cryptic messages including code words that I was required to decipher using special powers deep within me that couldn't be tampered with or manipulated) from disembodied voices over the phone line, from beings that existed in another dimension, and sometimes also from people who were unaware that they were giving me secret messages. Furthermore, I realized the Counsel of Light had deliberately scrambled a lot of different ideas and topics together so it would make no sense to anyone except to me—that is, after I painstakingly pieced the relevant pieces together using my inner resources, with the help of interconnectedness. And after I pieced things together and they started to make sense, then I could make sense of it for others. This whole enterprise was disguised as New Age self-help activities, and I was disguised as a reserved, struggling mother of small children, seeking said help. There was yet another layer for double disguise, just in case: a family melodrama involving a love triangle. And if there were something delicate going on, perhaps something of a covert nature, no one ever suspected because of the life trials and the drama occurring on the surface. (The perfect cover for a perfect counter-conspiracy, by the way.) Well, as I had already mentioned, I did try to tell my accomplices as much as I thought they'd fathom....

I imagined myself to be Neo in the movie *The Matrix*, when Morpheus offers him a choice between the red pill and the blue pill, between truth and illusion, only this wasn't a movie but real life, and I didn't think I was offered much of a choice in this particular situation: "Everything depends upon that first one," a secret message delivered several months before by my friend J. (unbeknownst to him) echoed in my mind. And because I was so inspired by my accomplices' brilliant examples, I placed secret, subliminal, consciousness-awakening messages in strategic locations throughout this book—which I am certain that "children" will be able to detect and decode much faster than their "parents." (Hint hint, wink wink.)

Even the blackbirds seemed to be in on this secret operation. (I wondered: did *they* know?) Anyway, no choice for me here—I was going through with my mission to find the truth. And as in any good story of real-world shadowy operations and multidimensional subterfuge, I became aware that—why of course—many obstacles would be placed in the path of those seeking the truth.

"You're here because you know something," Morpheus says to Neo in the movie. "What you know you can't explain—but you feel it. You've felt it your entire life; that there's something wrong with the world; you don't know what it is, but it's there, like a splinter in your mind, driving you mad. It is this feeling that has brought you to me. Do you know what I'm talking about?"

"The Matrix?" Neo asks.

"Do you want to know what it is? The Matrix is everywhere, it is all around us. Even in this very room. You can see it when you look out your window or when you turn on your television. You can feel it when you go to work, when you go to church, when you pay your taxes; it is the world that has been pulled over your eyes to blind you from the truth."

And Neo asks, "What truth?" Then Morpheus goes on to explain the illusion the world is living under, and so on.

Likewise, the Counsel of Light had explained to me that my soul pattern was about exposing the illusions and changing the systems of the world, and about breaking the rules: "Your life is dedicated to making the transitions between the old ways and the new ways. So it's not important for you to feel understood by those people who hold to the old tenets, who think the old ways are the best, because you're not going to fit into that system. You came to break that system literally." My heart had leapt at the sound of those words, especially the part about breaking the rules.

I was forever being taken by surprise by my identities—author, investigator of secrets, now also a deep-cover foreign-born operative on a highly sensitive mission. Who will I be next? Maybe W.'s telepathic powers were right all along—I certainly *had* been hiding something from him, from the world, from myself even, these long, long, lonely years. I must have given myself total amnesia!

Well, the Counsel of Light had certainly done their best to try to help me remember: "You chose this," they said when I was feeling my worst. "You said, 'Okay, I really know what I want to do here and I'm going to come in and I'm going to do it.' And it's because you're the one who's able to do it…You remember how creation flows. You remember how the ordination of the heavens feels. You remember what's going to be born here. You came here to activate the enlightenment of the human race. You know how to bring the new world order into being because that's part of who you are." Was that so? Well I must now try to make my mind remember.

Even Angelika helped me out, helped me confirm these suspicions a few months later when, around a year after we moved into the little house, she confessed with some trepidation that she had a very disturbing dream about me. In her dream, people in black ninja suits kidnapped and handcuffed me, tied a bowling ball on a chain to me, and pushed me off a cliff into the ocean. Being the good swimmer and diver she was, she dove in after me. "I went right after you, Mom," she said. "I put on my special Kim Possible underwater oxygen mask and dove off the cliff into the water. And with my sword I cut the chain and the bowling ball off you and brought you up to the surface. Then I fought off the ninjas and we were all safe." (Julianne didn't like to hear this story and had her ears covered the whole time.) When Angelika was born, I wanted to name her Ariel after the Little Mermaid, whose voice was taken away in the story. But that wouldn't do since Ariel was the brand name of a detergent in Germany. So W. and I named her Angelika Arielle, because she is an angel, a mermaid, and a lioness all at the same time.

Well, the Counsel of Light's wisdom and advice was encouraging, and the mysterious messages from others had enthralled and bolstered me, and the special assignment certainly sounded honorable and impressive—all of that was true—but for a long time I still wasn't certain that I was the right agent for the job. After all, I didn't consciously remember being commissioned for this assignment and I hadn't yet experienced the level of consciousness that was supposedly within. If it was there, why didn't I already have access to it? How could I know something I hadn't learned or experienced in this lifetime? And what were the illusions this world was living under and what was the truth? Well, I suppose that's what my special decoding abilities were going to be used for—for finding those things out.

I realized that the Counsel of Light had been right about my being too enmeshed in things to be able to see them clearly (and I was still enmeshed, but less so), like a fish in water, I guess. A fish swimming in water doesn't see the water and has no real distinction for it because the opposite, "no water," doesn't exist for it, until it's actually out of the water, or when It's so far in itself that it can see itself from outside itself. And, I suppose, how can a fish value and love and delight in water if it doesn't experience what it's like without?

But at the same time I didn't think they were right about my having had a choice in this secret assignment. When they talked to me a year before, in February 2003, they said that I had a choice as to how I would proceed. Free will, they had said. But I didn't see it that way at all. Free will? They had to be kidding! Free will had I? HA! It was my turn to laugh! I viewed my options as either: one, proceeding with this "extremely" important mission to its completion or two, folding—which to me was no choice at all. If I had folded I wouldn't have had any self-respect left and no one else would have had any for me either. I then would have wanted to die, and I probably would have begun hoping and praying for someone to come and save me from my broken life, my victim self. Eventually, who knows? I would have let some illness take hold in me, granting me my wish. So of course I went through with it. There was no other option.

Without a doubt, I wanted the enlightenment, the expanded consciousness. I wanted to jump right into the process so I'd have something to show for my work rather than living on faith that I'd get there someday, meanwhile having to stand up for myself on nothing but my word that I would do it, I would write that book on truth and wisdom. (Like most humans, I was addicted to needing to know things ahead of time.) But this expanded consciousness had its own timing, and also auxiliary learnings that came with it: what about patience, and compassion for myself and others? Did the level of trust in myself need to be deepened first? Was I learning how to ask for assistance? Was I learning to read signs and signals from the environment? Don't all these things take time?

But now, standing soaking wet in the storm, carried away into imagination by a blasting flow of rainwater, I was truly getting it. And indeed this assignment *was* important—it had something to do with humanity's origin. So I spoke to the universe, to creation, to interconnectedness, to the Counsel of Light residing in their other dimension: "I am here. I have shown up, as requested. What is it you want to say?" Then I continued my walk downhill to return to my car.

On the way, I suddenly remembered a seven-day creative workshop given by Ariel Spilsbury in Maui several years ago called "The Thirteen Faces of the Divine Feminine." The workshop was designed to assist with the balancing of the male and female energies within oneself, with a primary focus on the feminine aspects of consciousness. (A balance in your inner male and female aspects corresponds to a balance in the mind—*a very good thing*, I think at least—in spite of a famous governor's views on "girly" men.) This balancing work was accomplished through guided meditation, art, music, poetry, dance, mythic enactment, storytelling, impromptu plays, and sacred rites performed to invoke each of the thirteen archetypes of the divine feminine.

One evening, we drove up a windy road to Mt. Haleakala National Park to watch the sun set as well as the moon rise from the top of Haleakala volcano. We stomped up the rocky alpine desert trail, about a half-mile or so to the very summit at ten thousand feet. Though it was already mid-May, after the sun had set the temperature dropped quickly and even the heavy coat I had worn in Germany the previous winter didn't prevent the night chill from settling into my skin. Luckily I had Julianne, who was six weeks old at the time, all bundled up in one of those thick one-piece fleece baby buntings. I was nursing her and she had colic most evenings, making her impossible for W. to handle her for what would be several hours, so I took her most everywhere I went.

Some participants who hadn't packed a warm coat for this volcano visit borrowed long black capes with hoods to keep warm. The capes were part of Ariel's large exotic costume collection, in which we indulged every evening for role-playing and initiatory work—

declarations, King Arthur and the Holy Grail-type enactments. Anyway, we must have looked peculiar to the tourists hoping to witness a spectacular Haleakala sunset. They might have wondered about our group: four men and the rest women, one newborn. What were we up to? What were those black capes about? And why were we waiting for the moon to rise? Whoever paid much attention to the moon's comings and goings anyway? Well, I'm not so sure they thought those things, as those were my own thoughts.

But it was really that we were just a bunch of closet poets and gardeners, professional dancers, massage therapists, photographers, Reiki practitioners, and teachers (with my technical background I was the odd one out) gathered together to give homage to the moon and the energies it symbolized—the feminine energies. We sat on rocks, feeling on top of the world because we were doing something both important and cool besides—our part to restore balance to the earth by balancing ourselves first.

Once the sun set, it grew pitch black quickly. While we waited for the moon to rise, we recited poetry, said prayers, told stories and jokes, and shared hot cocoa from tall thermoses. We stayed about two or three hours, enjoying the vision of the moon and the millions of stars, the exquisite beauty and peace of this place. Julianne had no colic that evening; she was sprawled across my lap in a deep sleep.

Then when it was time to leave, we realized that not one of us had brought a flashlight, though there were sixteen of us—thirteen participants and three co-leaders. (None of us had cell phones either—this was 1998.) What, no flashlights? How could that have happened? Nice going, oh conscious ones, I thought to myself. Why didn't anyone think of flashlights? Duh! Who's responsible for this? My mind reeled on with judgments and complaints, for good reason too. (Doesn't it always have good reasons?) But more importantly, what were we to do now? It was so dark we couldn't see our own feet, and the trail sloped abruptly in some places and was strewn with sharp volcanic rock.

The situation definitely wasn't favorable. One could easily leave the trail and get oneself lost in the freezing night, stumble on sharp rocks and get oneself hurt, trip and fall on one's behind with a baby in one's arms. One could only imagine what a famous baby doctor would have said about this adventure one got oneself into. Would he have smiled a knowing smile and nodded his approval?

So. Well. We stood around for a while hemming and hawing and then a miracle occurred and we were blessed because one of the participants suddenly remembered that he knew what to do. We who had honored the moon and the stars and the earth had not been abandoned and our good fortune appeared in the form of an idea: Todd, a massage and cranial sacral therapist from Utah, pointed out that even though our eyes couldn't see, our feet would make up for it because they were connected to the earth. In the gentle, mindful manner of a massage therapist, he asked us to trust that our feet would know what to do; our feet would know exactly where to step so we could get down to the parking lot safely. Trust your feet, he stressed.

And well, we were open-minded, and a more open-minded group of people you couldn't find anywhere on that volcano. So we attempted to do what he suggested: we put our best foot forward, so to speak.

At first it was a little shaky walking down that path, trusting your feet to make the perfect next step, but I got into it after a while and it got easier and easier. (But first, I asked Todd to carry Julianne, since he was much more sure of his stepping than I.) In this way—by being open to new and empowering information—we transformed worry and anxiety into trusting ourselves. In the end, all sixteen of us made it down safely without leaving the trail, or having even the slightest mishap.

I hadn't known that my body had the capacity to perform such a feat, as no one until then had pointed it out to me. But I thought it was the coolest thing—my feet were somehow connected with the environment in this new and powerful way, even though I didn't know exactly how or why it worked.

And after I finished typing the last few paragraphs it suddenly occurred to me that this is exactly the way the process of reconnecting (to the inner core, to the interconnectedness) works. First, you learn about the possibility of it and when you try it, it's a bit shaky; you have some doubts. But if you're committed, you keep going. Even if it doesn't work well enough or consistently enough right away, you trust that someday your efforts will be rewarded. Eventually, you begin to experience results, which help you to have more trust in your inner self, helping you in turn to connect even more strongly. By then, you have begun the process of spiraling upwards. It begins to feel like you're on your wave, and things get a bit easier. And then, you learn to stay connected not only when things are going your way but also when the world appears to shoot its arrows at you (you've learned to *stay* on your wave). Finally, you begin to understand that even the arrows help you connect, and then you no longer view them as arrows but as they really are, as the truth: as the teachings and the learnings of your life. At this point you've learned to surf (to ride the crests of the waves), and you experience flow consistently—which means you've become the master of your life. (And surfing solves the problem, for the most part, of that bumpy roller coaster ride.)

So! Well! I didn't know I was going to write this last paragraph, but my hands just kept typing whatever happened to flow into my consciousness. And what's interesting is that these concepts jelled in my mind as I typed them; they weren't clear to me until I actually put them into form. Another interesting point: the previous few paragraphs, which were part of my environment at that moment, sort of jumped at me and inspired me to write the one thereafter. This is another example of my environment contributing to the writing of this book. Maybe even words or ideas or paragraphs themselves are self-reflecting and want to contribute to the creation of new paragraphs. Perhaps god (creation, consciousness, interconnectedness, the universe) exists in everything, living or not.

So when you are lost and find yourself not knowing in which direction to turn, remember that the things present in your surroundings—even your feet or hands or the paragraph right in front of you—are there to help connect you and guide you on your way.

∞

I had already been familiar with the concept of flow. Several years ago, not long after it came out, I read psychology professor Mihaly Csikszentmihalyi's book *Flow: The Psychology of Optimal Experience*. Others have also spoken and written about flow—that experience when everything seems to work perfectly, when things fall into place and you have moments of pure magic, creativity, and bliss. Some people have compared being in flow to becoming one with their experience or with life ("being at one with things"), while others call this experience "being in the zone." Numerous athletes, artists, musicians, and other creative individuals have described how they feel when they're experiencing this amazing state (calm, euphoric, clearly focused...).

Mihaly Csikszentmihalyi writes in *Flow: The Psychology of Optimal Experience*: "Flow helps to integrate the self because in that state of deep concentration, consciousness is unusually well ordered." (Well, I think the opposite of this is truer—when you integrate the self, your consciousness gets ordered and this helps create flow, or, you tap into the bigger consciousness that is well ordered.) "Thoughts, feelings, and all the senses are focused on the same goal." (You are congruent within, you are in tune with yourself, you have inner order.) "Experience is in harmony..." (Your outer experience will then be in harmony with this inner congruency because inner order creates outer order; what is within is without.) "When the information that keeps coming into awareness is congruent with goals, psychic energy flows effortlessly…" (When your thoughts are aligned with your goals, attaining the goals becomes easier. Also, congruence in thought and action means there is no resistance, and no resistance allows for flow and creativity.) In flow, "people become so involved in what they are doing that the activity becomes spontaneous, almost automatic; they stop becoming aware of themselves as separate from the actions they are performing…" (We are not separate from creation, from interconnectedness.) "The reason it is possible to achieve such complete involvement in a flow experience is that goals are usually clear, and feedback immediate." (Goals that arise from the inner core are clear as well as ordered and congruent and ordained, and the environment gives immediate feedback in the form of signs and synchronicities and insights.)

I have read definitions, descriptions, and anecdotal accounts of the flow experience but, so far, I'm not aware that a simple step-by-step method for effecting and sustaining this state in *all areas* of life has been made known. In the past, I had occasionally experienced moments of flow in my life, but in the course of my process of connecting within, following my inner guidance, and so on, I was learning how to sustain the flow experience. The following method worked for me. In fact that's how I learned it—it just started working: by being aware of exactly what I was doing that elicited the flow experience, I was learning a simple formula. This formula could quite easily be applied to access the domain of flow with increasing consistency, and, indeed, I experienced more and more flow not only in creating this book, but also in other areas of daily life and in relationships as well. For example, I was able to resolve disagreements or misunderstandings more quickly and easily, and the things I needed to fulfill my mission appeared when I needed them. Consciousness ("information that came into my awareness") further helped make it clear for me, helped me understand why it was working, the theory behind it.

The way to experience flow is to connect within by taking some time each day to be alone and quiet with yourself. Even fifteen minutes in the morning and fifteen minutes in the evening, and a minute or two a few times in between will help you reconnect. Next, you begin to pay attention to the voice that comes from this sacred space, taking a minute or two periodically during the day to just listen and notice.

Then you follow through on the guidance you receive from the inner core, which might include learning a new skill, trying a new idea, reading a book that gets your attention, as well as making note of insights or noticing other interesting things in your environment. It's a gradual process at first and it will take a commitment and some discipline, but you don't have to worry that you're not doing it right or that it will demand more than you can manage. You might also want to ask questions of the universe and request clear answers. Following through is an important part of the process, since it helps you become familiar with and then trust your inner voice.

Gradually, as you connect deeper and trust enough to follow through consistently, you'll receive more consistent and immediate feedback. Feedback can be in the form of a joyous, exciting feeling, or an amazing result or insight, which will then boost the trust in your self even further. Finally, you will learn to *stay* in the flow when you begin to trust yourself more than anyone or anything outside of yourself, even though you might have disagreements with others, even with those who are considered experts in their field. (I found it prudent and even *helpful* to take into account others' opinions and advice, but then after I let the information "process" in me, I followed my inner guidance when I was ready to do so.) You can be sure that this soul process will bring the right opportunities for advancement. So…the process of attaining creative flow is really the same process of reconnecting to the inner core.

The reason this process works for attaining the flow experience is: as you connect with your inner core, your soul gradually connects you to your original plan, your most authentic purpose for being here, meaning the deeper plan for your life—your soul's plan. When this happens, your inner life becomes ordered, your thoughts become aligned with that original intention and plan, resulting in more clarity and less internal struggle. Sooner or later you will know without a doubt that you're connected, because being aligned with your original life plan creates the consistent experience of flow with the mind, body, and soul, which transforms your life experience. Then gradually, the outer world gets transformed as well. A new world has been created.

In the beginning, the "ego," or mind can seemingly get in the way of this process running smoothly. But it isn't the mind that's the problem, but rather the conditionings and belief systems to which it was subjected. Those systems may need to be examined, and perhaps released. Perhaps the mind or ego isn't bad or wrong at all, and neither is it empowering to view the conditionings and belief systems as bad or wrong either. They're just ideas, that's all, ideas that can be released and replaced by more empowering, more truthful ideas—which is what growth and evolvement is all about. Or, as the Counsel of Light had stated: "Do you see that it's all about changing the mindset? Because if you don't, you have human limitation, and you're not going to be able to understand the truth of who you are if you look at it through human eyes." (If you only see things from the surface level, if you only pay attention to surface events, you won't see the bigger picture, the deeper story that's here right in front of you.)

For example, at the outset of my own process of reconnecting with my inner core and the creative energy, I learned that a writer's block (or any other kind of creative block) was at least partially if not wholly the result of the holding onto of thoughts, opinions, conditionings, superstitions, doctrine, and beliefs that are no longer valid or true; perhaps some never were true to begin with. This includes beliefs about the world, about yourself, about others, about anything and everything. Many beliefs, especially those you don't distinguish as beliefs or personal opinions but as "the truth," including those about yourself, limit and stifle creativity. For example, I would say to myself, "I can't write a good book, I'm not a writer," or "I have nothing to say and I know it too." Here's another good example that others might say: "She's from the East Bloc so what does she know about being personally responsible for her issues? Blaming others for one's fate is a cultural thing passed on from the East Bloc days."

Such thought and behavior patterns can lead to stagnation, depression, and sometimes even illness. Letting go of outmoded, judgmental thoughts and beliefs is the one way to free yourself of the blocks to the free flow of creative energy.

Fortunately, I had already let go of some of my baggage at such places as Landmark Education (formerly known as est), but still carried beliefs that inhibited my ability to write. For example, at first I had thought I was writing a children's book, which limited my expression because I filtered out anything that didn't fit that preconception. The ideas simply couldn't come through if I didn't allow them to. My soul wanted to express without any limitations, but I stifled it and got nowhere for a few weeks—therefore no flow. But as soon as I changed my mindset, the words started to flow.

Next, I worried that my writing was too arrogant and bold. I wanted to keep my ideas about the world and about myself to myself, didn't want to make waves, ruffle other people's feathers, or have others point and say, "Who does she think she is?" I was judgmental about myself—meantime no flow, no writing for a few more weeks—until I gave up those judgments as well and allowed my inner self its say. I even gave up the idea that I needed to downplay my so-called arrogance and then my writing again began to flow.

Then, for some strange reason, I had expected that I would have my first draft finished by Valentine's Day, because there was only so much time and energy *moi* was willing to devote to this project. I gave up that position in no time because it was absurd, and then I was rewarded with a new level of creativity and flow.

Then I didn't want to reveal unpleasant aspects of my story, until I realized this was selfish and petty of me and went ahead anyway. Shortly afterwards, my inner self came up with insights and new things I hadn't thought of before; many things about my life became much clearer!

Sometimes my inner self even surprised me with its vocabulary, which sometimes made me slyly look up words in the dictionary to make certain they were used in proper context. I admit I checked up on it from time to time, just to be sure it knew what it was talking about, hoping it wouldn't be offended by this lack of trust on my part. (There was just *no way* of keeping *anything* from it!) But it wasn't offended, I realized. It had room for my human frailties.

In fact, each time I let go of limiting thoughts, I was amazed with the insights I received about life. In other words, when I gave up my assumptions and judgments and expectations about what something was supposed to look like, how it would be done, what would be included, and by when, I then experienced a breakthrough and was rewarded with insights, creativity, and flow. More simply stated: when I let go of my expectations, I began to surpass my expectations.

And as time went on, my commitment and dedication to this project only grew. When I first started, I couldn't have imagined having to write a book on love and about how life works here, two hundred and some pages long—and very popular at that besides—before I could have expected some degree of comfort and peace in my life. It would have seemed like the project from hell—far too overwhelming to sign onto. Just take me now, I would have thought. So isn't it just beautiful that I was challenged with only as much as I could handle at any one time?

The Counsel of Light certainly led me on oh so delicately, letting me think I was close when all I had was "A Story for Julianne." "You're real close…Put in a few more ideas. Take the story and add a few more ideas about what happens as the protagonist grows and evolves. Expand it for more age groups," they said when I was still under the impression that I was only writing a children's book. Yeah right, a few more ideas…as if! And the Counsel, always supportive and helpful, further told me, "It's not like you're receiving an end product—you're creating it." (I think what they were really saying here is although I may have already thought things through and had these resources available to me in my spiritual bank account, I would still need to *transfer* those resources from the spiritual dimension to the physical dimension.) "And yet it doesn't have to be in any way intimidating for you." No, of course not, I thought. Nice of them to give it to me easy, though. So I just got on with it because I didn't want any edicts on stone tablets anyway.

But then, only several months later, I viewed myself as someone who could perhaps successfully complete this project. The Counsel of Light had said, "The connection to creation, to the life force, to all of nature, to the flow experience, to whatever there is, is a steady unfoldment regardless of what kind of energy system you are. Whether you're a leaf or a flower or a cloud or the sun or a human being, it's all the same." Yes, I can vouch for that, connecting to the interconnectedness within is a gradual, natural, organic, beautiful unfoldment.

This creative process feels really good too, like when you reach the summit of a mountain, or repel down a tall rock face, or when you're in flow and reach a new level of performance, or ace something challenging. The connection to the interconnectedness is the key to a magical life and the key to humanity's future. Our inner core that connects us to creation is the key to a new world.

Although some may be skeptical of my claims and may want to see "real proof," I can only offer my personal anecdotal experiences and cognitive awareness (with the help of the Counsel of Light's messages). My purpose is not to convince others to believe any of what's been claimed, but simply to share my story—what I learned and my interpretations of what occurred. I think the knowings and the wisdom came from the spiritual realm, the higher dimensions, the higher mind. I also think the principles presented here are, well, timeless.

But it isn't necessary to believe in these principles for them to work, just as you don't need to believe in gravity for it to work. Does gravity care if you believe in it? Just like gravity, creation doesn't care whether we believe in it or not—it's just there. But if we're aware of the interconnectedness we can begin to work with it, we can count on it to work. It's always there, always working anyway.

So I cannot prove what I write is so, but that's okay. I don't need to prove anything and I don't need anyone's approval. I am merely writing a memoir of my process of reconnecting with the infinite, one that is factual down to the core, but nevertheless it's still a story—my story. So you can decide, not I, which judgments and positions to let go of first, for I am only a storyteller. (Right now I can hear my inner child shouting with glee: "I will say what I want! I will say what I want! I will!")

Which reminds me: I myself would like to have a real explanation for what happened to the headrest of W.'s Volkswagen in Turkey, to be clear on the theory and method behind that, perhaps using the laws of physics and the principles of materials science, perhaps not. In any case, I am of the opinion that the headrest was tampered with and that someone somewhere has some explaining to do.

Truth and Illusion

TRUTH IS NOT DISCOVERED BY PROOFS BUT BY
EXPLORATION. IT IS ALWAYS EXPERIMENTAL.
—*Simone Weil*

The very next day after my epiphany in the rainstorm, I plodded up St. Joseph's hill a bit slower than usual. All this thinking and writing and being awakened in the wee hours of the night to take down the ideas and concoctions in my head that couldn't wait until morning was starting to wear me out. (A lot of my insights came to me in that drowsy floating state between sleep and waking.)

I suppose there's no surprise there—it had my full attention in the middle of the night. There I was, lying in bed, with no distractions. What else could I do? It was persistent too. Sometimes when I was slow to turn on the light, the thoughts in my head played themselves over and over like a broken record until I wrote them down. It certainly knew who was boss. Well, I really have no reason to complain because I appreciated the new ideas every night. The story kept unfolding and there was slim chance of procrastination slowing things down. It's just that I was tired.

While I walked up the hill, I tried to rest my tired, stinging eyes, glancing down at my boots. Then I asked myself a question that I tried to ask myself daily: Okay, so what's up for today? The Counsel of Light would have expressed that same question this way: "What is it best for me to receive now that will assist in the translation of truth into form?"

Suddenly, I almost stepped on a dead baby rabbit that lay right in my path, not a newborn rabbit but small, perhaps a few weeks old. Poor bunny, I thought. I examined it, wondering what circumstances could have brought on such a terrible fate. Using a couple of leaves, I moved it near the edge of the trail next to a fence and hid it, so the mountain bikers wouldn't squish it as they tore down the trail. Leaving the bunny behind, I continued my hike up the hill, keeping myself open to new ideas.

But the dead rabbit would not leave my mind and I remembered Mountain School commencement night the previous May, when my carpool partner Kari W. presented a unique project created for her daughter, Celeste. The project was conceived when the kids in our carpool, Celeste, Jagger and Julianne, became fascinated with dead animals. Their teacher Jill found dead animals on her mountain property—birds and squirrels and other small creatures—stored them in baggies in her freezer, and brought them to school for the children to study. The children gathered close in a circle around teacher Jill and examined the animals' little beaks and feet and eyes in detail. You could almost say that dead animals became something of the rage. For Kari too, in fact. When she and the kids spotted a dead animal on the road, she took photos of it for her upcoming project. (I can now imagine that if I were a teacher I'd gather my children close around me and we'd discuss such things as bird philosophy.)

Anyway, the annual Commencement Project was a requirement for being in good standing at the famous and popular Mountain School. We were reminded of this on different occasions so we wouldn't overlook its importance. There was, for instance, the long waiting list of new souls wishing to enroll in this special school the following year. But this wasn't an issue—many Mountain School parents were very well educated, owning impressive-looking homes furnished by Silicon Valley fortunes, and the Commencement Project was taken very seriously. Countless hours were devoted to creating memorable treasures like customized Native American wigwams, embellished with artistic and personal touches; photo albums complete with creative captions, exquisitely decorated; and other sentimental testimonials to their child's Mountain School experience for that year. Also, the special project seemed somewhat secretive. Some moms whispered about their creations when I sidled by them at school, perhaps to surprise the teachers and the rest of the class with their panache for things pretty and perfect on the Big Night, an adult-only event at one of the impressive homes. A themed pot-luck and festive drinks topped off this graduation celebration for parents; after all we were students in this school as well and had loads of requirements to meet—papers, monthly meetings, attending evening presentations given by authors and various child development experts, fundraising, maintenance of the grounds.

However, Kari didn't keep her project a secret like some people, but had revealed it and, as soon as she did, began to be supported in it. People supplied her with information on dead animals witnessed in the area and in no time at all, the leads began to pour in. For example, on Highway 9 one mom spotted a super specimen of a raccoon, which Kari and the kids then tracked down and documented. Well of course, tell someone about your project and suddenly everyone wants to be a part of it. Isn't that always the case?

Anyway, with Commencement Night coming up so fast, the pressure to complete her project was on. With only several days left, it required a stepping up of her efforts: on one occasion she zoomed from school into town to purchase a disposable camera, then zoomed back into the Los Gatos mountains to return to the site of the crime, so to speak, so that the requisite photos could be taken. Dead animals had become something Kari you might say suddenly looked forward to.

When it was her turn for Project Presentation on the Grand Night, Kari had passed around for our perusal a twelve-month calendar of these photos and chronicled the story behind each one—the site where the animal was found, the children's views on the cause of the deaths, that sort of thing. This made everyone laugh so hard I thought we wouldn't get over it that night. Everyone that is, except for one person who happened to be a trauma nurse by profession. To a nurse, death was obviously not a laughing matter. Kari's attitude was different though; you might even say refreshing. As a single mom—her ex-husband was an ex-convict and a drug-addict who never paid a penny of child support—she had learned not to take life too seriously.

But today was my day for dead animals, I thought as I walked up the hill. (Perhaps also it was my day not to take life so seriously.) I also thought my children would like to see that cute bunny rabbit and help give it a proper funeral: we'd dig a hole in the yard, have a ceremony with flowers from the garden; I'd ask my kids to say a few words before we covered up the bunny, we'd say our goodbyes. It would be a teachable moment; I'd think something up.

So on my way back downhill, I decided to take the bunny home with me. Strangely, it wasn't lying where I had moved it near the fence but exactly where I had originally found it, a couple of feet away. Did someone or something move it back? Anyway, I took off my fleece jacket and wrapped it in that. I carried the bunny carefully but casually, trying not to draw any attention so no one would think I was walking off with something suspicious. I worried though that if I tried to appear too casual, as if I were simply carrying a fleece jacket I had taken off, the bunny would tumble out and land at someone's feet. On the other hand, if I carried it too carefully, as if I had something wrapped up in my jacket, well, people would think, perhaps a ranger would show up, someone would suspect something wasn't right; you just don't know. So I tried to walk the fine line between nonchalance and negligence.

There had to be, I suspected, some important reason, other than burying it, for why I had come across this poor creature—at least that's why I think I stole away with it. But what was it? Off the top of my head I didn't know, so I asked the bunny, "Dead bunny rabbit, what is it you want to teach me?"

Well, everything that's alive will die sooner or later. And though the young bunny was in its element, far from the dangers of moving vehicles, it wasn't safe even here. A couple of small sharp pebbles were pressed into its belly and one of the legs seemed to be broken. I hypothesized that it could have been hit by a mountain biker tearing down the hill. Or maybe the rabbit, in a devil-may-care attitude, raced straight into the path of danger—what squirrels seem to do sometimes. It wasn't fair that it went like that, that it went at all. I felt for it, contemplating the ruthlessness of nature and existence and fate. But you never know when you will go. Did the rabbit know what was coming? (I'm demonstrating here how sometimes you have to get past all the silly thoughts to get to the good ones.)

Anyway, all this got me started and I thought about the illusion of safety. Although we try to think about safety, assure ourselves we always stay safe and maintain control over our existence, can we really do that? I was pondering these questions and then immediately after that, something clicked in me and I had another one of those "ah ha" moments where suddenly everything became clear: I had already written a short story on the illusion of safety, but I didn't know what to do with it, what it was for, or where to put it, as I hadn't yet thought of discussing safety in this book. And if I were to, I would need it to tie in somehow. So now here was the tie-in: the dead bunny rabbit I stumbled upon that morning showed me not only that that story belonged, but exactly where it belonged as well.

The idea that things I "randomly" came across in my surroundings were guiding me was confirmed to me once again, and also that my book was developing itself with the help of my environment and my expanding awareness.

While I am contemplating these things, I am very conscious that my mother-in-law, when she reads this book, will say, "*Siehst du, die war immer ein bisschen verrueckt!*" ("Don't you see? She was always a bit Nutty!" Luise, I know you will laugh with me here, I think?) My mother-in-law has a good sense of humor and loves to laugh, as does my own mother, although neither indulges this humorous side of life.

So I took that bunny home and hid it under a bush right outside my front door. Later, when my kids came home from school, I went to show it to them but it wasn't there. Did someone steal away with my bunny? No, it couldn't be. I looked around under the bush and found it had moved (again) a couple feet away from where I had placed it. Was someone or something playing tricks on me? I don't know. Anyway, here's that story on the illusion of safety:

We live in a world where it's incontrovertible that safety is an illusion (I refer again to the dead bunny). Safety can be intended and strived towards, but it can't be guaranteed. During the course of writing this book, it began to occur to me that perhaps the only security we have, the only thing true, the only thing safe, comes from interconnectedness. (The word interconnectedness could be replaced with creation or God or All That Is with essentially no loss of meaning.)

What happened was that when Julianne was in her last year at Mountain School, the tires on my station wagon got quite bald. I drove extra cautiously when it rained because I didn't trust them. It was definitely time to replace them, but I also had to consider our finances. W. had been out of work for several months, had informed me that we were running out of money, so I delayed purchasing new ones. But one day, after dropping off Jagger and Celeste at Jagger's house after school, I noticed that one of my tires was completely flat.

I was seriously annoyed, especially because I knew I'd have to deal with the flat myself—I knew that W. wouldn't come to rescue me. I didn't even bother to call him, so thick and icy was the wall between us. Just a month before he had made me change my own oil and filter which—after consulting him on how—I did for the first time ever. (Thankfully, he walked me through the process, watched over me and told me exactly what to do.) Fed up with me because our savings were being depleted and I wasn't looking for regular work, he had informed me that my vehicle from then on was my own responsibility.

He was particularly irritated with me then because he had already told me more than once, in case it went in one ear and out the other, that my chances of writing a successful book—children's or otherwise—were the same as winning the lottery. "Nothing personal," he said, "but any new author's chances of writing a successful book are the same as winning the lottery." (And who was it that said that the chances of winning the lottery were the same whether or not you bought a ticket?) Were the things people prophesied about you likely to be true? He had a point, of course, and he also knew how to cause a panic in me. This point in particular terrified me because it was reasonable, it was well-grounded, and many would agree if pressed for their opinion. But what could I *do* with other people's opinions?

Anyway, that's why I preferred to change the flat by myself and forget him. So first I hunted down the street for a jack that would work because I couldn't find my own; it wasn't where I expected it near the spare. Then I loosened the screws, jacked up the car, and took the flat off. A man who drove by stopped and helped me put the spare on and tightened the screws. In about half an hour's time, it was all done. Then Julianne and I drove home.

That evening when I related the story to W., he told me to get myself four new tires in the morning, which the next morning I did, exactly as instructed. He advised me on the make, the model, the price, everything. I wasn't going to argue with him when it came to tires. I didn't have all the necessary distinctions to make an informed or wise decision, and I trusted W.'s judgment on mechanical and automotive matters completely. At the tire store I felt like an informed consumer and knew exactly what I needed—very good quality steel-belted radials, tires to last me for quite some time.

How would you go about choosing tires anyway? What would you look for? What factors would need to be considered? How could you make an informed decision about anything important in life if you didn't have all the necessary distinctions? I was glad I didn't have to make these decisions on my own, that I had help all around me.

The next morning the Italian tires were put on and then I drove off to Santa Cruz. It was a crisp and clear winter Saturday, a day I had off from my family, and I was on my way to hear a friend give a talk on raw food. With brand new tires on my car, I felt free and comfortable and drove as fast as the traffic allowed—as is my usual style on the hilly, meandering way to the coast. Then, going about 55 mph around a blind curve, I noticed that the vehicles ahead were completely stopped. I slammed on the brakes and came to a screeching halt barely a couple centimeters from the car in front of me.

Evidently only seconds before, there had been a four-car accident in both lanes just two rows ahead. Thankfully, it wasn't very serious. The vehicle damage was significant, enough for a car or two to require towing, but the passengers seemed to be okay. People shut their engines off and got out of their cars to peer at the damage and to socialize while waiting for the traffic to begin flowing again. I heard some folks congratulating each other on their good braking. The first thing I did—secretly, of course—was to congratulate my new, full-treaded tires and also, thank my old tires for going when it was time for them to go.

This car incident had been the *third close call* with vehicles that month. (The other two times, people had made left turns at lights without seeing me coming.) Something was definitely going on with regard to safety and security and it certainly had gotten my attention.

So thank you, dearest bunny rabbit, for going when it was time for you to go.

∞

The issue of safety and security came up again in the latter half of June 2004, when my children and I were visiting my parents. An interesting news story on the Yahoo Internet site—a Reuters' *Oddly Enough* article about a friendly dog that prevented a killing spree—caught my eye when I "just so happened" to check my email remotely. I emailed this news item to J. to show him that there definitely were positive shifts occurring in the world (though it sure didn't appear that way) because I had heard, through W. of course, that J. was inclined towards depression. W. had found this information out when he had a lunch meeting with J.'s wife (those two!); they had apparently discussed how both of us were similar, amongst other things.

The news story went like this: a Canadian man who was known to be mentally disturbed was intent on killing as many people as possible in a Toronto neighborhood, apparently so that he would be placed into prison permanently. (Makes you wonder whether incarceration is an effective deterrent. Perhaps this man thought he would suffer less in prison?)

His car was found loaded with weapons and ammunition—six thousand rounds, along with two rifles, a shotgun, a semi-automatic pistol, a revolver, an air rifle, a few knives, a camouflage mask, and some netting—according to Toronto police. Setting himself up in an east-end park to load his weapons, he then planned to drive around shooting. But while at the park, he was approached by a dog that started to play with him, and evidently this encounter with the dog "melted the man's heart," which then led him to turn himself in to the police. The man was a pet lover and he figured that since there was such a nice dog in the neighborhood, the people there must be nice too and he wasn't going to carry out his plan.

In my view, the "mentally disturbed" man allowed himself to connect to his heart through the simple act of relating with a dog that just so happened to show up in his environment. His heart responded to the dog and then guided him on what to do next. The inner message was clear; he knew what he had to do and he followed through with it immediately.

It isn't that difficult to connect with your heart. If an angry, mentally unbalanced criminal ready to bring down as many people as possible can do it, anyone can. This heart connection is what will bring balance, peace, and harmony to the world. When you connect to your heart, to your sacred space, you connect to all of creation, to the interconnectedness between all beings and things—which will assure that what you do will benefit all. What more can provide safety and security?

∞

There was nothing safe or secure about my writing a book, but I longed to trust in the security that comes from within, that comes from the deepest spaces of the heart, though for the longest time even I was painfully aware that my writing sucked. I mean that my early drafts were pretty lame, as well as being under a hundred pages. But, just because it wasn't good yet, did I need to give it all up? No, I would not, could not give up—so much depended on it. And my writing—like most anything in life—got better in stages. The Counsel of Light themselves even spoke of this, er…I mean read from my record that I'd work on my writing style, which of course I did. They told me that I had a high capacity to write but who could tell, judging from my early work. And bestselling author Anne Lamott in her book *Bird by Bird* says that early drafts can be awful, so I felt better, made an effort, and developed that capacity just like they said I would.

To help me in my process, I solicited the advice of a friend from college who happened to be a science writer for a national weekly news magazine, a playwright, and a soon-to-be novelist. Even though on the whole, Vernon thought my earliest draft was well written, he said there were some very small language issues. (He was too kind.) Vernon requested I pick up a copy of Strunk and White's *Elements of Style*; "both guys taught at Cornell, by the way," he added. Unfortunately, this advice just didn't seem to fit into my process at the moment because I wasn't about to get a hold of some English style manual and study it—who has time for that when you've got a book to complete A.S.A.P., when you know you can't putter around anymore because everyone's on your back about it?

I mean when you receive emails—I have them in my inbox still—relayed to you by W. from "people he knows who know me" (or at least they think they do), an array of messages strung together from nameless sources advising me on my life: "I hope she will grow up soon," "She needs to stop blaming others for her lack of happiness and success," "It takes more than a normal life story to succeed," "The big challenge lies elsewhere, and that's why you keep yourself writing and rewriting," and "You occupy yourself with unimportant things" (like chauffeuring my children to swimming and choir practice, for example)—it does motivate you to complete that book of yours with a resolve that's beyond the normal.

I keep myself writing and rewriting? Well at that point I mostly had been adding pages and pages to my book. For all they knew though, I could have been lying in the sun, baking cookies, or plotting to undermine dark renegade ET forces. And now that I think of it, isn't writing and rewriting typical and necessary for a writer?

I occupy myself with unimportant things? Isn't helping to bring love, truth, and wisdom to the world important, especially now at this time in humanity's development? What about the value of exposing the world's illusions? The value of connecting people to their intuition, to their soul's purpose? And who was responsible for making whom happy? Immature and irresponsible was I? Immature indeed.

Not long afterwards I received another email from W.: "You know, you are usually taking the position that you are the one who is superior because you know better than others. Actually since I met you.

"You are elusive, don't explain yourself very well, but are certain you have something others don't, because they don't get it or are "closed-minded."

"Over the years you changed your direction many times, after you've always pursued the current idea very strongly (which, by the way, is not a bad quality in itself). However, none of these ideas were carried on to completion or success. You later explain that it wasn't the right thing anyway. But the current thing was finally it. This is the pattern that I'm suggesting you look at for a while."

"Yes, I understand this about myself," I emailed back. Well, of course he was right about my needing to look at my direction and my patterns—here I was examining those things.

One evening when I dropped off the kids at the townhouse and asked for my monthly check, W. said, "Be an adult, Christine," referring to my lack of responsibility for my own upkeep. "It's time your mom learned to be responsible," he said to our children in the next breath.

And of course I wasn't *now* about to teach him not to say these things in their presence, as my pointing out such things was often a sore point with him. He did things *his* way, it was *his* decision to tell the children what he thought they ought to know, and I wasn't about to tell him otherwise. "You're not my mother and you can't make me," he had often said, and I had agreed with him on both counts. Well, I have to admit I also had made decisions without his input, which he felt was hurtful and selfish. I tried to remember to include him, but my mind just forgot, as though I had a mental block against it, or something.

Actually, I wouldn't want to make him do anything against his truth anyway. What someone does has got to arise from inner inspiration and inner urging rather than outer forces. And likewise, he couldn't make me either—why should I have gone to work when I was on an important mission, when according to higher sources I was sitting on a pot of gold? When I had unlimited assets available to me in my spiritual bank account? Would I have felt all safe and secure in some loathsome job somewhere?

Yes, that's how it was with us. Sometimes the hate and pain was expressed with words, sometimes with silence—which he wasn't pleased with either, because, of all the things he didn't like, he hated being ignored the most. "You ignore people, you ignore me, you ignore your mother, your sister, everyone," he said. Another typical phrase was: "If you were right you'd justify yourself, you'd say something back." It made me think that he liked to argue just for the sake of arguing, as though it were recreational, like some sort of game, or even an art form. "Your eyes become so green when you get angry, I love it!" he would often say when we were still together, the same eyes that used to make him dizzy. At other times he laughed when I got angry, which only got me more frustrated. It might have been fun and games for him at times but not so for me; I never did understand the game.

But what could I have done about this writing project? How could I have justified what wasn't complete yet, or hadn't been looked at yet, or whatever? What could I have said besides "I hear you and I'm working on it"?

My side of the family joined the chorus as well, trying to challenge my determination to follow through with my mission. My Mom called many times while I was writing and in her motherly way repeated how she had cleaned houses to help pay for my college expenses—and all for nothing. One of my brothers also concurred, she said. Even though this education had happened over twenty years ago, it didn't matter. With all these degrees and qualifications behind me, I'd be credentialed enough to make informed choices, you would think. Besides, I *was* using all my education and experiences and this is what it happened to look like.

Next in line was my brother-in-law, Chris. Apparently, Chris was recruited to cross-examine me during a restaurant meal my children and I shared with his family, when my sister Lydia was in the Bay Area on business for her company. He had come along to watch their baby while she went on her appointments, and also to check me out: "What are you doing with all your free time?" he asked.

"Writing a book," I answered. Back in March 2004 I didn't have the audacity to say, "I'm here on a mission to shift the existent paradigms, to break the rules that no longer serve humanity, and to ground truth onto the planet, and the way I'm planning on doing all that is by writing this book." Would he have believed that I was on a highly sensitive mission and had all these important assignments? Plus, would he have known what a paradigm even was? (Well, I myself didn't *really* know what a paradigm was until I started doing the difficult work of taking them apart.)

"Why can't you do this writing as a hobby?" he went on.

"I suppose when I am a grandma and I have time to knit I will have time for hobbies. But right now I have no time for hobbies of any sort."

"How are you supporting yourself?" he said, intent on discovering something—I don't know what. Well, he was obviously onto something; I did after all have secrets. But his line of questioning wasn't even in the ballpark so my secrets were safe.

"W. is supporting me right now, until the time when I can support myself," I said.

"Why is he supporting you?" Chris was obviously curious about this particular point.

"Because he's a man of integrity," I said.

"Will you be able to support yourself and your kids with the money you make from writing some book?"

"Yes, I will, if it's a bestseller I will." (I suppose that telling someone you're going to do something is a pretty safe way of making yourself stick to your word.)

Back home on Long Island my inquisitors sought W.'s counsel and then reviewed my case amongst themselves. After a few weeks of careful deliberation, Chris advised that I seek gainful employment posthaste.

Well! Who would have known that nestled between Cold Spring Harbor Laboratory and Brookhaven National Lab was this other Long Island think-tank, a husband-wife team of life coaches and consultants? Certainly not I.

My sister Lydia then called a longtime mutual friend, Steve, with whom I chatted about philosophy and personal ambitions, hoping to get him to convince me to look for a job. One of Steve's hobbies happened to be amateur astrology; perhaps he could see in the stars that I needed to look for work was what she, with her little game, had in mind. "The book is not going to make it, Steve. Everybody says that, including W.'s mother and aunt, and they read the first draft." (Well, that wasn't entirely true. W.'s father wrote me that he thought it would be *ein Renner* (a winner) if I continued to work with it. And W. himself hadn't read it, didn't want to read it. "I'll read it when I can buy a copy of it at the bookstore," he said. A good thing too; a part of him—the inner powers part—must have known that I didn't need anyone throwing any monkey wrenches into my mission before it was complete.)

But Steve, who had known me since my first job as a process engineer and also was acquainted with my astrology chart, dismissed her argument, saying, "If anybody's going to make it big, it's going to be Christine. And I don't mean anybody in the family. I mean anybody anywhere."

Also, a friend's husband asked his wife why I was writing a book about myself. "Why is she still doing that? Isn't that being a bit self-indulgent?"—this coming from a man who owned well over a dozen very expensive, collectible guitars, that if sold at a famous auction house could buy you a nice townhouse. Well, there's nothing wrong with having all those great guitars, especially when you actually play guitar, but this is such a good example of human nature—we project onto others what belongs to ourselves.

Even my own kids got into this little game, and why not? "Mommy, when can we get a bigger house? We hate this house!" they'd whine about our rental. Normally competitive with each other in typical sibling fashion, they joined forces on this issue. "We're always bumping into things and hurting ourselves because this house is so small!" (Of course not because their attention was focused elsewhere and they weren't looking where they were going.)

Plus, Angelika made bets with both W. and me on whether my book would be published. If so, W. promised to pay each girl one thousand dollars. Her gambling with me was more conservative, first betting twenty dollars that I wouldn't be published, but after I agreed she reduced her bet to five dollars. Smart girl.

Many people in my life were worried about my life plans. I admit I was baffled myself, even while writing this book. But it sure felt like it was a case of my word against W.'s, his reality versus mine, and since the outer evidence of success wasn't visible yet, it was "them against me" for the time being. "I hate you, Mom," Angelika said to me one day. "You make Dad do all the work. When are you going to make money?" Pretty strong opinions for a then nine-year old. Children of course expect instant fruition; mine did anyway.

My response to all this? I felt that the answers didn't lie in what my mother wanted me to do, in what my in-laws wanted me to do, in what W. wanted me to do, even though he often had good, sound, logical points. The answers didn't lie in what all of them were trying to coerce me to do! I tried to be with all this drama with little or no loss of power or inspiration. I tried to let go of all the complaints, saying "I'm working on it. A book takes time…" I brushed all these things off because I had the advantage of knowing things they didn't know and had more important matters to occupy myself with (trying to figure all this out, trying to make sense of it).

Even J. offered his two cents on my book, after asking how it was coming along: "Why don't you leave some material for the sequel?" (This was merely ten months after my writing began to flow.) He's clever, though. How could he know there would be more than one book?

A couple of months later, about three years after our coffee shop meeting, I finally had the nerve to tell him (in an email of course) that he was an important character in my book. This he was flattered about, but also I think it made him a bit nervous. He asked whether his name was mentioned or "just a general description of his person."

"General descriptions are not that interesting," I pointed out, "You really need to add details in order to bring a story to life. I discovered that pretty early on."

"Is there any intimate information?" he asked.

"You mean, for example, about the time you paraded around in front of me with nothing but a skimpy towel around your behind? No, I didn't write about that. This isn't that kind of book."

"That's not exactly what I meant. One of the residual effects of overprotective parents is my noticeable suppression of certain types of information, especially that concerning personal doings. I'm very protective of my personal life," he emailed.

"I had overprotective parents, too, so I have a particular sensitivity when it comes to personal privacy. I hope that reassures you. Besides, this book is about letting go of all that baggage from the past, about being free from those conditionings that make you overly sensitive about your life. It'll help you with that," I answered.

"But there can be a domino effect that impacts more than just you or me. This is more of what I mean."

"Yes, exactly, that's what I mean, too—it *will* have a domino effect. It will impact the world, and that will be good—you'll understand all this when you read it. We are on the same wavelength!"

"It's not that I keep it to myself so much as I try to limit its exposure. I'm just not comfortable having it put out there in this fashion. No matter how things have turned out, this was a messy and difficult set of events that occurred, unfortunate as it is."

"So philosophical you are! And you seem so wary. Do you not trust me with this task?" I asked, having a little fun.

"I'm not judging your ability; it's just that I'm inconceivably wary at times," J. emailed.

"Yes, you are. It's good to notice that. Also, I want you to know that you are very brave. If I didn't feel connected to my inner self and to interconnectedness, if I didn't see that there was a bigger picture to the events that transpired, I could imagine that I'd be pretty freaked out. But this is bigger than any of us involved, and our role in it is a contribution to the world. You could share it, and it would be healing for others as well. I don't have a choice about it, and you can't make me not write it." (Not to mention that I *already had* his permission—it's just that he wasn't aware of this on his most conscious level yet.) "Besides, do you realize how silly this conversation sounds in reality? I am a nobody, having no connections in the publishing industry, and not even a writer by trade or background, with the odds of getting published staggeringly low, and you're worried about the world finding out something I write about you?" (I was having a little fun now!)

"I would ask that family names never be mentioned, especially because of my kids. They have nothing to do with this. My family should not be involved. What has happened has happened. Why it has happened is for each individual to search out for himself if he so wishes," Jon responded.

"Jon, there's no reason to put in family names—what would be the point? This isn't reading for little kids but when they're older why in the world would you want to keep it from them?"

He didn't respond to that. A day later I emailed Jon again: "Well, anyway, good luck in your endeavor." But he didn't respond to that either! He was so serious sometimes, and didn't ask what I meant. I would have told him; I mean I would have told him *something*, as I still didn't have the complete picture. I still had to be careful about what I revealed to people prematurely.

Later when I asked him why he had been so serious (usually, he liked to joke about most anything), he emailed, "This is a serious time in my life. I'm trying to figure myself out. You were commenting on that this last week about your needing to focus on you and what you're doing. After yesterday I see that for myself as well."

"That's good, actually" I replied, glad to have made an impact in his life. "I'm pretty close to figuring myself out, but a book is a major endeavor. That's why I need to focus my time on it. It won't get done by itself." (Those unlimited resources that I had in the spiritual dimension still needed to be transferred into the physical.)

What I have been trying to show is that I hadn't even had a chance to work on my book for a whole year, in addition to taking care of my children during summer vacation, after school, etc., and the pressure to complete it already and to do it well was intense! I suppose I should have been flattered by such high expectations of me.

Well, given these high demands, this unrelenting pressure, this special form of encouragement, and the high stakes besides, I decided to take the quick and easy route. I'd immerse myself completely in the process, developing my writing ability as I went along, and oh, also by picking up elements of style and grammar from random books—fiction, even—that seemed to jump at me as I walked past them at the library. In this way I learned what I needed all at once, because I needed to teach myself how to write good books and I needed to do this fast. And who could go wrong with using Michael Crichton's book *Travels* as a fine example of a personal narrative, an account of his life adventures from medical school student to suspense novelist? This book my friend Marianne recommended to me. So even if I didn't know everything, even if I didn't know how I was going to get it all done, it didn't seem to matter since I had my inner guidance and also had people who supported me with empowering information and encouragement at exactly the right moment. The interconnectedness was clearly working.

My playwright, soon-to-be novelist, friend Vernon encouraged me with his comments on an early draft: "First of all, congratulations—on everything. I know how difficult life changes can be and what kind of courage is required to find your true calling and pursue it. Almost everything in our society is geared toward making people conform. I just went to my twenty-fifth high school reunion and saw firsthand what happens to people who give up on their dreams. It's not pretty."

Vernon also advised me to logically organize my material into chapters. "The good news is that having a science background really helps with knowing how to organize things. Many writers couldn't reason their way out of a baggie because they have not been taught to think logically. Fortunately, being a smart, well-educated person, you have all it takes to develop an organized theme that can tie together what you are saying. With that in mind, let me take the liberty of suggesting that you create a flow chart that outlines the steps required to say what you want to say. What is the main point you are trying to make? What are the logical steps in that argument? Write them down. Each one will become a chapter. Then edit your manuscript so that your wonderful stories and observations support the points in any particular chapter. At the end of this process—which I'm confident will be easy for you—you will have a well-organized, but still compelling book.

"I hope this helps. If you decide to give it a shot, I'd be happy to take a look again. Or feel free to ignore it all. I'm just a pasty-looking guy who sits in front of a computer all day, after all. Vernon"

Vernon's advice was fine in theory, but how could I organize my life into neat, well-defined chapters when I didn't have things figured out yet, when I didn't yet know who I was? My life felt like one long trudging journey to me, with its one constant underlying theme—what was it? Oh yes, I soldiering on seeking something just beneath my comprehension, allowing myself no say whether I felt like it or not, striving to always move forward, each outcome a stepping stone to the next, having the feeling—knowing, really—that in the end I will prevail; I will triumph! It will be worth it!

Furthermore, I thought it would be way more interesting, more fun, more like me, and perhaps easier, too, to let my inner self organize my book, there being a natural order to the universe that ultimately is more beautiful and more logical than the rational human mind on its own could ever conceive. So I didn't do a flow chart, couldn't have done one anyway even if I had wanted to. Rather, I followed my inner guidance moment by moment and discovered what was next for me one day at a time; I let things flow. And I let myself be surprised.

∞

Sometimes it appeared that I didn't have a whole lot of security and support from the people around me, the outside world. That's when the connection to my inner core (and interconnectedness) was particularly helpful. My inner core provided me with inner support in the form of confidence in my abilities to keep manifesting, and the wisdom to see things differently and move things forward. (I mean that my inner self supported me while I was *still under the illusion*, at times, that there wasn't a whole lot of support available to me from the outside world.)

Of course it's great to be materially and emotionally supported when working on a project that takes time to manifest. Children especially need long-term, unconditional support because they take a long time to fully mature and because they respond immediately to their perception of the level of support they receive. The following story illustrates this point and is part of the wisdom that helped get me through those illusory times:

At the end of March 2004, I had scheduled a swim meet for Angelika on a weekend she was to be with her dad, forgot about it, and informed him about it a little late for his liking. W. had already planned a hike for that Sunday and wasn't happy about having to be at a swim meet. Since I was in error, I proposed a possible solution by suggesting he do both: they could hike in Morgan Hill (a great place for hikes) right after the event. I volunteered to take her to the meet in the early morning, with sandwiches and drinks and all her things. All he had to do was show up at the meet with Julianne mid-morning.

But he didn't approve of the idea and Angelika had to choose between the swim meet and hike, between swim meet and dad, which made her feel very uncomfortable. I called him to discuss how Angelika was affected (she was crying), but he was too annoyed with me to have a constructive conversation. We put the phone down, resigned to our natures. But an hour later he called back while I was soaking in the bathtub and asked for information and directions to the meet. (Well, one thing I know about W. is that he usually comes through in the end.)

I was very pleased with this change of heart and asked him to arrive by ten, to support her in the breaststroke and the backstroke, her strongest events. Angelika was a star breaststroker and had advanced fast in her times, but seemed to have hit a plateau lately. I had a hunch this was because she didn't feel very supported by her dad. I let him know this, but he didn't see it that way. "Everybody hits plateaus after a while," he said.

The next morning we called his cell phone around 9:30 to make sure he would be at the meet by 10:15, 10:30 at the very latest. He said he'd try to make it. At 10:32, Angelika's 100-yard breaststroke race came up.

"Where's Papa?" she asked with concerned voice as she took off her parka and put on her goggles. She had been looking forward to his arrival all morning. I tried to support her as much as I could: "I'm sure he's on his way. Maybe there's traffic. It's just not like your dad to be late for anything; you know he wants you to do your best…"

She stepped onto the starting block and at the sound of the buzzer, dove in. I was mentally with her all the way, cheering her on. But her strokes seemed labored, as though she were swimming in a pool of molasses. I saw and felt her fatigue and had the strange sensation that I was watching a slow-motion video, like those on TV during the Olympics. After swimming the four laps, she climbed out of the pool completely out of breath and sighed, "I did my best." She was four seconds over her best time.

W. arrived with Julianne and a friend several minutes after the race was over. Annoyed, I said: "I see that supporting Angelika is not on your agenda." But then I noticed I felt embarrassed at my reproachful remark, and let the whole thing go. Besides, he was here now, and the 100-yard backstroke was coming up in about half an hour, her next strongest event. Then like a perfectly supportive father, W. discussed Angelika's goal with her. They agreed she'd try to cut two seconds off her best time.

I watched her as she prepared to get on the starting block: she looked excited, lively, and uplifted. With all of us cheering her on, she dove in and this time, no longer swam like she was exhausted— she was jamming. Then she won her heat and cut six seconds off her record. The plateau was gone. Like the Santa Cruz fog on a good September day, it vanished in midstream, dissolved by the warming rays of the midday sun.

Of course it's important that children feel supported, especially during what they perceive as challenging times. Being supported is a wonderful thing, but if you don't have consistent support or when the support doesn't seem to come in the form you think you need, you can get support from within. You can get the energy and the excitement necessary to complete projects and fulfill dreams from the connection to the universe through your inner core. In this way, you'll get what you need so you may carry on.

But I learned something else that same day that helped me expand my views and ideas about what I thought support actually was: if W. had simply acquiesced to the schedule change or if he had arrived on time as I had wanted him to, I wouldn't have learned how immediately, how significantly children are affected by their perception of support. How children act and how well they do is clearly affected by the level of their support structure, perhaps more than we think. In fact, I wouldn't have had the opportunity to learn about any of these things if I had done things right and given W. enough advance warning about the meet, or if W. simply let me off the hook, because then I wouldn't have been there, none of this would have happened, and I probably wouldn't have bothered to ask the many questions I had been asking myself. And after I thought about these things I realized something even more important: W.'s part of the deal in this so-called drama, his contribution, his life purpose, the role he agreed, a long, long time ago to play with me, was to help put me into challenging situations so that I would learn what I needed to learn so that I could then share it with the world. And when I got that, I sat down on the lawn of Morgan Hill High School and cried. (And from then on, I saw him differently as well.)

∞

Meantime the pressure to complete my project did not let up. When I thought I was close to showing my work to an editor for inspection, W., at the children's Zone champs swim meet in January 2005 asked, "So when are you going to generate some income?"

"Maybe in a month or so I'll be done with this draft, and soon after I'll work towards getting a book contract," I answered. He seemed glad it was nearing completion; everyone wanted it to be completed, including me. But of course I wasn't anywhere close. I had yet to discover who I was—the piece of the puzzle the Counsel of Light had been asking me for years to find—and there would be much more material to synthesize and understand after that.

"Well someone I know who's been through publishing told me that it takes three to five years," he said.

The next day I emailed W. and asked, "By the way, who told you what takes three to five years?"

"A friend of Otti apparently published three to five books, fiction and nonfiction, but he had had a tough time making a living so he gave up a career as a writer and instead does it as his hobby. It took him years to get to market, but then no one invested millions on a marketing campaign to push his books. These days books are not conceived "the old way." Most of the successful ones are "planned developments" for particular target audiences and then pushed with elaborate marketing campaigns. There are too many books out there that a non-pushed book goes under in the noise," he replied via email.

He had been telling me these things ever since I took the book idea seriously and now he finally discovered firsthand proof. These remarks used to frighten me and cut like little daggers in my heart, but by this time they no longer had such an effect. I could shake off the anxious feelings faster and faster and now, thanks to my strong relationship with my inner core, they even amused me somewhat. (Wow! More material for my book!)

"Oh, I can assure you my book is not done the "old way." That's the last thing you'd call it, actually. And it's definitely a planned development since it was actually planned way before any other book out there," I emailed.

"I don't think you understand; it's not the writers who plan today's blockbusters, it's an army of marketing people and project planners…High-volume stuff that needs huge investments is not just happening by accident but is planned before the creation. Basically, you first find out what the market would absorb, then you create that. You have been out of working life too long to understand how things work these days. I hope you are one of the few who will 'win the lottery' anyway." (I so liked what he wrote here and I thought: Give me more, baby! Your brilliance astounds me!)

He tried hard to get me to understand his points, which, actually, I did. But would he have understood my points—that my book (as well as mission) had been in the planning before "the creation" too, that I seemed to have my own army of "project planners" that used to work with me, that it was no accident or coincidence that this was now the case, and that the conventions and rules did not apply to me because I came to break the rules? So did he, by the way, and he knows it, too. So did Jon, and I'm pretty sure he knows this about himself, too. We all came to break the rules.

∞

Besides being encouraged to complete my book not long after I started it, another pattern I noticed was that things that didn't have anything to do with me were unfairly attributed to me. For instance, when my kids and I visited my parents in the suburbs of Buffalo the summer of 2005, I worked on revising my book. I set myself up cozily in my parents' dining room, a chandelier over my head, and worked a few hours each day.

One morning Mom came down from her bedroom while I was eating breakfast alone. She came into the kitchen in a way that reminded me of famous TV detective Colombo, a contemplating and searching look on her face, as though something was up and she was determined to get to the bottom of it. Then she asked me why there were so many ducks loitering in the backyard that morning. "We never have ducks here. We get a lot of geese all the time but never any ducks. And there were fourteen of them this morning; I counted them. They were all in the backyard, hanging around together. When you visit we have ducks. That's very strange," she said in Polish while staring at me.

"Well, Mom, I was writing about ducks yesterday, that's why they were here," I blurted out, because actually I had revised my bird philosophy the previous evening and briefly thought about ducks.

"Imagine, fourteen ducks in the backyard, that is a first around here…" she went on and on as usual. The things I got blamed for! (Another thing: I certainly wouldn't have thought of actually counting the ducks, but I think if I had, I would have found that she had miscounted and there were but thirteen ducks in the backyard that morning.)

Anyway, what matters the gesture of pulling down a shade or two when the whole roof of your house is uninsulated and the heat beats down relentlessly into your space? Might as well just fling the windows wide and embrace the heat, let in some fresh air, pull the blinders off, and accept the inevitable. Accept it all and see what this is all about—this is how I felt about my "mission" by then.

And just as older dogs teach puppies who it is they are and cats teach new dogs in the house who it is that they are, every one of these people was helping me learn who I was in the face of all these circumstances, and eventually, who I was in essence.

∞

As I have already mentioned, I trusted my soul, my intuition to synthesize my material for me and take me to my next step. I also discovered that my capacity to write and to write well grew by quantum leaps once I really "got" who I was—that's basically it. And I learned who I was not all at once but gradually, by putting the various pieces together, as though I were cracking a mysterious code. During this time, I was also slowly realizing that this whole project, my entire life, and this whole earth experiment, was less and less crazy than I had thought it was. And it became clearer and clearer to me that the *support for this project was everywhere.*

Incidentally, most enlightened folks realize that critiques aimed at them often have little or nothing to do with them, but instead reflect the fears, misconceptions, proclivities, or unexamined conditionings of the critics—usually unknown to them. Their critiques often reflect the fears and illusions about their own maturity, about their ordinary life stories, about their own survival, and so on. Another way of saying this same thing is: one has a tendency to put down those things one most dislikes in oneself. That's why author Don Miguel Ruiz, in *The Four Agreements: A Practical Guide to Personal Freedom*, says never to take personally criticisms pointed at you.

This applies to any judgments or critiques that target individuals, groups, or ideas, including those of professional critics, commentators, and experts who shape culture or opinion, be they conservative or liberal, men or women; it's all the same. Your judgments have more to do with your own fears and unexamined conditionings or the fears and illusions present in mass-consciousness, rather than with the true heart of humanity, or even your own heart. There are exceptions, of course, such as when a teacher critiques a student's work objectively and constructively.

And this reminds me of Jem's song *They*:

> *Who made up all the rules*
> *We follow them like fools*
> *Believe them to be true*
> *Don't care to think them through*
>
> *And I'm sorry so sorry*
> *I'm sorry it's like this…*

I'd like to add my own words here:

> *And I'm so sorry too*
> *It's true, we agreed to this*
> *Now that we know the tune*
> *We can transform it.*

Balance

The Sunday evening after the heavy rainstorm and the bunny, Julianne and I drove to Lisa's house to pick up Angelika from a play date with Lisa's daughter Ciara, arriving just as the Academy Awards show was beginning. I recalled that yes, I had happened to hear someone somewhere mention the Awards, but I wasn't clear about the details of when, or the channel, or which movies were up for awards, and I didn't think I had seen any of them. But now the show was live on Lisa and Frank's large screen TV in their comfy family room just off their newly remodeled kitchen. Lisa, a movie buff, was already lounging on the sofa with a wine cooler in her hand while Frank completed the cooking for dinner, which smelled wonderful. Anyway, I must have looked hungry because Lisa asked, "Why don't you all stay for dinner and watch the Academy Awards with us? We're having Indian food."

"Yes, thank you, we'd like that. I love Indian food," I said. My kids of course wanted to stay. Lisa and Frank had four children and a dog to play with, a big happy family atmosphere. And since it meant I wouldn't have to cook, I gladly accepted the invitation. We sat in front of the TV with plates on our laps, eating curries and basmati rice and some kind of yummy Persian dish, sipping our drinks. I felt comfy-cozy and contented. We had buried the bunny that morning, Julianne and I. The issues of life and death and the illusion of safety were behind me and I could relax now. Or so I thought.

But it wasn't long before I began to notice more patterns as I sat with my eyes glued to the television. (For those on assignment investigating things, this must be the sort of thing that comes up a lot.)

First, I noticed that almost all of the movies up for awards were about war or violence—some historical, some fantasy, but war just the same. One movie was about the Civil War, another about warfare in middle earth, others portrayed combat on a ship, pirates in battle, duels in the East, and also, violence in the family. The war/violence theme was glaring.

I thought about this and then it began to occur to me that within all of these conflicts was the original and most important war: the war within the self, the inner war that could end all others if it were resolved. And it became clear to me that this war within, this deeper war, is responsible for all other acts of duality, struggle, or disharmony, and that this principal war is the outcome of a separation that will finally begin to be resolved, because we are not so divided from one another as we are from our own true selves.

Below is another good example, in the form of a song, of the struggle within that manifests itself as a struggle without. The ending of this song had been playing in my head for quite some time. I caught the last few lines on the radio: "You labeled me, I'll label you. So I've done the unforgiven" is what I thought I heard and later emailed to Jon, asking him to help me find the song's title. But Jon is good with music; he emailed the lyrics to me in no time. Anyway, it's very simple, I think: inner turmoil creates outer turmoil. Turmoil in the spiritual realm creates turmoil in the physical realm. Turmoil in your inner life creates turmoil in your outer life. What's inside will be outside. Another way of saying the exact same thing is: as above, so below. The song is titled "The Unforgiven" and is sung by the band Metallica. Here is a short excerpt:

> ... *They dedicate their lives*
> *To running all of his*

He tries to please them all
This bitter man he is…

…What I've felt
What I've known
Never shined through in what I've shown
Never free
Never me
So I dub thee unforgiven…

Pretty cool words, and somewhat similar in theme to Jon's song "Reality"—which is also about breaking free from societal conditionings and trying to be yourself when the pressure to conform is intense. Metallica's lyrics exemplify not only the external struggle between what's in our heart ("our truth") and societal expectations, but also suggest a deeper internal struggle: the struggle between the left and the right brain, between the rational and the emotional, between the mind and the heart, between the male and the female aspects within. An example of this is when you're under pressure to make a difficult choice, the mind can go back and forth, so what are you to do? How do you know what's correct and true for you when there's a split between your mind and your heart and, at times, a split seemingly in your own mind?

Ever since I began the process of connecting within, I found that that the inner voice of the soul is often inspirational, animated, and uplifting, as well as being consistent; it doesn't go back and forth, but tends to be constant for weeks, months, and even longer, while the mind can change its position many times and sometimes even hold contradictory viewpoints at the same time. (My inner core guided me to stay focused on my mission while my mind held contradictory viewpoints about it—some lofty, some rational, and some fearful.)

As often happens in these inner conflicts, the rational prevails because the rational is expected and validated in our society, and to a variable extent the entire world. We have been conditioned to think rationally; it's part of the current paradigm and affects every aspect of life. For example, most people in my life wanted me to use my formal education and get a job in engineering or in environmental work. This is rational; it makes sense, and it would be recommended regardless of what country or hemisphere you live in. I also have been handed clippings of articles from prominent newspapers that claim that following your heart will not pay the bills. Everyone seems to know this, and very few question it. When you need the money, it would be very hard to win against this thinking. And because it seems easier to go along with the crowd and not make waves, you go against your heart, thereby creating inner conflict—like the one that Metallica's song shows so well.

Another way of saying all this is: the biggest spiritual battle goes on in your own mind. And it is also true that the biggest political battle goes on in your own mind. Actually, the more I think about it the more it seems that the spiritual is the political and the political is the spiritual, manifested. To me, they seem to be interchangeable.

This may help explain why religion and politics often are so enmeshed. The separation of church and state might be another illusion, and perhaps even part of the problem. What I mean exactly is that the separation of the *spiritual* from the *mundane* is part of the problem. But then again, it's also true that the church and spirituality often have little to do with one another, which is another interesting point to ponder. Anyway: what kinds of spiritual forces (or political forces, since they're interchangeable) are running this country? What kinds of religions and governments run this planet? What values are promoted in our name?

But frankly, I'm not very interested in religion or politics, as my focus and insight are on the individual. I can speak with authority about my own experiences, having made myself into a guinea pig for the ideas presented here, and also because I feel the individual (or more specifically, the inner realm of the individual) is the only place a difference can be made that can then affect the larger world. The raising of individual consciousness, individual inner change, and personal accountability is the only thing that will transform the future of humanity.

Well, I hope Mr. Metallica doesn't mind my taking the liberty to use him as an example for individual inner change. Maybe if this author of "The Unforgiven" could let go of his past, release his "failures" and disappointments, he could move on, be himself, and follow his dreams with new enthusiasm and power. What is he, in his forties perhaps? The perfect time to have these matters arise. And if he's older then so what? It's never too late to begin. So you get another chance, Mr. Metallica!

Well, it's not so easy to let go, that's the problem. But maybe there's a really good reason for that too. Perhaps once Mr. Metallica understands his particular situation from a deeper perspective, forgiving and letting go, even forgiving himself, will be as natural and as easy as breathing. The resentments he may be holding onto in the meantime just might have a purpose—to remind him that there's still some unfinished business, perhaps to help him learn an important lesson. But if he forgave simply because it was required of him, because someone somewhere once told him it was the moral and right thing to do, and he didn't bother to examine and understand his situation from a deeper perspective, well, it would have been very nice and generous of him but I think he might have missed out on learning something really valuable. Plus, would it have been real if he forgave half-heartedly, as an empty gesture? Would the difficult situation have served its purpose if the deeper lesson wasn't learned? And wouldn't he then continually *attract* the difficult or unresolved situation to himself, over and over and over again, until the lesson was learned? Similar to what actor Bill Murray experiences in the famous movie "Groundhog Day," where his character, a cynical, acerbic, and self-consumed TV weatherman Phil Connors, trapped in a blizzard in Punxsutawney, Pennsylvania, relives the worst day of his life over and over again—groundhog kidnapping and suicide included—until he gets it right: until he learns to take advantage of his unique position, experiments with the rules of existence, then finally connects to his heart and discovers his authentic self. So Mr. Metallica is a smart guy—he's writing songs and examining his life.

Furthermore, the things he might learn from striving to understand his life from a deeper perspective, from his willingness to examine things and inquire within, might be exactly what he needs to restore peace and balance for himself, and is what the world needs right now as well. It might be why his psyche is resisting the half-hearted gestures and is holding out for the fuller experience of the learning. And when he learns what he is here to learn, it will change his perceptions about the people in his life, about the world, and about himself. Learning is about changing the mindset and expanding consciousness. And when consciousness is expanded, something new becomes possible that wasn't possible before: the block to creative energy is dissolved, the energy starts flowing, the struggle within is diminished, which allows him to receive the gifts of the universe, as well as being more free to be his authentic self.

This is a fine point I feel I can rightfully sermonize upon: forgiveness. Although my highest philosophy included forgiving and forgetting, I had gone through a stage where I carried around a bit of a grudge because I felt hurt and betrayed. I had sent out poisonous thoughts, little fuck yous here and there. It wasn't until I examined my issues from a deeper perspective and received some amazing insights, that I was able to naturally and easily let go and be free—because I had begun to see the blessings in the original (though awful) experiences. (Like, *thank you so much* because I learned something so valuable from that experience you helped create for me.) From anguish to gratitude, you might say.

"Creation doesn't care about the feelings, it wants to give you perspective on what's real. And the feelings are just a part of the picture and it doesn't mean that it's real just because you're feeling it. There are a lot of other elements that you may not be seeing," the Counsel of Light had tried to explain to me, but I didn't understand, not until now anyway.

So life is really about learning and creating opportunities for changing the mindset (which is what growth and evolution is about). And learning of course frequently occurs by making mistakes. For example, when I thought I was writing a children's book and was mistaken, I learned something important I probably would have missed had I been correct to begin with—this misconception helped me learn how the flow experience works. And at Angelika's swim meet in Morgan Hill, when I wondered why W. had to be *so* difficult, what I learned once I examined the situation was *so* amazing. There is perfection in the divine design; there is perfection in everything, even in people being difficult, even in being mistaken, even in unforgiveness.

Myself, I forgave my parents for their parenting mistakes years ago once I learned where they were coming from; after that I forgave society once I saw the bigger picture and stopped blaming the system, and I forgave myself just recently, once I learned the truth about myself and my life (that is, once I changed my mind, my beliefs about things). As soon as you learn the lessons you're here to learn, you can forgive and let go easily and naturally, making peace with yourself and others. Once you get to the truth of your life, the learning process stops, because you got what you came to learn. This opens the door for the flowing of grace.

Making peace in your mind is part of the process towards higher consciousness. The mind can judge and weigh pros and cons; it can go back and forth. The brain itself consists of two parts, a left brain and a right brain—perhaps that's why it's easy to feel a split within the mind. But it's not easy to feel a split within the heart. The heart has an affinity for inner truth and protects you from compromising your truth. The sacred space is the gateway to wisdom and ultimate truth. And according to what I learned from Father Charlie Moore, the heart remembers and this remembering and inner knowing can override and transform false beliefs held by the mind. In other words, the voice of the heart is a good built-in detector of nonsense.

Connecting to the inner core also seems to restore a balance between the left and the right brain that allows the two parts to work together better. This then creates a balance between the rational and the creative, between logic and imagination, between the male and female aspects within. When someone asks me which side is "better," I say that I prefer to use both sides of my brain equally and simultaneously; I would rather not have to choose between the rational and the creative. I have respect and appreciation for both and know that one without the other is incomplete, is broken. I mention all this because I actually heard some "right brain-reformed" individuals proudly announce that someone who develops his creative side "does damage to his left brain"—as though that were a good thing. I can understand that there's been a push in our society towards right brain creativity lately, but it shouldn't be *at the expense of* left brain reason and rigor.

When your mind is aligned with your heart and soul (when there is inner congruence, inner balance), there is a natural alignment with your purpose in the bigger design. Then fewer conflicting messages come from within the self, allowing inner wisdom to be more easily revealed, and you are no longer so easily manipulated by your fears or by false or disempowering beliefs, because your wisdom and understanding overrides them. This is inner power. It's also my understanding of the process I went through as I connected within: that as I reconnected with my inner core, my mind was balancing itself and aligning with my truest self. The Counsel of Light had said, "You come out of polarity by coming into unity within yourself."

Perhaps chemical or organic changes occur in the brain during the reconnection process. In my own experience, I had many headaches several weeks in a row, during which thoughts of a balancing taking place in my brain kept popping up in my mind. Once I realized I was reconnected to my inner core though, the headaches disappeared and I noticed that from then on I had fewer conflicting thoughts. In fact, I almost forgot what it was like to have any conflicting thoughts in my head at all. My mind doesn't "chatter" as much anymore, and there are times when I wait patiently for my next thoughts: what will I think of next?

Returning to my thoughts about Oscar night: I knew by then that the environment always gives us messages and wondered what Hollywood was communicating with the films it produced and selected for the 2004 Academy Awards. It's true we're in a time of war, but why all those movies? And the songs, the wailing, yowling, whining songs—what were those all about? Sting, the song-king of melancholy (W. had pointed this out to me years ago), the king of tragedy and loves lost (one of his songs is "King of Pain") was a featured performer. The other artists wailed through their songs as well. What the hay? Well, perhaps I don't know my music—I shall ask country folk—but that was my perception anyway.

I also perceived some unease around the Academy event, and even sensed a palpable air of discomfort in the attendees. Okay, so the entertainment wasn't exactly light-hearted and uplifting, that's for sure. And then, the movies, the songs, this whole event, it all started to remind me of someone. I kept seeing his image in my mind's eye, flashing repeatedly across the big screen like a subliminal message. Strange, because I'm not strongly visual and rarely see pictures in my mind. Also, I prefer to avoid him, even though he happens to be our leader right now. I should explain here that I'm predisposed to shunning him because…how shall I put it? Well, it's because he and I, we just don't resonate together! That is, at least not yet. And by the way, I've done such a great job of avoiding Dick Cheney that if he were to stand in a police lineup with a number of his peers, I wouldn't be able to recognize him. Needless to say, this TV experience—war and

George W. Bush—wasn't exactly what I had envisioned for myself sitting so comfortably, so soon after the bunny's funeral.

A few days later, the Academy Awards still on my mind, I was driving and scanning radio stations and came across Howard Stern's program. I rarely tuned into his show but listened in that time because Mr. Stern was complaining about the curtailment of free speech in our country and about some government agency trying to get him off the air. Since I considered freedom to be a principal desire and quality of the soul, and the Counsel of Light had mentioned that standing up for my own self-expression was my main learning here—I listened in.

Mr. Stern had a few good points: no one around him, not even the station bosses, had the courage to stand up for the right to free speech, and the government officials supposedly in charge of his special case would not or could not provide him with straightforward answers as to what Mr. Stern was or wasn't allowed to say on the air. Mr. Stern also complained that basic American freedoms were being eroded under the guise of fighting terrorism and no one did a whole lot about it. Those in charge have contrived situations and have been taking away our rights on the pretext of protecting us. (I will concur with Mr. Stern here and also add that, being majorly disguised myself, I have been becoming quite skilled at recognizing covers and disguises.)

Give up freedom in order to be secure? But that's like *so contrary* to what I have strived towards in my life; it goes like *so against* what I have been experiencing during this mission, and it goes against the principles I have been formulating. I have a major issue with this because for me, freedom and security go hand in hand. Well, perhaps I'm wrong, but my experiences have shown me that the greatest protection comes from the interconnectedness accessed through the inner core, and the greatest freedom comes from the same source as well. Freedom and security both come from within. So bless your heart, Mr. Bush.

On another radio news program a day or two thereafter, I heard of an environmentalist who had tried to board an airplane but was denied access because his name was on some sort of government no-fly list. Exactly what he had done wasn't mentioned, I don't know why, but I suspect he must have earned someone's contempt, or the contempt of some multinational corporation. In other words, he was probably not an average recycling Joe but someone who had made waves and then got arrested.

With regard to environmental issues, I try to be responsible for my part. I even go around at parties collecting empty bottles and cans, placing bags with "please recycle" signs in strategic places. Sometimes I root through messes and retrieve other people's cans. If we can't put our own trash in the right place then where are we? Is it any wonder, the shape of the world? And doesn't what we do and how we do it reflect the state of our inner world? That's why I admire those who have the courage to take the extra step and act on behalf of others, and nature, and life—like that environmentalist on the no-fly list.

Anyway, it seems that no one is immune to anything now. Things have gotten so imbalanced that even recycling can get you into trouble—which is what happened to someone I know. An instructor of environmental studies at San Jose State University reduced, reused, recycled, and composted so thoroughly that the total amount of garbage he generated each week—stuff like plastic wrapping from pasta, band-aids, worn-out baggies, etc.—fit into a lunch bag, which he then discarded in a city trash can. He didn't use his weekly trash service, decided that he shouldn't have to pay for it, and for this he earned the contempt of the system. Imagine the reaction of the industry when you inform them you no longer need their service, the number of cans you put out is naught, so would they please stop sending bills? He made the front page of the San Jose Mercury News a few years back. An article stated that he was making appearances in court.

Why was it such a big deal, to have to go to court over this? He was but one person, a very likable person, funny too. But I suppose when you upset the status quo you can expect consequences. I suppose also that they didn't want any templates established, didn't want his unique soul blueprint, his particular energy pattern grounded into the earth's grid system or something. And the guy on the government no-fly list was giving off energy patterns too, as was Howard Stern. Well, that's always the problem because an individual can only do so much, and then he is subject to being singled out or dragged into the courts or something. But an individual can establish the groundwork and the gridwork for new energy patterns to emerge and flourish. Individuals who do something new, who create new templates *can* be very powerful indeed.

I realize that the point of mentioning these problems—war, terrorism, fear, environmental degradation, the erosion of constitutional freedoms and basic human rights, government priorities being driven by forces other than public interest—is to remind us that, at least on the surface level, this world looks like it's in serious trouble. (Just as I had thought I was in serious trouble.)

But luckily, everything isn't how it seems on the surface, as vision only goes so far. There could be a deeper perspective here, another way to look at these things: perhaps all of this has been designed for us to experience and learn from because in this world of duality, we learn through contrast. To see an image, for instance, you need both light and shadow. Using this analogy, how are you to discover who you are and learn the deeper truths about yourself unless you experience who you are not? How are you to discover who you are in the face of challenge (that you are a hero, for example) if you don't go through challenging situations? How are you to know anything fully unless you know its opposite as well?

By the way, Father Charlie Moore had mentioned that right/left brain imbalance is *the* root of humanity's problems. He implied that our brains had been designed with this imbalance so that we would be more easily manipulated and controlled, by buying into false beliefs given to us by the "false gods." But I feel there's a deeper (and more empowering) explanation. When you accept that we actually *chose* our life situations, a deeper explanation can emerge: we chose to buy into the false beliefs so that the game of duality could be played. In other words, buying into the beliefs that each of us had bought into was a requirement for playing this earthly game fully—for the learning experience of it.

Perhaps life on earth is an illusion after all—an old philosophical saying that has eluded me for a long time, as I kind of bought into it and kind of didn't. Not that it's not real—the earth is real and life on earth is for real and the trees and the mountains are solid and real and so are puppies, and the problems of the earth and its peoples will not simply disappear or get resolved with the wave of a magic wand or through simple affirmation, without us taking action and doing the work. As individuals we still need to do what we can, leaving the rest up to interconnectedness. What I mean is that life on earth is pretend; we've been pretending to be something other than who we really are, so that we can learn through *firsthand experience* who we really are. And I don't include just myself here, I mean all of us. I remember the Counsel of Light explaining to me: "You're a barometer for what's happening in the world." (I am using my understanding of my own life to help me understand what's happening in the larger world.)

And if you look deeper, say from the perspective of the soul, you begin to see instances of other things happening, things that aren't so apparent. For example, it's always darkest before the dawn. Also, it's clear to me that the human soul wants to be free to express; the soul is freedom itself. And when personal freedoms are suppressed, the possibility for the greatest freedom is set forth. Eventually, the soul will win out—there isn't really a question about that.

Anyway, how was I to learn the truth about W.'s soul agreement with me if I didn't experience difficulties with him? How was I to learn who I was in the face of challenge if I didn't experience any? And how can a fish value and love and delight in water if it doesn't experience what it's like without?

What I am trying to say is that there are gifts even in the hard times, even in terrible things like fear and terror for they too offer something, like a chance to completely "lose control" and break free from self-imposed limitations and societal conditionings. And doesn't fear sometimes keep you on your toes and help you do your best? The right proportion of confidence and fear expedited my process and strengthened my drive and resolve to have this project, my contribution, shine in the end.

∞

At the end of January 2005, I awakened from a dream where I was scrambling across a craggy landscape that looked like the aftermath of a mountain explosion. Large boulders and slabs lay all around me in complete disarray, as though they had fallen from the sky. Crevices wide enough to fall through stymied your path; you had to watch your every move. I was stepping through the wreckage, hopping from boulder to boulder, headed towards a city that looked like ancient Rome. Then when I entered the city through the front gates, I saw lions living among the people. Lions loitered in the courtyards, on the piazzas, and the verandas. The people hummed about the city guardedly—quite understandable, given that you could never be sure what a lion might do. I too walked around feeling a bit guarded, and slipped away to a safe place while still going about my normal business. I was with a Hispanic woman. She had been stopped for questioning at one of the city's checkpoints—this was a common thing. And as I was waiting for her, I awakened.

After I recorded this dream into my journal, it occurred to me that the people had learned to live with the lions; the two had coexisted. And perhaps after a few generations, it became the only way they knew how to live. They had learned how to walk, what to do, what to feed the lions; they went about their daily business taking certain precautions and thus, were relatively safe. And then, the lions didn't seem so much like lions anymore. They mostly lazed around, swishing their tails.

A few weeks later, as I was entering my lion dream into these pages, the song "The Lion Sleeps Tonight" was playing in my head. I had heard it on Greg Kihn's radio program on KFOX that morning. Mr. Kihn was running an on-air contest where listeners were asked to call in with the name of a song and the male artist who sang the highest musical notes. His radio partner, Chris Jackson, then played the suggestions on the air and checked the highest notes on his piano. I think "The Lion Sleeps Tonight" won the contest with a high C note. Steve Perry, one of my favorite male singers, had been out in front until then.

Perhaps this dream was showing me that indeed, we're living in very interesting times. Perhaps also it was telling me to keep going with my mission and to coexist with my fear. Maybe so.

Well, I feel that the time is ripe for the collective soul to emerge, and for us to discover who we really are. I also feel that the time is past for just puttering around. We've experienced the extremes of disconnection and duality, and it's time to connect within and finally figure out, from a deeper level, who we are and to see what's possible. Who are we, and what is our purpose for being here at this time? What is next for humanity? Perhaps we'll choose to play a whole new game.

All it would take—and I am in line with the Counsel of Light and with Jon here—is for one individual to begin this. Someone needs to act as a catalyst for the possibility of freedom and truth and self-expression and unity, someone who is already set up in a high position. Perhaps Mr. Bush? Well, I happen to think George W. Bush is fulfilling his soul contract—which is to help awaken the people from their ages-long sleep—very effectively, despite it not appearing that way on the surface. The way I see it is that Mr. Bush has been waking people to the truth of their individual responsibility, their individual role in these unique times, and what can be more important than that? (Just as W. has been helping me awaken to my own responsibilities—here I am being responsible, diligently writing this book, trying to make sense of what's happening in the world from a deeper perspective.) In fact, George W. Bush and Osama bin Laden have been playing a game that will ultimately bring the greatest peace this planet has known, for this is the way it's been divinely designed. I wonder if they know these wonderful qualities about themselves? Anyway it's true: Bush *is* on a mission from God.

Certainly, events have been heating up on the earth's stage between, it seems, the forces for life and those for total annihilation. Local as well as world events seem to be increasingly confusing and crazy. But maybe all this serves a bigger purpose. Maybe we've deliberately designed it this way so that we don't look anymore outside of ourselves for guidance and answers, but that we find them within. This makes sense because as fragments of the Creator, each of us has our own unique role to play (which can only be found by looking within). Perhaps part of the divine plan is to help us discover first-hand who we are in the face of these world challenges. Perhaps we're being prompted to connect within and find the truth and wisdom and balance that lie there for ourselves, so that these qualities can spill over and benefit the rest of the world. Because these deeper levels of awareness connect to the memory of your individual life purpose (the part that only you came to bring), to Creation itself, by playing your part you will help everything "click into place"—which is what will bring ultimate resolution here. The Counsel of Light had said that in the divine design, everything's already been taken care of, so there isn't any need to worry about anything. It's just about connecting within, connecting to interconnectedness and playing your individual, unique role. Then what you do not only benefits yourself, but all of creation as well.

And let's say you did just that, you connected within and followed your inner guidance. Would you then discover, say, that at the level of essence, who you are is a pushover who needs rescuing from this crazy world? I think not. It isn't what I discovered for myself, anyway. In fact, I have a sneaking suspicion that rescuing victims is not part of the divine plan, and that prayers asking for rescuing will not be answered.

On the other hand, I'm sure that prayers for understanding and empowerment will be answered. Prayers in accordance with the laws of the universe and questions in accordance with the creative process (the spiral of spiritual growth and evolution) will be answered, not those that perpetuate the very conditions from which we wish to be freed. What you feed grows, what you focus on in your thoughts, intentions, and actions grows. When you are willing to participate in the process of growth and evolution through the raising of your own consciousness, creation will respond with ways that support that process. (By the process of evolution, I don't mean Darwin's adaptation, but growth and expansion in spiritual awareness and experience.)

This is because human beings were made in the essence of the Creator; we are fragments of the divine source, and source is not a victim. Divine beings are not victims in need of being rescued; they can rescue themselves by participating in the creative process of expansion and evolution of consciousness—which is how they will save themselves and their world.

Individuals who raise their consciousness (who expand their understanding of life) often then separate from the herd. But following the herd is not a good idea anyway when the herd is headed in the direction of danger. When you respond from inner truth rather than reacting to controlling external influences, you will separate from herd mentality. You will then no longer participate in the world's craziness, thereby doing your part to reduce it.

Creation grows and expands and we, as part of Creation, were designed to do just that. So the point is to be willing and to accept the challenges of life and that is the most important part of the for-mula of success. Be willing and the rest comes much more easily. And this, I feel, is what's occurring on the earth right now.

∞

In summary, it's the raising of individual consciousness, the rising up on the spiral of evolution that will make the difference for the individual and consequently, the world. Individual inner change through connecting to the interconnectedness within will elevate the world.

I suppose now I ought to say a few words about my understanding of the "new world order," given that the Counsel of Light had brought up that topic. The same reasoning, of course, would apply here as well: the new world order isn't something that can be imposed from the outside. Order can't be legislated or commanded into being, and that's not how it's been ordained in the divine design. The struggles and chaos in the outer world today merely reflect what's happening inside many individuals. You can't have outer order where there's struggle and confusion within. When there's no longer any struggle inside, there won't be any struggle outside. Only then will a new world order arise. Therefore, a new world order begins with having order within your own self first; it's an inner individual thing that will grow and become outwardly apparent once more and more individuals participate in their own spiritual evolution.

So people really need to do this for themselves. Inner order and inner unity can only be attained by connecting to the intercon-nectedness within. This is also the only way to access your truth, wisdom, light, and the awareness of your personal divine design, the design that you, along with the Creator, originally ordained. Getting in touch with your inner core and thus your personal divine design provides balance and inner unity, which, in turn, results in outer unity.

As individuals, we can choose to consciously evolve sooner rather than later. The soul is timeless, but we, as humans, can fulfill our personal divine design sooner or later, with a lesser or a greater amount of struggle—the choice is ours.

An excerpt from the song "Closer to the Heart" by the band Rush expresses this challenge quite clearly.

> *...Philosophers and ploughmen*
> *Each must know his part*
> *To sow a new mentality*
> *Closer to the heart...*

Nurturing and Sustaining

As I strengthened the connection with my inner core, I began to contemplate how to teach children to live closer to the heart, so they can access their creative and expansive selves more easily, as well as grow emotionally and spiritually. I further considered how we learn to be guided by our inner self in a world so distracting and overwhelming, that demands so much conformity from early childhood on. How do you nurture these inner strengths and qualities in children?

Observing my own daughters, I found the connection to the inner self is already there; it's as innate as breathing and doesn't need to be taught. My contribution then is to help guide them in their process of growth, and to help them recognize and honor this heart connection and encourage its development.

In September 2003, when Julianne was in kindergarten discovering her talents, she excelled in enhancing her drawings with imaginative details—striking geometric patterns, brightly-colored butterflies, beautiful flowers, and other things she saw in her imagination. These little details made her art unique and her own.

In December, she was chosen to be student of the week—a big event for kindergarteners. As part of that important affair, she was given a homework assignment where she had to describe all about herself on the "all about me" poster, including drawing a picture of what she wanted to be when she grew up. She drew a singer holding a microphone. Angelika sings well, and has been singing ever since she was about five months old (but that's another story). Julianne admires Angelika, but such obvious copycatting bothered Angelika. "Mom, tell Julianne to stop copying me!" she would say over and over.

"I'm not *coffeeing* you!" Julianne would loudly protest.

Anyway, Julianne had worked for hours on this poster that represented her, cutting and pasting pictures from magazines: photos of dogs and flowers for things she likes, of cactus plants for things she doesn't like ("because they poke me"), many, many pictures. She drew the family members, and I helped measure her height and noted the other vital statistics. It was Sunday evening, shortly before bedtime. The poster was almost done, a poster any parent of a kindergartner would be delighted with. But there was just this one little thing: the drawing of the singer—which she had drawn and erased three or four times—wasn't right yet.

"I hate the hair and the eyes! I can't draw them good!" she started to cry. "I want to draw as good as Angelika!" Already at the tender age of five there is such intense self-evaluation.

I tried to make things right. First I explained that her sister is three years older and that's why she draws better but that didn't help; it just made matters worse, judging by the increasing volume of her outburst. Next I tried another tactic: "It looks very good to me. I like how you drew it so pretty…so let's finish your poster. It's time to get ready for bed." But now, both inwardly and outwardly furious, she shoved the poster away and it flew to the floor.

She was on a fast track to a screaming tantrum. (She had been called a "screamer" by some parents at the Mountain School.) It didn't take much to push her to that place of terror somewhere in the mind. I dreaded this; once she got started, she would carry on for a while, an hour even. But it was too late—she had started sobbing in those forced yet frantic sobs. I was frustrated, almost in terror at the thought of this, and I felt my inner strand of patience getting thinner and thinner until it would snap and I would start yelling too. But that wasn't my intention. I was tired and just wanted the poster done and her in bed.

Not knowing what to do, I stopped myself to think (or rather to *not* think, to just be still and connect to my inner self) and looked at her. And in that moment I remembered who she was. "Oh, I get it," I said. "You want to make things beautiful, and you're not going to be happy with it until it looks beautiful to you." I simply explained what I saw, what popped into my consciousness, because it wasn't my job to fix everything for her, only to get it, to get her (to communicate what I observed), and to help her make sense of her emotions and desires.

She heard me; with her sobbing so loud I was amazed that she could, but she did. A big smile came over her face and the tantrum lifted miraculously. I picked her up and hugged her. "You little perfectionist," I said, and tickled her until we both laughed. Then we sat down and practiced drawing the eyes and the hair just right—the way she wanted. A few minutes later the poster was done and she happily jumped into bed, totally self-satisfied.

In this example, even frustrations could be viewed as valuable opportunities in disguise because they offer insights into who the child is, for under each disappointment there is a vision, a yearning for something grander than what currently exists.

As I contemplated what I had learned, I thought of the steps each child would go through on her path. As she went from childhood to adolescence to adulthood, she would naturally grow and expand in her awareness and in her sense of self, which I realized I could help nurture in various ways. For example, at bedtime I will ask each what touched her heart that day, what she learned or discovered. I will ask about her fears, hopes, and dreams for the next day, and for the future. Knowing that this heart and soul connection will become stronger through awareness of it, through communicating and sharing it, I will encourage each to pay attention to the voice within, especially when choices are to be made. Teaching children how to make choices is, after all, an important part of parenting.

To be able to mature to a balanced, whole person, a child should learn about all of her four levels—the physical, the mental, the emotional, as well as the spiritual. Even though she might not be able to articulate her feelings or the sources of her frustrations well, creating a safe place where the inner voice is acknowledged and nurtured will help her understanding grow. And as she learns to respond to and take care of all four of her levels, I know that she is living fully. Of course, being an example of this yourself is the best way to teach it, as is sharing experiences and learnings from your own life, even those learned through difficulty.

So I will try to create a daily opportunity for freely expressing from the soul and learning from sharing. I will also trust the process of life to take each one where she needs to be in each moment, for only she can forge her own path. I will fully trust her process of unfolding, for she is the one who chose her life plan.

Well, I say these things now but am fully aware that this is an ideal to work towards, a guideline for cultivating this connection. I still reserve my right as a parent to guide and set limits when necessary. Issues always come up and they need to be dealt with according to your best abilities in the moment. Matters like sibling rivalry, picking up after themselves, becoming responsible inhabitants of this planet, are things that need to be addressed by teaching and example, often over and over again.

As children mature, the more personal responsibility they demonstrate, the greater the freedom that can be allowed, as freedom and individual responsibility go hand in hand. The ultimate goal then is to have young people learn to act according to inner truth rather than to the myriad of confusing societal conditionings. By learning to distinguish their own truth and direction from the directions encouraged by cultural beliefs or icons, I feel their potential will be realized faster and easier, and they will experience greater joy.

Ultimately, my intention is for the child's self-esteem to arise from her heart connection, and for her to define success on her own terms. When she taps into her inner core and trusts it, she will trust *in* herself, not in some quality or attribute *about* herself, like her ability to do or to have something—which naturally varies from moment to moment. There's no substitute for trust in the deepest self. It is essential for living life fully.

Who knows where life will take her if she stays true to herself and follows the guidance in her heart? Who knows what will be possible for her and her world? (I am thinking how I wish I had had this larger awareness when I entered college, instead of having to figure this out later in life. But then again, I wouldn't be writing this book and I'm really enjoying it right now...)

After all, isn't this what we want by the time we're adults? Don't we want to really know ourselves, to trust ourselves, and to use our inner guidance for the betterment of our personal lives, the community, and the larger world? Don't we wish to unleash our hidden potential and fulfill on the part of the design that only we came to bring? In times of transition, wouldn't it be reassuring to be able to trust in the unfolding of our lives? Wouldn't that make life more joyful, full, and adventurous, and at the same time peaceful? And when it's time to leave this world, wouldn't it be comforting to know that your life was complete, that you had no regrets? What would this world be like then? Better functioning, I think.

Superconductor

After what had happened in merely a matter of months, I was only motivated to connect further to become an even clearer conduit of creative energy, to see what would be possible continuing on this course of listening within for guidance. I had a sense this was only the beginning and I wanted to see what was next, and how far I could go.

With a pounce onto my chest, our kitten awakened me from a dream the day I was revising this chapter. In my dream, I was on my way to Alaska as a passenger in what looked like a new, comfortable European-style city bus. I was aware that I've never been to Alaska, only to Canada, and I was thinking that going to Alaska would be just as easy as going to Canada.

The bus traveled through a picturesque, green valley in between beautiful snow-capped peaks, maybe ten miles from one side to the other. The valley reminded me of Davos, Switzerland, still snowy in the higher elevations though it was almost summer. The bus meandered, switchbacking up an incline, went here and there, stopping in many places for passengers, taking its time. Impatient, I asked a passenger sitting next to me how long this trip to Alaska would take. "It'll be around four hours," she said.

Four hours? That was way too long for me! I wanted to get there sooner! I explained to her that if I drove my own car, it would take me only two hours. So I decided to get off of public transportation and drive my own vehicle. I pulled the signal to stop and got off the bus. That's when the cat woke me up.

So if the key to memory and the key to dreams is metaphor, was this dream telling me to forgo mass transportation or public direction and follow my own, to power up my vehicle and drive up the spiral of evolution? Furthermore, I understood that Alaska doesn't have to be viewed as some destination or end point because in reality, once you get to Alaska there's a whole new, big wonderful state to explore.

With a new level of enthusiasm I began to do a second meditation (a grounding meditation) to strengthen my connection with the heavenly dimension and with my environment, so as to help clarify and completely unveil my mission for this lifetime. (The "heart and soul" meditation connects you to your inner core, while this grounding meditation helps to further strengthen the "vertical" connection of the above with the below.) At least twice a day, I practiced a simple three- to ten-minute exercise for this purpose, an exercise slightly modified from one I had learned in the Soul Recognition Workshop.

Standing with my feet shoulder-width apart, my hands hanging loosely at my sides, my knees slightly bent, my eyes closed, and exhaling slowly, I'd imagine energy or sunlight flowing from the sun (or source, or the dimensions above) down to the top of my head, entering my body at the crown of my head and going down through my body in a line as straight and as coherent as a laser beam, down my spine all the way through to the bottom of my feet, to the core of the earth. Then inhaling slowly I'd imagine this energy reflect back up from the center of earth, through the bottom of my feet and the rest of my body to the top of my head and back up to the sun or the higher dimensions. I would repeat this several times, imagining the energy or light flowing up and then down; inhale energy going up, exhale energy going down, with a short pause at each endpoint, and sometimes as long as I could hold it. (Alternatively, I sometimes imagined this energy going out to the universe with each out-breath and coming back into my inner core with each in-breath.)

I'd do this exercise expecting the connection to both my physical environment and to the heavenly or angelic realms to strengthen and the energy to flow in between with more clarity and ease. This grounding exercise, as well as paying attention to my inner voice throughout the day, helped deepen the connection to the interconnectedness and made the inner guidance clearer. It was a simple practice I could do anywhere, but it seemed to do the job.

I didn't practice traditional eastern meditation as I wasn't comfortable sitting Indian-style. Some people can sit with their legs folded neatly under, hands resting comfortably on relaxed knees, palms up, but I always felt weird and out of place. My legs would make a forty-five degree angle with the floor, and my back, which normally gave me no issues, would need support. Instead of relaxing and meditating, my attention would be focused on trying to relieve my discomfort.

"You're just inflexible," W. used to say. "And women are supposed to be flexible." I knew exactly to what he was referring—the inflexibility in some of my joints and of course, my stubbornness. But I thought my inflexibility was an advantage, part of my uniqueness. Why would I want to change a part of myself I felt right about? Maybe that explains why I never really got into yoga: because for the time being, it was important I be inflexible about certain things. At least that's what I told myself.

After beginning the regular practice of connecting the levels above with the levels below, I noticed that people approached me more often on my daily walks up St. Joseph's hill. This was now the middle of March 2004, a few weeks after the rainstorm and the bunny and the Academy Awards and it felt like my first draft was coming to completion. People I had seen for months who, except for an occasional greeting, normally paid little attention to me were now getting off their bikes or interrupting their jogs, asking why I carried a pen and paper with me, whether I was a poet of some sort. I would respond that I was writing a book, and then we'd discuss creativity and intuition and topics of that nature. I noticed that they also happened to be involved in creative projects and second or third careers. Was I now sending out the energy patterns of a creative individual? This was also a sign that my connection to the outside world, to people, was increasing, though I hadn't been working on it in the normal ("horizontal") way, but was merely strengthening my connection between heaven and earth—my "vertical" connection, as the Counsel of Light had called it.

Incidentally, two or three days after being asked that "poet" question I awakened around four in the morning feeling an urgency to write. The words spilt out of me and I scribbled the following composition. It's slightly embarrassing, I'll admit, but I include it here anyway; what's a little more soul-baring when I already feel so deeply exposed? One can discern from this piece of verse insightful glimpses into the state of my emotions, body, and psyche at the time:

> I want it but I won't go to bars and look for it—because
> I know they'll only leave me low.
> Doing it by yourself isn't very satisfying; I'd rather there
> be a body, somebody with me.
> If I were in New York I'd call an old friend, a navy pi-
> lot, wouldn't matter to him if he were with someone or
> not.
> I want it with you, but I'll admit that's crazy and be-
> sides, your conscience is pulling you otherwise and I
> don't even know what that is anymore—my conscience,
> I mean. Haven't for a very long time.
> I don't know where it exists or whether I call it by a dif-
> ferent name.

So I keep myself going—listening, writing, and taking care of the children, for I know in the end it will be worth it. Won't have it be any other way.

The pendulum of my psyche swung between this longing for connection illustrated above and, increasingly, moments of delight and deep insight and, sometimes, occasions of still being on the brink of insanity and despair. In other words, between longing, joy, and terror, between those three points. I had those three degrees of freedom available to me.

I am also embarrassed because part of this is nonsense—I don't know this about my pilot friend, or that I'd call him even if I *were* in New York. This happened many years ago, before either of us was married. But I wasn't thinking about what I was writing, I just wrote my reckless thoughts and my involuntary, visceral feelings, is all. Anyway, people can decide what they want.

∞

There are probably many ways to connect within but what felt best for me was to link in as directly as possible by doing the heart and soul meditation. No special positions requiring flexibility or props such as candles or altars were needed, and I liked that; I could connect in anytime and anywhere. The Counsel of Light gave me this meditation early 2002, back when I felt most awful and confused. Practicing it is what started my upward spiral; it helped me pick myself up. I think right here is a good place to include Flo Aeveia Magdalena's understanding of the Counsel of Light, since it is she who channels them: "The Counsel is the body of light, order, and truth that emerged directly from the Monad (God) to direct the free-will experiment. The Counsel is God's/Goddess's right-hand organization, consists of twelve original points of reality, and is the sustaining body, so to speak, of your universe. The Counsel is your energetic stability, that which provides a knowing of 'home.'"

To do the heart and soul meditation, I would lie down and put my left hand on my heart and my right hand over my soul seed, which is in the center of the breastbone where the ribs meet. I'd imagine a figure eight of energy going under and over my left hand in a circle clockwise, then under and over my right hand in a circle counterclockwise. (Together the two circles formed the figure or number eight—which stands for infinity.) The figure eight of energy would thus connect my heart with my soul. I also imagined that this energy represented love or essence, which I think made the meditation even more powerful.

After doing this meditation for a few minutes, I'd often feel a very subtle but pleasant sensation in the center of my chest. I'd repeat this exercise a few times a day during the most challenging times, and I even meditated by imagining I was meditating, while cleaning the house or taking a hike. Learning to recognize the feelings associated with this meditation helped me discern which messages came from my heart and soul (usually feelings of love, passion, excitement, joy, and expansion). This exercise helped me feel better rather quickly as well: my heart comforted my soul by giving it love, and my soul, getting love, opened up and began to offer its wisdom, which in turn inspired my heart to give more love, inspiring more wisdom from my soul, in an affirming upward spiral.

In this meditation, the heart symbolizes present life, and the soul past lives, other dimensions, and your infinite life. When you access the soul, you begin receiving in the present the wisdom from all past lives, all aspects of yourself, so that your innate wisdom becomes increasingly available to you now. Also, when you do this exercise, it becomes easier to settle into the body, it helps calm the mind, it helps stop the craziness and the worry. Calming the mind and placing your focus on your heart and soul connects your present life with the wisdom of your infinite life.

The Counsel said the following about the heart and soul meditation: "See, human beings think if they pay a lot of attention to problems that they'll solve the problems; even though they know that it never works, they keep doing it. Ha ha!" (They laughed again lightheartedly here.) "So what we're saying to you is stop doing what's making you crazy. Put your left hand on your heart and your right hand on your soul and make the figure eights. Okay, now what's that going to do? It's going to bring the love—you have love in your life and you have people who love you and you understand what love is—so love connects to the soul, which connects back to the love, which connects to the soul, which connects back to the love. Okay, what's that doing? It's bringing the answers that you're carrying from your deepest soul into your heart to fill you with love and feed you so you're less afraid. Then the love feeds the soul and says: 'Give me more understanding, give me more connection.' The figure eight is infinity—it brings you the wisdom from before time. It helps to support you; it helps to clarify things; it helps to bring things into resonance; and it provides you with an opportunity that's absolutely amazing, because you don't have to try harder; it's all done. It's absolutely done." (My understanding is that the hard work for humanity has already been done, the struggle will diminish; the rest has to do with connecting, following inner guidance, and receiving the wisdom.)

"When you're human, pain and suffering is the way it is. You have pain and suffering because you're human," they repeated for extra emphasis. "So connect and go into the wisdom because if you don't, if you try to live your life trying to be happy humanly, it's going to suck."

Doing the meditation often and as described will bring the quickest results, even if you don't believe it will. In fact, believing doesn't seem to be an important factor here. (Believe in nothing is what I would tend to say, and if there's anything I'd have a tendency to believe in, it would be in nothing and in the nothingness that takes you into the realm of creation.) Of course, in the beginning when things are going a bit slow, it does take a commitment to continue the practice when the results aren't apparent yet. But this is true for most anything worth doing.

The Counsel of Light also acknowledged the benefits of the martial arts, saying, "All the martial arts, whichever they are, they're all about coming from the space of the *chi*, which is the life force inside that's connected to the wisdom, the life force that lives through the wisdom; it's all the same." Practicing the martial arts is a way to connect to and increase life force—which in oriental medicine runs through the meridians of the body—for the purpose of healing the body and increasing the energy level and general well being. They also indicated that the heart and soul meditation would provide more of an "instant wisdom hit," for my purpose here wasn't so much to "work with my *chi* but to work with the wisdom that comes from universal *chi*."

As further ways to connect with the inner self, they also recommended being in nature—for example hiking, spending time in a forest, near the ocean, or near running streams of water. I found that listening to music, soaking in a bathtub, or any activity that calms and feeds the body and soul was also helpful. I'd also recommend connecting to heaven and earth through the grounding exercise while listening to Sarah Brightman's "In Paradisum" song from her *Eden* CD. When I did that, I felt the *chi* energy moving through my internal circuits like streams of subtle sparks going up and down my spine. All this simply suggests that loving yourself by being good to yourself and feeding your inner self is the best way to improve yourself and consequently your world.

∞

Spirituality, I have learned, is not about rigid beliefs and formal practices, but about connecting within and discovering your truth, raising your awareness, and being on the upward spiral of the evolution of consciousness. Adding the spiritual level to the other three levels—the mental, the emotional, and the physical—completes the picture of life so that all levels can be attended to on a daily basis, promoting a balance between them. This will result in a balanced individual, one who plays with a "full deck," who lives life fully and reaches his or her potential more quickly and easily. The soul's energy after all is the energy of your potential.

Living fully entails being connected within, having your feet firmly on the earth while receiving guidance from the higher realms. Once you're connected, there isn't a whole lot that's more rewarding. And once you're truly connected, it is done. The daily practices are no longer required because they have become integrated into your being; you're just living that way and it's natural. In fact, I found I was connected even though I missed a day or more of my practices, and later, even if I missed many days (once I learned how to "surf"). After a while, it didn't seem to matter anymore that I wasn't meditating, as I would still experience the benefits of it (flow, insights, synchronistic events). Even when things weren't going my way, I still felt connected, more balanced and aligned with myself. And as time went on, even the things that really used to unbalance me (for instance, my kids) had less of a capacity to do so, and I was able to feel balanced again much quicker than before.

In your heart and soul lie the memories of the purpose you came to fulfill in this lifetime, including the promises you made to yourself and others. These memories can be distinguished from ordinary thoughts because they feel inspiring and uplifting, whereas judgmental thoughts and conditionings often feel constricting or limiting. But even these help you connect because releasing old judgments and conditionings and asking the universe for wisdom and a higher-level understanding of their purpose might be the next step in your process.

If you take care of your inner self first, everything else in your life begins to fall into place, although this requires some constancy, of course. It requires you to be consistent in giving the inner—the deep levels of awareness—at least as much attention as the outer, which means that the guidance within is at least as valid as outer influences.

You will find your own pattern as you begin to strengthen your connection. And you strengthen your connection by following through on the inner guidance and inspiration with constancy. Then from the synchronicities you experience, your observations about what happens around you, and your insights, you will begin to synthesize the information you receive, or rather, your superconscious mind will do it for you, pretty much automatically. (That is, if you avoid artificial sweeteners such as aspartame that have a tendency to dull nerve endings.)

The resulting confidence gained from this process will, as a side effect, also help you achieve secondary life goals more easily. So instead of working hard at the qualities you'd like to exemplify (such as being more assertive or courageous, patient or forgiving), or the qualities you'd like to be free from (such as shyness, procrastination, or even some extra weight), or worrying about a hundred different things you must remember to take care of (which will only make you more crazy anyway) take care of this one thing first—your connection to your inner core. This inner connection will help you progress as easily and as directly as possible.

Although some self-help books suggest that you challenge some aspect of your personality or ego, such as the angry or selfish part, the part you're ashamed of or have regrets about (because you feel you "should" be a certain way), this will not help but only magnify any inner discord because…what you focus on grows. When you fight some quality about yourself or put something down, the problem will seem to get bigger, the craziness will get amplified. When you focus on worry or challenge or on controlling your "faulty ego," those things too will grow. Fighting a war with your ego won't bring inner peace. The Counsel of Light never indicated that the problem was the ego, and I don't see the ego as the culprit here, but blaming the ego seems to be the rage these days. What a bunch of baloney that is! Well, as I had already mentioned, a lot of what we've been conditioned to think is for the birds.

You experience life through your observing ego mind, and it is through your ego (consciousness, awareness) that you express. For example, when you have an idea you wish to manifest, then the ego takes a hold of this idea and initiates the process; the ego focuses on the process. What a wonderful thing! Without an ego observing and aware, where would you be? It's just that the ego has been burdened with distortions and half truths—the should and should nots, the rules, beliefs, regulations, conditionings, dogma, superstitions, doctrine, what's right, what's wrong—and that is the problem, not the ego itself. Our conditionings and belief systems get in the way of our connection with creation and our beliefs get in the way of our intuition. As John Mayer so eloquently sings, "Belief is the chemical weapon for the war that's raging on inside."

The following is a good example: In 1999, four plainclothes police officers drove an unmarked Ford Taurus through the Soundview neighborhood of the South Bronx, a poor, working-class neighborhood noted for drug trade. During their routine patrol, they noticed a black man loitering in the vestibule of an apartment building, which one of the officers deemed suspicious: "He was just standing there...What's this guy up to?...All right, definitely something is going on here," the officer thought to himself. They stopped the car and two of them approached the black man, Amadou Diallo, a recent immigrant from Guinea who peddled socks and gloves on the sidewalk in lower Manhattan. Diallo got scared at the sight of two very large men approaching him (who wore bullet-proof vests beneath their sweatshirts), ran up the stairs towards the door of his apartment, and put his right hand in his pocket as though he was trying to dig something out. The policemen saw the man begin to raise a black object toward them that looked like a gun. Next, one of the officers fired a number of bullets into Diallo, the others following. They kept on shooting, believing that the bullets ricocheting off the walls came from Diallo's alleged gun, until they shot forty-one bullets, killing Diallo. After it became silent, the officers climbed the stairs and discovered a wallet in Diallo's hand.

It wasn't the police officer's *intuition* that had him react and shoot those first bullets. His intuition hadn't failed him. Rather, his beliefs about black men, what they carried in their pockets, and the powerful fear this engendered in him, made him shoot at Diallo. The police officer's beliefs and the subsequent fears got in the way of his intuition. What brave souls though, Mr. Diallo, and the four officers as well, to have chosen their life plans (their soul contracts) so as to contribute such an important spiritual lesson to humanity through this hard way.

John Mayer expresses his feelings about beliefs in his song titled "Belief":

> *... We're never gonna win the world*
> *We're never gonna stop the war*
> *We're never gonna beat this*
> *If belief is what we're fighting for*
>
> *What puts a hundred thousand children in the sand*
> *Belief can, belief can*
> *What puts the folded flag inside his mother's hand*
> *Belief can, belief can*

Taking care of this fundamental relationship first—the relationship with your inner self—will help calm the ego and bring it into balance. But I did mention that we needed to buy into the beliefs in order to play this earth game fully and convincingly, didn't I?—so that we could play the game and learn the lessons not through theory but through actual experience. But at this point in our collective history the learning has been done; the hard work has been done, and the rest is all about connecting, the Counsel of Light explained. (And indeed, my connecting made the hard work of writing a book much easier.)

∞

The reason that connecting to the inner core works is that the inner core is connected to the energetic field around you, to your immediate as well as your extended field—which is All That Is. You connect to source first through your core. Then as you relate to this connection in the moment, you are supported in what you are doing because when you're connected, you are in alignment with the experience of the destiny you planned for yourself together with the Creator. Then you experience a level of cooperation and cocreation that isn't possible when you act from personal decisions alone.

Further, there is an order to the universe and to how we experience this destiny. The way to experience your soul's plan is not to decide first what you want or what you don't want in your life. You don't ask for what you want and then expect to receive it, believing all you have to do is negate all those annoying, unruly thoughts that indicate to you otherwise—if you only believed better, or visualized better (meaning, made yourself see things that aren't there). You also don't do it by setting intentions and forging ahead with hard work, which would be very logical. Rather, you get to know your inner self first by connecting with your heart and soul (lower level with upper level, present life with infinite life, respectively). You get yourself connected and aligned first.

"This alignment has to do with you and your Creator, your plan, your blueprint, your destiny, and therefore your life, but not your life first…You listen to the vibration from your inner core and you let the vibration express and then integrate the expression into every moment of your experience through the breath," said the Counsel of Light. In other words, you feel and listen to the guidance within and act upon it and put everything that comes up for you through this process. Because of your connection with interconnectedness, you'll get exactly what you need in the moment because the core knows what that is, your mind doesn't. It will come as soon as you let go (of whatever you may need to let go of) and let it come. Then you live this way moment by moment and finally, your outer life gets ordered.

"It's very important that you let go of what you want so that it doesn't drive you in a direction right now, so that you don't stop the future that would be best for you in ways that you have not yet understood. So it's letting go of the control—that's what the time of rendering is about—let go of the control of what's happening. Let the events and the interconnectedness all around you start working and rest in that knowing," said the Counsel of Light to me back in March 2002, when my life was definitely not in control. And after a while, I did let go. And when I worked within the order of the universe, I had miracles and magic occur that wouldn't have been possible had I worked with my will alone.

"Consequently, you don't have to worry about and solve all the problems you're worried about right at this moment. You don't have to worry about what to do next week, even tomorrow. So instead of worrying and asking questions about your survival and the outcomes you want, you might ask yourself, 'What am I being told today? What am I aware of right now? What is the next step for me in this moment?'" Connecting within, breathing deeply, and calming the anxious thoughts going out of control is the way to be in the moment.

"You realize that when you are in the flow of the oneness yourself, it supports everybody, it supports everything—and that's what you came to teach in a literal way—that if one is in the experience of one's own destiny, the blueprint is clear, the foundation is strong, the awareness is direct, and everyone benefits. There is nothing left out of the equation," they said. If you live in tune with yourself, creation supports you because you live in accordance with the creative process of all life and with the laws of creation. Then you're not fighting inner conflict and you experience more freedom from conditionings. You'll also be immensely gratified with the results because they are consistent and congruent with what the heart wants. Your dreams and heart's desires serve a wonderful purpose—to get you on the path of your true potential.

In 2005, I finally was beginning to understand what the Counsel of Light told me during my first talk with them in 2001: "You will teach your children to be free of the world's edicts and dogmas and how to be in love, which provides them entrance into whatever it is they want in the world and in their lives because they don't have to think about it. If they love automatically, then they're safe and people love them back. And then the environments that your children and your family are in are much more sustainable, much more open, much more cooperative, and much more acceptable. You know there's a yearning that you have just to have this kind of life and that's why you have it—because you're here to live it that way. You wouldn't have it if you weren't here to live it because the yearning is what's coming, not what's missing."

Furthermore, when you are living in accordance with these principles, it's much easier to let go of expectations that things have to be a certain way *right this instant,* and just be in the moment. Zen, Buddhist, and New Age philosophies teach detachment, but detaching isn't easy to do, especially if you have a huge, huge dream that things be better here for your family, for yourself, and for everyone. But it's easier when you know that this process will bring the results that right now are but dreams in your heart, especially when you begin to see results that indicate progress.

Well here is a good example: I wanted this book done fast, but there were many problems with it and I didn't know how to solve the problems. I didn't always know what I was doing or why I was writing what I was writing and that was kind of scary. But I connected within and worked with it moment by moment. Often I skipped over the parts I didn't know how to solve (for instance, the passage on the illusion of safety) and worked on the parts I was inspired to work on in the moment. By the time I came back to the problem areas, I realized the problem had either worked itself out, or I now had the capacity, some new knowledge or insight, to deal with it more effectively. I didn't have to consult an expert or try to solve it in the ordinary way, as in "I see this problem so let me at it and we'll see who wins." I didn't need to tough this out too much and thank goodness too, because it was difficult enough without having to plow through this project using sheer mental and physical resolve. So I am grateful that the insights and ideas just came into my mind at the right moment through the interconnectedness. Besides, I couldn't have done this book in the ordinary way, like a term paper, if I had written an outline and figured out beforehand what I was going to say, or if I had followed conventional rules of writing. Rather, this worked because I was willing to listen for inspiration from my inner self and then be disciplined enough to follow through, even in the face of challenging circumstances. Thus I discovered that the most important part of the formula for success is to be willing to accept the challenges that life places before you and all the rest follows so easily.

An excerpt of a quote by W. H. Murray (*The Scottish Himalayan Expedition*, 1951) says this well: "...the moment one definitely commits oneself, then Providence moves too. All sorts of things occur to help one that would never otherwise have occurred..."

So wherever you may be right now, whatever the situation, trust that the knowing inside will get you through it, the inner connection will guide you to the next step in your process. You don't have to know anything, you don't have to do anything or be anything that you don't already have available to you in the moment; you're already connected to your next step even though you might not see it yet. And if you don't see the next step, you might need to take a small step out—a small leap of faith or inspiration—and then you'll see it, and someone or something will catch you when you take that leap. (And…if you just so happen to flip your bouncy seat in the air—like Julianne did that once—there'll be someone there to catch you.)

The Counsel of Light explained how this internal guidance system works for finding your direction: "So, for example, when you're walking down the street and you realize you don't know in which direction to go, the input from the physical world and the input from the spiritual world starts to marry inside you, so that when you start to move, you're moving in the physical world as a result of the spiritual world. The spiritual world (the level above) corresponds to your inner guidance, your dreams, and spiritual guides. The physical world (the level below) corresponds to your sensory perception, your vision, awareness, consciousness, and body. It's the integrating of you and the mixing of those two levels together that you do automatically; in other words, you're taking the above and below and integrating them within you, that allows a third, center level to be born: your soul expressing itself in the world." (You don't have to think about all this theory in order for it to work, your mind does it automatically.) "Your soul's energy and expression is the energy and expression of your potential, the expression of your unique design in the world, because this vertical connection with the above and below is what aligns you with the blueprint that you're carrying—with the core of your decisions and choices from your blueprint, which honors the original agreement you made."

Furthermore, your soul expressing itself in the world is what brings the dimension of heaven to the earth, allowing you to experience more flow and ride the tops of the waves. Then you resonate with the unique, pure clear essence within, and you become a conduit for bringing heaven to earth. And when you live as though your soul comes first, when the relationship with your own self comes first, you begin to, as they say about the power of distinctions in Landmark Education, "put your hands on the steering wheel of your life, rather than holding the rearview mirror and trying to drive."

Simply said: if you don't follow your heart, you aren't likely to experience much happiness. As the Counsel of Light put it, "If you don't cultivate that inner space, if your soul doesn't get expressed in the world, then the outer world will be a reflection of the non-cultivation of that inner space—in other words, a lack of joy and happiness—because you wouldn't be cultivating that which makes you happy in the inner, deepest, and truthful realms. The result would be more unhappiness." It makes sense that you cannot continually go against your heart and expect to be happy.

Besides cultivating a strong connection with my inner self, I allowed myself to be in a state of inquiry and exploration, to have an open mind, and to change my mind about things when necessary. (This openness is what helped me generate new ideas and insights.) The Counsel of Light had said: "The more you allow yourself to be in a state of not knowing or inquiry (as opposed to already knowing), the more you open to that upper level or that deeper place to start putting information and energy and remembrance and direction and wisdom into the center level." Further, they added: "It's important that you realize that you can be manipulated and that it's time for you to decide not to be manipulated and as that unfolds you're calling into being a real truthful and valuable system of responsibility for yourself."

During this time of intense cultivating and keeping an open mind, I would occasionally half-awaken in the middle of the night feeling very elated, but also really confused. All kinds of ideas ran through my head, wonderful, ecstatic ideas it seemed, but I wasn't awake enough to be able to even pick up a pencil. And by the time I fully awakened, except for the elated feelings, I remembered very little from my experience, or at least nothing I could articulate into words. This occurred, I think, because the "computer files" or "tapes" in my subconscious were being rearranged for more efficient systems operation and were therefore down for a few hours in the night. Perhaps this was also a part of the "clearing out of the cobwebs in my closet?" Perhaps my subconscious was being reprogrammed so that my brain would act as a better receiver and transmitter of energy and information? Well, that *would* be helpful in this line of work, wouldn't it? Anyway, if this sort of thing happens you shouldn't be alarmed.

After I realized that I was integrated (one morning I woke up and my mind said, "You are integrated!"), this third level of soul expression was consistent and reliable and I no longer awakened (much) at night or had to soak in a bathtub or hike for inspiration or to solve a problem. I then had the capacity to access information and inspiration at any time, not only while meditating or trying to be in a relaxed brain-wave state.

For example, on New Year's Eve 2005 I called my friend, Steve, to wish him happy New Year. He didn't pick up so I left a message on his answering machine, including my telephone number this time, even though I knew he knew it; he had called me several times in the recent past. I just did it automatically, without planning to do it. Steve called about an hour later, glad that I had left my phone number as he was housesitting at his sister's and didn't have my number with him. (This kind of automatic behavior is distinct from hearing the inner voice and then responding, but it's also part of the flow experience and helps things run smoother, even the little things.)

I think the Counsel of Light explained these ideas when they said: "When people live from their core, everything they do is lived in order and in harmony with All That Is, because that's where Source is contained, in a sense, in the consciousness." When your soul is connected to Source, to creation, it supports everything and everybody, and everything and everyone in your life is taken into account, without you having to figure things out. What benefits you benefits everyone else, because everyone is also part of the Oneness. How could it be otherwise? "You are getting the keys to the kingdom, the secrets of how life really works here," they had said in February 2003, but these things didn't make much sense to me until I actually experienced the interconnectedness and the wisdom on a more consistent level. Only then did I put things together and begin to understand.

So now I'm going to suggest that you are in the life situation you're in because you are the one who has the wherewithal to pull it off, and if you follow your true course you will succeed, because you are the one who wrote the story of your life. As a result, you'll start having a life that really excites you, where your deepest longings get fulfilled. There is nothing wrong with wanting certain experiences and things in your life. Desiring a more fulfilling life is also not the cause of suffering. Disconnection with the inner self, with the interconnectedness is. (But as I already mentioned, we chose disconnection, we chose the human experience in order to learn through direct experience. Because how can a fish really delight in water if it doesn't really know what it's like without?)

There aren't any victims or perpetrators, only disconnected actors on the stage of life, learning and experiencing evermore the truth of existence. Suffering isn't a requirement for existence here—not anymore anyway—but it sure is the quickest way to learn. Being on the learning curve of life can be quite fun, can actually be a blast once you get into it, I discovered. You can also erase karma easily by letting go of tired, boring, worn-out beliefs and judgmental attitudes toward yourself and others. Because once you learn what you came here to learn, it's done. Once you change your mindset, the learning has taken place; the karma is burned off. You then no longer attract the experiences that will continue to try to teach you. Once you learn the lesson, the teaching of that lesson stops. It's simple, though easier said than done, of course.

In the process of connecting to your inner self and to all of creation through your core, you will become a superconductor of creative energy, a form of energy that is both alternative and renewable at the same time. (Quickie definition of a superconductor: having no resistance to the free flow of energy.) Furthermore, you'll become a high frequency resonator as well. Then you'll be living in the flow consistently and surfing those waves. So don't count on a humdrum existence from this point on.

By the way, there really isn't any separation anyway, it just appears that way, but you might have to play with this idea for a while to really get it. You were always connected, only the purpose of the illusion was to learn through direct experience. You've been playing your part in the divine design without even realizing it (well, perhaps George W. Bush is the exception here, because he obviously knew). And now is the time to see all this and to come together with yourself and others. "The coming together of the ages is the bringing together of the wisdoms that each person has had in all of his incarnative history, or herstory. It's time to bring it together and have it all at one time and awaken to it, not to have fragments of the self in different aspects non-orienting, in a sense, but rather to experience a deeper and deeper foundation where the commitment is experiencing its, what you might call, resolution... It's time to come together," said the Counsel of Light to me back in March 2002.

We are all included in the divine design; we're not in this or in anything on our own. We are not separate from the interconnectedness of All That Is, from Oneness. We just thought we were because we deliberately gave ourselves amnesia to be able to buy into the world's belief systems and conditionings to then play this interesting earth game with complete conviction for the learning experiences that will benefit the entire universe. In other words, we chose to come here to this planet called earth to serve the universe. After all, the microcosm can't do anything without affecting the macrocosm, and the macrocosm also affects the microcosm.

"Interconnectedness, Oneness—that's really all there is. Nothing else can substitute for it; there is no other answer," the Counsel of Light had said. And there's no magic answer or magic pill or magic remedy—there's only the magic process.

"WE LIVE IN AN INCREASINGLY CONNECTED WORLD....
SOMEDAY YOU AND ALL YOUR STUFF COULD BE
CONNECTED ALL THE TIME FROM ANYWHERE.
BEING CONSTANTLY CONNECTED CAN MAKE WORK
MORE PRODUCTIVE AND DAILY TASKS EASIER..."
—*From the Communication exhibit at the San Jose Tech Museum*

(I love it when things can be interpreted at a surface level and at a deeper level and be valid and true for both!)

Revelations

No, the game never ends when your whole world
depends on the turn of a friendly card.
—Alan Parsons Project

It's been a long journey and, as usual, I have been contemplating things. I have also been asking Julianne about her hopes and dreams and what she wishes to learn and discover.

Since I began her story, Julianne has gone to gymnastics class, and practiced her cartwheels and headstands. She has created beautiful art with her watercolor set and markers. She's been exercising the neighbor's dogs, wearing them out for their owner by making them pull her while she's on roller-skates. She explored ancient ruins and pyramids in the Yucatan. She helped make homemade jam with plums picked from teacher Jan's orchard. During ball games at school, she's chased after boys who stole away with the ball. She's gotten herself written up by fifth-grade conflict managers for hogging the tetherball during recess. She locked herself and the kitten in the bathroom—to have sole custody of it, no doubt—at least while she's bathing or brushing her teeth. (Meantime, to the tune of Berlin's "The Metro" Angelika sang, "I remember searching for the perfect cat, riding on the metro...") She's gone on neighborhood treasure hunts, collected landscape rocks, flowers, twigs, lemons, garden slugs, nails, construction wood, and who knows what else with her friend Michael, then arranged it all in an elaborate display on Michael's wagon. Well, at least that's how *I* saw it. According to Michael, however, they had collected fox heads, the tails of dead rattlesnakes, and fought off the dragons. She's been going to swimming class, of course. And it's all been an adventure to Julianne.

∞

One evening not long after I wrote these concluding paragraphs to "A Story for Julianne," I began to teach my children about getting in touch with their hearts and listening to their inner voice. I was barely able to say a few words before Julianne stopped me mid-sentence, "Mom, I know what you're talking about!" she said excitedly. "I do listen to my heart!" And I believe her.

My efforts hadn't escaped Angelika either. Around the house, I have been finding pieces of poetry, songs, and secret love notes to friends written in her handwriting. One day, she handed me a sheet of paper on which she had written two sentences, asking me to put them in my book. I hadn't been sharing my writing with her and didn't know what I was going to do with her sentences, so I put them aside on my desk. But after writing this paragraph, I know they belong right here: "It doesn't mean you're perfect. It's just about your talent and your self."

As for me, I learned a few things as well. I discovered that my life had been unfolding exactly as I had originally planned it, so that I could grow and evolve as much as possible. My true course was to disconnect, to experience what that was like, and later, to go through the process of reconnecting step by slow step so that I could teach myself the process first, and then be able to teach it to others. External forces hadn't caused my life challenges, there were no enemies, and change didn't just happen for random reasons. I had actually designed my life, along with the particular challenges I would face, in complete cooperation with creation so that I would finally connect with the dreams in my heart, discover who I was, and contribute my learning to the world. And I learned that challenges that cause reactions of despair, sadness, and even terror help us connect, help us evolve new pathways in the heart, help us discover our true self, our essence, and open us up to more compassion and love.

In the place between existences, along with creation and those who conspired with me, I had planned to place myself into a situation where I had no choice but to call upon my inner resources, because it was definitely time for that. Holding on to what I already knew held down my progress, so I had designed a difficult situation where I *did not know* anymore what to do; I *had to* look deeper—which is what allowed the most growth. The design also ensured the following outcome: I could be more conscious, more compassionate, more free, more joyful, and more fully alive. A perfectly designed plan, for in the design the outcome was assured.

Sometimes, the most direct way to the light is through the dark. And for some of us strong, stubborn, and arrogant know-it-alls, it might be the only way.

Okay, I had (reluctantly) admitted earlier that I was arrogant, but since then my sentiments about that have also changed. Now, I am grateful even for my arrogance, as well as for my stubbornness, my naïveté, my selfishness, and my dauntlessness, for all these qualities of the ego have served me well. I am also grateful for my clarity and my purity, as this perfect combination and proportion of qualities has helped me fulfill my mission to humanity.

I am grateful to all the people who helped shape my life. To my mother and father I am thankful for the character they helped foster in me so that I could go through with my mission to the end. I thank my parents and my siblings for understanding that I needed to go far away to grow up independently, so I could become the person I needed to be.

I am grateful to my friend Stacey for recommending the two courses that helped shape my life and gave me a profound "shot in the arm," and for asking me to connect within, to be in nature, and to listen to spiritual music. I benefited a great deal from others' input, and hers was totally brilliant.

I am grateful to all my co-conspirators in this drama for leaving me to myself even though at the time I thought I really needed you, for in your absence I came to find myself, and with that I came to understand that we have indeed been keeping our promises to each other.

I am thankful to W. for being my partner and for initiating this adventure with me. I know you loved me so much that you did everything within your power just so I would have a real chance at finding myself and fulfilling my mission and commission to the world. Although I might not be able to keep *all* my earthly promises to you, I will keep the promises we made to each other in the spiritual dimensions: I will help you find your light! I will help you find your self! I will give you the detailed, clear directions you always wanted and I will show you every step of the way. I will illustrate, with examples, every step of "The Way."

I told W. before we separated that he had played his part perfectly. But then again, this was exactly what was needed to assure the outcome of this assignment. And *who else but* W. could have played his part so perfectly? W., if they gave Oscars up in heaven you'd get one for one of the finest performances in one of the greatest leading roles ever!

And I am grateful to my friend Jon, who is here at this particular time to make sure that the job is complete! He knew exactly when he could have been of service, and when he needed to leave me to my own devices so I could find myself and find my own way. Jon, you gave me courage to persevere and you supported me in ways you couldn't have known, and for this I thank you.

Both of them helped me find myself. To tell the truth, I'd be surprised if both have not served on the Board of the Counsel of Light at one time or another.

I am also grateful to the Counsel of Light, without whose help I couldn't possibly have completed my mission. I understand now that you in your other dimension were (and still are) a key and necessary part of this plan—a part of heaven coming to earth. This story wasn't just about my searching for my personal life plan, as you had said. I am also grateful because I know this work of love is a gift from you, a gift from Creation.

As I said, the design was elegant and perfectly orchestrated, and we pulled it off with everyone's cooperation. W. didn't know what I was talking about when I told him that he had played his part perfectly, but after he reads this I think he'll get the picture. I hope he also realizes that the *way* he played his part was perfect and crucial to fulfilling this mission of revelation—and the completion of duality—to humanity. The same is true for Jon: as W. himself had communicated in the subject line of his email to him, Jon has indeed done his job well.

∞

We are here to learn and expand our consciousness, which is what will create a new world. The spiritual realm, when understood and integrated into everyday experience, brings heaven to earth. And now is the time to bring heaven to earth. It's time to come together in cooperation through the interconnectedness, through the oneness, and it's definitely time to use our wisdom from all aspects and all dimensions and have new kinds of experiences on this planet. As the Counsel of Light said, "It's time to come together." They are not alone in saying this. Madonna expresses these ideas well in her song "Ray of Light":

> ...*Faster than the speeding light she's flying*
> *Trying to remember where it all began*
> *She's got herself a little piece of heaven*
> *Waiting for the time when*
> *Earth shall be as One*
> *And I feel like I just got home...*

Spiritual growth and evolution occurs more quickly, easily, and painlessly when it's done consciously and intentionally. Because either you'll teach yourself new things, or the outside world will try to teach you, and it's a lot easier and far more comfortable when you teach yourself, that's for sure. There is also no other place in the universe where you can learn your lessons so quickly or so thoroughly. Spiritual growth and evolution is the goal and destiny of all souls, and life on earth provides many opportunities to accomplish this rather fast. But no need to worry or despair about any of it. As Kierkegaarde so brilliantly stated, "The self must be broken in order to become itself, but quit despairing over that." Well, the self I think has already been broken, been separated, so that part's already done; the hard work is complete. The rest is just about reconnecting and becoming. As the Counsel of Light said to me: Relax, because everything's done. Just connect within.

This reconnecting and the freedom it provides is what the soul longs for and what living life fully means from the soul's perspective. It's also what gives joy, what allows for full potential, and what supports life and all of creation.

In fact, it's a good idea not to pay too much attention to what's going on in the world, as if the outer symptoms are indicators of the future or of personal future happiness or future desolation. The last shadows of the old game, the old world, are being played out right now. Instead, using the soul's discernment, trusting the inner guidance, trusting the divine design, and looking through and beyond day-to-day happenings will help bring the soul's potential to the present moment. Everything is already woven together, and in the design, the outcome is assured.

Interestingly, I didn't focus on love as much as I had originally thought I would when the Counsel of Light first asked me to "write a book on love." But that's okay with me because love is what has made this whole journey worth it; love was the only choice for me. But that's because, from what I now understand, love *is* the only choice.

So, yes, I was protected but at the same time I had to grow up fast, which was a challenge for me. I was an old soul, going back to the beginning of it All, and I had to help in the way that someone has to help when the children don't know the ways and the ins and outs of the universe in which they live. And I had to help care for and pave the way for my brothers and sisters, as first-borns often do. Yes, I am a woman, but whom were you expecting anyway?

∞

I suppose now is the time to finally address the question of my identity. Well, I always thought that thirteen was my lucky number, and I always liked the number twenty-two. For one, I was born on March 22nd, and my vehicle driver's license number is A6662266. I used to wonder what those numbers meant. Stacey used to tell me that I was always a spiritual warrior, as I had already mentioned, it's just that I was very much misunderstood. Now about that number twenty-two: recently while purchasing a book over the Internet, I just so happened to discover that twenty-two is "the master number that reflects power on all levels and the ability to change the course of history." Wow, now that seems good and fun, no wonder I like it, but what does the number sixty-six mean? Another quick look on the Internet showed that numerologists realize that any doubled number is a master number, but it isn't clear what some of the higher numbers hold and mean. "No doubt time and greater awareness will help solve the keys to interpreting the special missions of the owners of master numbers 44, 55, and beyond..." is generally the accepted idea. Special missions? Greater awareness? Well now, those are confirming ideas. And perhaps I am helping create what the number sixty-six actually means right now, by writing this book?

By the way, at the time of completing my first draft, I had had this driver's license number for thirteen years. It had been assigned to me when W. and I first moved to California, and I didn't return to the DMV demanding that it be changed. I'm not sure why. Well, on some level I must have known that the universe was playing some kind of joke on me. I also thought it would be interesting and funny to have it: look at me, I have this number A6662266 and see if I care, I'd think as I handed it over for identifying myself. Anyway, it served as sort of a conversation piece. Some bank tellers and store cashiers joked about it with me. "That's an easy number to remember," one woman pointed out, and I agreed that for that reason alone, it couldn't be such a bad number. Others would frown and I'd just smile a knowing smile. But I didn't know then that there would be so much more to this story than I could have ever imagined.

> BUT DON'T BE SATISFIED WITH STORIES,
> HOW THINGS HAVE GONE WITH OTHERS.
> UNFOLD YOUR OWN MYTH, WITHOUT
> COMPLICATED EXPLANATIONS...
> START WALKING...
> YOUR LEGS WILL GET HEAVY AND TIRED. THEN COMES THE MOMENT
> OF FEELING THE WINGS YOU'VE GROWN, LIFTING.
> —*Rumi, translated by Coleman Barks*

What more can I say, besides what is the story of *your* life and how does it go from here? But tell me something, dear reader, has the light begun to dawn on you yet?

∞

Well, things weren't clear to me just yet either. There was more that needed to come to light regarding the mystery of my identity. Then the following story, "Duality Is Born" by Toni Sar'h Petrinovich, was emailed to the Soul Recognition email discussion list (a group of around seventy) in August 2004. Toni Sar'h Petrinovich, who has a Ph.D. in metaphysics and is a Soul Recognition Workshop facilitator I haven't yet met, was guided by her intuition to share it with the rest of the group. I read her story then and found it interesting, then forgot about it. But then I remembered it again mid-January 2005 because I had a hunch that her story might be useful, in some way, to have in my book. Luckily, I found it quickly because it was still in my "sent items" folder. I remembered I had emailed a copy to Jon. And as I was entering Toni's story into my book, the light began to dawn on me and I knew without a doubt that it belongs right here. This short story comes from her 2002 book *The Call—Awakening the Angelic Human*:

"Duality Is Born"

It was only a few days into THE beginning that God realized that there was a necessity for a meeting of all of the angelic realm and a consensus reached if duality (one of His better creations) was going to succeed. He sent out a memo letting each of the cherubim, seraphim, thrones, powers, archangels and angels of all degrees know that a meeting was being called in THE BOARD ROOM and that a great decision was to be made.

The entire angelic realm showed up on the appointed day (of course, since they only know the Divine Will) and each angel was intently curious about what the question was going to be that could be SO important that God would call every single angel into this meeting. They were arranged by rank with the most important archangels seated nearest the throne of Almighty Source. Everyone was there—Uriel, Metatron, Gabriel, Ariel, Raphael, Michael, Lucifer, Samiel—all of the mighty names appeared in person to sit next to the throne of God as He called the meeting to order.

"We have before us a very grave decision. I am going to need the help of every angel of every rank. It seems to me that there is a piece of duality that has not been created and I am not going to create it myself. It takes something and someone much more important to create this piece. It has to do with the Planet Earth in the Milky Way Galaxy that is going to form in another several billion years. This planet is going to be the home of a particular creation that is going to experience duality for Me. And there is the rub. I AM ONE and I need to be dual to create the opposite so that the creation which will be called Man will be able to learn by contrast how to experience the Love that I AM." All of this God said and not a single angel spoke a word. You could have heard a pin drop (if there were a pin TO drop) it was so silent.

God continued, "I am calling for a volunteer. I need one angel, most likely an archangel, to hold the opposite end of the energy vibration that is known as Love. I need an angel who is strong enough, bright enough and who loves Source enough that it can hold the opposite end of the energy spectrum that will be called Fear. This angel must be capable of enduring endless hardship, be hated by mankind as the most abominable entity imaginable, have horrible actions done in its name and be thought of as the ruler of a place mankind will create called Hell. All of this must this angel do out of love for mankind so that my second finest creation (angels being the first) may come to know what Love really is, experience a polar world and allow Source to truly experience ALL."

After this last part of the announcement, a loud shuffling of chairs was heard as many of the angels of all ranks and dominions left the Board Room Chamber. No one wanted to take the part that would be opposite of Love for that would be like taking the part that would be the opposite of God. By the time silence was again "heard," there were very few angels left and only a handful of higher or archangels. Some of the cherubim and seraphim had also stayed though they were of no mind to take on this part in the Divine Play.

God sat looking at what was left of the "staff" and held the Divine Space for someone to come forward. And then a voice was heard. It was a mighty voice, one like the north wind when it blows through the tundra in Alaska through the wet, cold nights. It was the voice of Lucifer. "I will play this part with you, Oh Mighty One. My love for You and my love for your creations knows no bounds. I KNOW that I AM strong enough for you have made me that strong. I KNOW that I have enough love to hold the opposite energetic end of Love for you have created within me ever-enduring Love and I will not forget Who I AM for I AM You—as are all of your creations. I have the strength, the brightness, the might and the courage to hold the opposite end of Love with you, God, for all eternity if that is what is required."

God was SO pleased. His best, his brightest, his bravest archangel was going to take the job and hold the opposite end with and for Him. He had really created WELL! It looked like the Board Meeting could come to an end and God was about to adjourn the few remaining members when it became apparent that Lucifer had another few words to say—and these words were to Archangel Michael. "Michael, my brother," he said, "I have one reminder for you before we part. I am going to a place where you cannot go. I am going alone. We will meet many times before this Play is over. I ask that you remember that we are the same every time you see my face. I ask that every time you raise your sword at me in the name of Source, you remember I AM Source. If you will remember to do this, mankind will learn the lesson of contrast more gracefully and my job will be made easier. Will you agree to this?"

And Michael, as great an archangel as Lucifer himself, knelt on one knee before his Mighty, Courageous Brother and bowing his head, he said, "Yes, I will agree. Give me your blessing before we begin our roles in this Divine Drama." And, as Lucifer placed his hand upon archangel Michael's head, the horns of triumph could be heard blowing throughout the entire Universe for now God's plan was complete and mankind would be born—born into duality, into a world of polarity, so that Source could experience what it is like to be separate and then, once again, become One.

I really like this story, and I like the way Toni Sar'h Petrinovich emphasized the "BOARD ROOM" aspect of it as well. (If I were to add anything to this story, I'd say that in order to appear at this

"Board Meeting," the angels had to interrupt their important work of harp playing, wing polishing, and cloud fluffing.)

Toni describes the angelic-human mission in her book:

At this time of the earth's great transformation, many of the angels who work with the earth's plane have requested and been granted the opportunity to share soul fabric with certain human beings. This sharing is in full agreement with the soul design of both the human and angelic planes and is in response to mankind's silent request for additional assistance during this transformation.

...In this framework, then, certain human beings have agreed to share soul essence while the human is on earth. This allows the angel to record in its own soul fabric earthly illusion of reality as experienced by the human and usually creates within the physical being a more altruistic desire regarding his or her life's intention. That is not to say that this human appears as a deeply spiritual being or even wishes to live life in that manner. It only means that there is a certain drive from within to do things a bit differently than usual and to have more distinct experiences. Some of these experiences may be outside the purview of the politically correct mass mind and often are. Yet, it is only through this consideration of rebellion that the angel and the human will coordinate the knowledge and skill desired to be registered in each soul.

...The soul may be shared wholly, in large part or only a fraction. I have seen variations of this theme that surprise me daily. Remain open to what the next evidence may bring. You, too, will all ways and always be surprised.

Toni says that you might be an angelic human without sharing soul fabric, you might share soul fabric and not feel the calling of the angelic humans, and you might share the soul fabric *and* experience the calling.

Expanding on these ideas, my current understanding is that angels have balanced aspects of the female and the male in them—they are whole and complete in that sense. Human beings on the other hand have accepted a feminine or a masculine polarity. In other words, when Creation originally separated into individual sparks called souls, these souls were again split into two—into the female and the male half, into soul twins. I suppose that I share the soul fabric of this famous angel with the other half of my soul, my male counterpart, and I am sure that I have already met him. I think though that he, as usual, doesn't know this on his more conscious level yet. Well, anyway, here I am world: Lucifer, at your service. (Yes, Lucifer, the one whose name means "bringer of the light.")

Interestingly, Jon's house number used to be 866, and his phone number at that time was 866 plus the triple sixes if you added the four numbers using the simple rule for numerology. I also think W. shares the soul fabric of this other, you might say rival, famous angel. That's one reason, I suppose, they also didn't exactly get along.

Well, these revelations certainly explain a lot of things to me. It explains why my mother had a strange issue with my reputation. I suppose that she viewed me as someone who was up to something mischievous, even though in reality I was innocent. It explains why some of my friends' husbands viewed me as a "bad influence" on their wives, my friends. Imagine that. Of all people, me—pure, sweet, innocent Christine, and such a good student too. If only my school-teachers could see me now, making waves, raising havoc wherever I go. It also explains why I so often felt like I didn't belong here on this planet. But now I do; I so belong. And the way I see it, I am unifying now. Because as Ariel Spilsbury used to say, innocence unifies!

Interestingly, around the time when I synthesized these ideas, I received in an e-newsletter to which I subscribe a channeled message declaring that, "for the first time in ages the light balance on earth is greater than the darkness." I'm not exactly sure what this means for us here or the accuracy of this observation, but it sure sounds good to me. Yipee!! Woohoo!! My reading of this also coincided with my despair vanishing because I finally understood my role, and that of the others, in this divine drama.

∞

At the beginning of February 2005, I had another call with the Counsel of Light through Flo. They said, "Well, hello! How are you? (Chuckle, chuckle…) We feel that we have been basically walking beside you all of these months and years as you have unfolded the destiny of your consciousness and as they say in your society, com-mitted it to paper. (Ha, ha.) It is not like we are coming to you from a long distance or from not having been in connection because we have been with you in each phase of the journey and it has been a beautiful process to observe because you've had a very strong and very committed awareness that this journey for you was as important as any other spiritual journey that you will take—that this is really in some ways the crème-de-la-crème because it's the integration of all of the consciousness that you've come to bring as well as being the space of intention that will carry you forward into the future… You've been writing just as much about the collective consciousness as you have about your own experience…" Then they basically told me to continue doing what I was doing.

I think I understand it all now: we have been living through a time of rendering, as the Counsel of Light had said. And in my experience, everything was up at once so I could help with disintegrating the parts that aren't real, the illusions. What's left now is the essence. It was a close call (whew!), but now I've got myself back. The truth has set me free. And the truth shall set the others free as well.

"Who's to say what will happen?" Jon emailed me when we first connected in response to my question, "Do you know what's going on here?" "I am sure you and I will respond to the moment," he continued. "This is a potentially very volatile situation that must proceed with caution. I am very attracted to your aura."

Ha! No kidding. Who *was* to say what would happen? This *had* to proceed with extreme caution. We *did* respond to the moment. We played all of our parts well. All of us did.

∞

As usual, I thought I was done, that this was it, and during my next phone call with the Counsel of Light (via Flo…) mid-June 2005 I had expected "well done" compliments from them but instead they said, "What we want you to understand is that this is much bigger than you. It's much bigger than what you think, what you believe, what you've come to understand and convey through your own channels and experiences. You've come here to truly download lots of information to humanity…

"This is the moment when the freewill experiment is abating. We're beginning to come into the superconsciousness point where we're moving from freewill kind of experiment to choice of intention. We're moving from a place where we have been kind of gathering understanding to a point of initiating and intending that understanding to be utilized in a way that changes the world order and changes the qualities and the vibrations through which we're functioning. So you're at a place where you're saying it's your turn to actually look through that window of consciousness where you see All That Is. It's your turn to embrace all that you have not felt comfortable or ready to embrace—and it's fine that that was the case because now, of course, it's the time to get it and that's great.

"Your lineage and origin has to do with the planetary configuration of the third dimension. Now that means that in a very literal way you've come here to scribe wisdom, you've come here to write it, you've come here to clarify, and you've come here to shape-shift the illusion of how the dynamics of science and of metabolic understanding, cellular integration, medical experience, holistic energy work, the consciousness of how it all fits together—how all of that is viewed by humanity. So you're not just here to help new-agers find a particular level of understanding and awareness in a world that doesn't quite get it; you're here to change the world that doesn't quite get it so that the consciousness has a place to balance itself, has a place to ground itself and is fully in alignment with the truth of All That Is, simultaneously with experiencing what it's like when the wisdom is present in the moment...It's about what you're carrying and who you are and how what you're carrying is going to serve consciousness, how it's going to bring forward lots of information and lots of cohesiveness..."

Well of course I know they did not mean genetic or familial lineage as probably many people would assume, but *soul* lineage. Intuitively, I got immediately what they seemed to be referring to, but it took a little while for things to sink in, for me to accept this new information, and to get confirmation from the universe as to my understanding. Anyway, this message from the Counsel prompted me to remember a vision I had during my Soul Recognition Workshop experience when I was under deep hypnosis. In this vision, I was on the earth during the time of Christ. Specifically, I was at the Crucifixion and had the feeling that I was a disciple of his, a female disciple, the one who had been known to have a bad reputation. And even though it was dark and stormy and I saw the cross and knew what *that* represented, I was aware of feeling peace that evening because the design had been fulfilled, the prophecy was fulfilled. And although it looked like a tragedy, I felt enveloped in the deep peace of this knowing.

I let this new information sink in for months and I began to suspect that the three of us—W., Jon and I—had played starring roles in the leading drama of that time. I think we were part of the key figures who helped fulfill the design of the Crucifixion and Resurrection. I also suspect that old story isn't exactly the way it's been passed down in written form either—about any of us—and that we were very much misunderstood. For instance, back then, as in this lifetime, I was born four years before them—to help prepare them for their roles. Further, I understand now that, when you have the extremely difficult and delicate divine task of "betraying" another, to manifest *that* in the physical realm, it certainly helps, for one thing, to have complete conviction, great internal strength, and also, a love triangle. I'm also aware that founding a genetic lineage was not part of Christ's soul plan and mission back then, and that the bloodline that some people have written about involved the other leading character, whose soul lineage goes back to Archangel Michael. (After the Big Event, the three, along with a few others, escaped into France, where they lived for a while before continuing on with their missions.) It's clear in any case that Christ's mission involved teaching humanity about our immortal soul, that we live again and again, and that the kingdom of heaven is within. Perhaps more about this will be coming out in the future, perhaps not. Anyway, a good book on this topic has already been written by Flo Aeveia Magdalena (it was received through Flo, channeled from the Counsel of Light) and it is titled *I Remember Union: The Story of Mary Magdalena*. It's a story about the lives of Jesus, Judas, and Mary Magdalene. The story begins before their births, when the Counsel of Light discusses with them their individual soul plans, and it ends with them promising to return 2000 years later, when the light of Christ would bear its fruits. I think I'll need to spend my time "scribing wisdom."

…have I been wrong
have I been wise to shut my eyes and play along
hypnotized paralyzed
by what my eyes have found
by what my eyes have seen
what they have seen? …
—Natalie Merchant, *Carnival*

∞

So although this memoir is about me, at the same time it's also not about me. What it's really about is all that is, interconnectedness, creation, and oneness—which is, as I said, humanity's destiny. It's about bringing heaven to earth, the other dimensions to this dimension; it's about the golden age that's coming, our potential and our birthright. And it's about everyone having the same creative power and potential—through the sacred space—as the masters and the angels.

We all have a part and a stake in this hologram of existence. As they say in this new millennium, "We are the ones we have been waiting for." But please don't take my word for it: inquire within.

I think my parents will be surprised by this book. They have no idea. It's like the time they came to my high school graduation: they sat in the audience, probably wondering when the evening would be over. They hadn't been informed that I would deliver the valedictory address, and they must have been surprised. Life is so full of surprises.